The Complete Book of
JAPANESE COOKING

Other Books by Elisabeth Lambert Ortiz

THE COMPLETE BOOK OF MEXICAN COOKING
THE COMPLETE BOOK OF CARIBBEAN COOKING

The Complete Book of

JAPANESE COOKING

ELISABETH LAMBERT ORTIZ
with MITSUKO ENDO

Drawings by MARION KRUPP

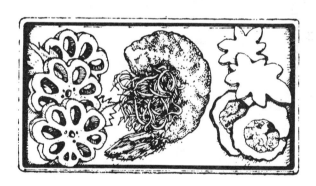

M. EVANS AND COMPANY, INC.
New York, New York 10017

M. Evans and Company titles are distributed in
the United States by the J. B. Lippincott Company,
East Washington Square, Philadelphia, Pa. 19105;
and in Canada by McClelland & Stewart Ltd.,
25 Hollinger Road, Toronto M4B 3G2, Ontario

LIBRARY OF CONGRESS CATALOGING IN PUBLICATION DATA

Ortiz, Elisabeth Lambert.
The complete book of Japanese cooking.

Includes index.
1. Cookery, Japanese.   I. Endo, Mitsuko, joint
author.   II. Title.
TX724.5.J3073   641.5'952   76-16008
ISBN 0-87131-212-3

Design by Joel Schick

Manufactured in the United States of America

987654321

Contents

Foreword

Ever since the years when I lived in the Far East, I have wanted to learn more about the elegantly distinctive Japanese cuisine. Having traveled since childhood, I grew up knowing the kitchens of the Caribbean, India and China. But it was not until I was married, and my husband was sent by the United Nations to Bangkok, Thailand, that I was able to visit Japan and familiarize myself with the cuisine. Welcomed into the homes of Japanese friends, I experienced the delights of the Japanese kitchen; I thought each dish was a work of art.

My husband had been assigned to accompany Mr. Yutaka Kubota, a noted hydraulic engineer in Japan, on a trip surveying the tributaries of the Mekong River for the UN Mekong project. Later when we visited Japan on a holiday, Mr. Kubota and his associates not only introduced us to restaurants representing the whole spectrum of Japanese cuisine, but also invited us into their homes, where they fed us, and answered my questions about the kitchen with kindness, patience and accuracy. They drove us to nearby places of interest and sent us traveling by train to distant parts of the country. On train trips, we became acquainted with the lunch boxes that are sold in Japanese railway stations, miracles of well-flavored and garnished rice. And our friends saw to it that we stayed in Japanese inns, helping us to be travelers, not tourists. We also met members of the Japanese press and radio and television journalists who appreciated my interest in their country's cuisine and went out of their way to help me.

On subsequent visits to Japan I learned more about the country through an old friend, Val (V.J.G.) Stavridi, then head of the UN Information Center in Tokyo, who was generous enough to put his considerable knowledge of Japan at my disposal. His was valuable assistance, since one must have some understanding of a nation's cultural life if one is to understand its kitchen.

I remember with gratitude the kindness and helpfulness of Ambassador Extraordinary and Plenipotentiary Masahiro Nishibori and Mrs. Nishibori, and of Mr. and Mrs. Kan Akatani, who were then with the Japanese Embassy in Bangkok. And I remember dinners at the Embassy with pleasure.

On my return to the U.S., I was deeply involved in a study of the kitchens of Mexico, the Caribbean and South America. Ironically, this project brought my attention back to the Far East because the cuisines share culinary roots. Along with the Spaniards, the Portuguese played an important role in the Far East during the 16th century, when they first introduced foods from the New World.

It was my friend John Clancy, test-kitchen chef for the *Time-Life Foods of the World* series who, as we worked together on the food of Latin America, rekindled my interest in the Japanese kitchen. I owe him a debt of gratitude.

It was a fortunate moment for me when I met Takashi Endo, now Deputy Chief of the UN Radio Broadcasting Service. His wife, Mitsuko Endo, is a gifted cook who offered to work with me on a book which would bring the Japanese domestic kitchen within the reach of Americans. We spent a happy year cooking together. Afterwards I cooked again alone in my own kitchen as I felt it important not only to be able to cook the dishes Michie (Mitsuko Endo) and I had tested together but also to know how to buy the necessary, often exotic, ingredients from local Japanese stores. I invested in some Japanese cooking equipment and have found it useful for all kitchen purposes, no matter what the cuisine.

Michie has painstakingly checked all the recipes to make sure we have interpreted the cuisine faithfully, and I can only hope readers will enjoy the food as much as I, and my husband and friends have.

Elisabeth Lambert Ortiz
NEW YORK

Acknowledgments

I would like to thank the friends, old and new, who have given me such generous help with this book. To no one is my debt more profound than to my collaborator, Mitsuko Endo, who truly opened the door of the Japanese kitchen to me, and to her husband, Takashi Endo, ever ready to help with language problems, and to their children, Taketo and Yoko, who helped evaluate our cooking.

I have lost touch with many Japanese friends from the past, and I hope they will forgive me. My thanks to Mr. and Mrs. Takeshi Fukui, Mr. and Mrs. Hirofumi Shinozuka, Mr. and Mrs. Tatsuo Shiraki, Mr. and Mrs. Naoya Yoshida, and Mr. and Mrs. Katsumi Shiraishi for having encouraged my initial interest during visits to Japan.

I would like to give very special thanks to my friend Dr. Alex D. Hawkes, the noted botanist and cookbook author, who has been unfailingly generous in helping me identify Japanese herbs and vegetables.

My thanks also go to Miss Yoko Yoshida for secretarial help.

The Complete Book of
JAPANESE COOKING

Introduction

Japanese cuisine, characterized by foods with a natural taste and appearance, is the most elegantly simple in the world. The whole aim of the kitchen is to enhance the intrinsic qualities of whatever is being cooked, and to serve it in bowls and on plates that add a grace note of beauty.

Equally characteristic is seasonal feeling, which the Japanese call *kisetsukan,* an appreciation of foods appearing at their appointed times in spring, summer, autumn and winter. There is also an appreciation of how foods are best eaten at certain times of the year. A Japanese summer noodle dish, eaten out of season, will chill one to the bone on a cold winter day, but will wonderfully refresh the wilting spirit in August.

Although not particularly ancient, the Japanese culinary tradition developed during long periods of isolation from the rest of the world; and perhaps for this reason it is fundamentally unlike any other cuisine. Japanese cooking was influenced by China in the 8th and 9th centuries, when chopsticks and soy sauce were introduced. Buddhism arrived from Korea in the 6th century, influencing the kitchen considerably since the eating of meat was discouraged, and again in the 13th century from China with the introduction of Zen Buddhism, which insisted on strict vegetarianism. In the 16th century the Portuguese brought in *tempura, castera* (sponge cake), and a number of root vegetables such as potato, taro and sweet potato, as well as pumpkin, from the New World. In the 19th and 20th centuries the kitchen was influenced by the West in general, but especially by France, and vegetarianism was dropped. But essentially the Japanese kitchen remains what it has been since its earliest times.

Since food was cooked over charcoal until comparatively recently, techniques of cutting were developed to make foods cook quickly. The technique of cutting on the diagonal produces a greater surface area exposed to the heat, and it is also very pretty to look at. Cutting *ichōgiri,* ginkgo leaf, is another example: cylindrical vegetables are sliced thinly, then the slices are quartered, giving the fan shape of the ginkgo leaf. Then *rangiri,* which is to cut on the diagonal, give a half turn to whatever is being cut (a carrot for example), then cut on the opposite diagonal into 1-inch pieces. And *sasagaki,* which is to cut in slivers, like sharpening a pencil, is useful for vegetables like burdock root which take a lot of cooking. These simple techniques enhance the appearance of the finished dish and make possible very precise cooking times since each piece will be done at exactly the same time. Since knives and forks are not used at table and everything is eaten with wooden chopsticks, meat and fish are also cut into bite-sized pieces for cooking.

Foods are washed more often than in the Western kitchen, not only before cooking but also to stop the cooking process at a special point. And washing just-cooked vegetables preserves their fresh green color, a technique probably borrowed from the French. Much attention is paid to small details such as cutting off the tips of shrimp tails because they have a high water content and will splutter when fried.

This meticulous attention to detail characterizes Japanese cooking; in fact, a little work in this cuisine may improve one's general cooking skills. But it would be unfair to give the impression that the cooking is tedious, or that one needs a stop watch to do it well. So much is prepared ahead of time, cooking time itself is so short, and so many dishes are served at room temperature, that assembling a Japanese meal can, with practice, be quite relaxed.

The Japanese meal structure is different from our (Western) own. There are many one-pot dishes cooked at the table and served with rice, that provide a whole meal. Of these, *sukiyaki* is perhaps the best known. More often the courses are presented all at once and eaten in no particular order. Traditionally, diners sit on cushions around a low table, about one foot from the floor. Each person is served the whole meal in individual bowls or plates and platters. Unlike the tableware of the West, Japanese dishes are often oblong or square and beautifully decorated. For a main meal there is always rice, a soup, a vegetable, salad or a pickle dish, fish or shellfish, and a meat or poultry dish, all served in small portions. Desserts are not intrinsic to this kitchen, although there are a few. Fresh fruit is a more popular choice, and anyone who has ever eaten a Japanese white peach will understand.

Sake (Japanese rice wine) is slightly warmed in tiny *sake* cups, and may be served either with the appetizers or, for festive occasions, throughout the meal. Wine is becoming increasingly popular. A dry white is perhaps the most suitable, but that is a matter of taste and one should experiment. There is also excellent local beer. Western pre-dinner drinks have become very popular. And then there is the green, unfermented tea that is served plain in tiny bowls and is light and delicate in flavor. There is always a teapot on the table, and when guests come to call they are always offered tea with a snack.

It is not considered impolite to be a little noisy with soup, or a bowl of noodles, and it is good manners to lift the bowl with the left hand when negotiating hard-to-manage food like noodles or bean curd.

Michie has worked out a group of menus to help in the planning of Japanese meals. I have put the recipes into Western categories into which they fit quite neatly. There is an alternative, more traditional, way of classifying Japanese food, by the cooking method, which gives one considerable insight into the kitchen. It is indicated in the recipes.

The system of classification is as follows: *Aemono* are dishes of mixed vegetables, fish or meat, cooked and mixed with a sauce. *Sunomono* are foods, salads basically, in a vinegar dressing. *Yakimono* are grilled or broiled foods, *menrui* are noodle dishes, *gohan* are rice dishes, and *sushi* are vinegared rice dishes. *Agemono* are fried foods which of course include *tempura,* and *nabemono* are the one-pot dishes which include *sukiyaki. Nimono,* foods cooked in a seasoned liquid, are what we would call stews. *Mushimono* are steamed foods, and *sashimi,* sliced raw fish, isn't cooked at all.

I have written the recipes in detail so that anyone unfamiliar with Japanese cooking can follow them and feel confident of good results. The technique, for example, of turning up the heat to high before standing the rice to steam in its own retained heat, may seem unnecessarily fussy, but it does produce a rice of just the right consistency. It holds together so that it can be eaten with chopsticks, but is also nicely fluffy. Many apparently trivial cooking details that one might be tempted to bypass are in fact vitally important.

Almost all the recipes serve four instead of the more usual Western six. Japanese recipes fall more naturally into this pattern. Michie and I found that these amounts allowed flexibility and could be halved or doubled successfully.

The one single thing that distinguishes Japanese cooking is the use of seaweeds. Instead of chicken, veal or beef stock, *ichiban dashi,* a very subtle stock known for convenience as *dashi,* is used not only for soups but as a cooking liquid. Made from *kombu* (kelp) and flaked *katsuobushi* (dried bonito), it is extremely easy and quick to make but does require strict timing as overcooking spoils the flavor. Its poor relation, *niban dashi,* is made from the leftover ingredients of *ichiban dashi* enlivened with a little extra bonito. A weaker stock, it is used for *miso* (bean paste) soups, and for cooking vegetables. *Nori* (dried laver seaweed) is used principally as a garnish, and *wakame* (lobe-leaf seaweed) is used in soup and other dishes. These, together with kelp, make up the principal trio of seaweeds. They may seem strange at first, but are very easy to get used to as the flavors are all delicate.

The soy bean plays a dominant role in the Japanese kitchen. It comes in the form of *shōyu* (soy sauce), *usukuchi shōyu* (light soy sauce), *momen tōfu* (bean curd), *kinugoshi tōfu* (silky bean curd), *yakidōfu* (broiled bean curd) *koyadōfu* (freeze-dried bean curd), red and white *miso* (bean paste), and so on. Despite their common origin, the products of this versatile bean manage to be very different.

Rice is almost as important an ingredient since it may be eaten at any meal and often is. It also produces *sake* (rice wine), the most popular drink and widely used in cooking, and *mirin* (sweet rice wine), used exclusively in cooking.

Noodles, thick and thin, of wheat, buckwheat, devil's tongue root plant, or soy bean gelatin are also very much present; most of them seem familiar since the wheat noodles approximate our own spaghetti and noodles.

JAPANESE COOKING EQUIPMENT

Buying some Japanese cooking equipment is very worthwhile, although any reasonably well-equipped kitchen will have all that is needed. You may want to add: a *suribachi* which is a serrated earthenware mortar with a large wooden pestle (*surikogi*) that makes grinding nuts, sesame seeds, or anything else, remarkably easy. Chopsticks, useful cooking as well as eating utensils, should be used to scrape down the sides of the mortar. They also come in handy for a variety of tasks from stirring eggs to checking the oil temperature for deep frying. A *shamoji* (wooden spatula) is good for stirring cooked rice as it does not break the grains. A *donabe,* a flameproof earthenware casserole, only needs the usual care of starting it off on low, not high, heat. A series of bowls, available in Japanese stores, is excellent for serving: tiny ones for sauces and garnishes, medium-sized ones for soup, large ones for rice or noodles, and all can be used for other foods. A *tamago-yaki nabe,* the Japanese rectangular frying pan for omelettes, while not indispensable, is worth getting. Rolled omelettes, which the pan makes easy, make an excellent accompaniment to drinks even when a Japanese meal is not being served. I do feel strongly that a small kitchen scale is handy especially as small scales for diet purposes are available at very reasonable prices. However, I have given alternate measurements for foods, wherever possible, for people without kitchen scales.

Another useful piece of equipment is the simple grill that is used on top of the stove; there are double ones for fish as well as single ones.

As for ingredients, no foreign kitchen is better served in America than the Japanese. The list of stores selling Japanese food and cooking/serving equipment grows, and the range of foods available also grows. I've provided a list of larger stores throughout the country as well as a glossary explaining both food and equipment.

There are rather nice bonuses that come with Japanese food. It is easy to cook, and most of the recipes take only a short time to prepare. It is also low in fat, and if I am any example, can be quite slimming.

Cutting Techniques

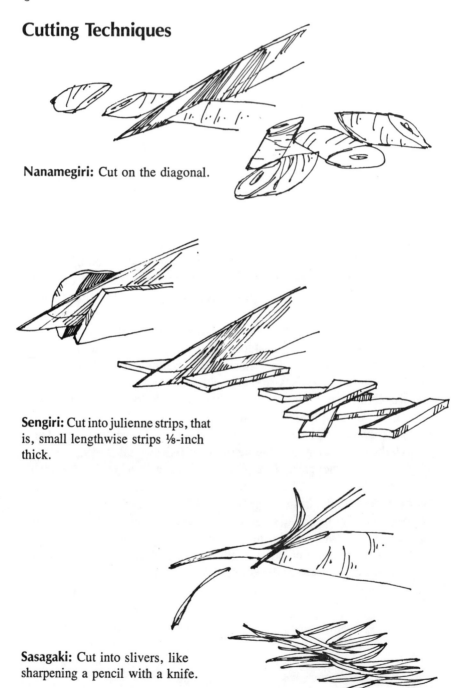

Nanamegiri: Cut on the diagonal.

Sengiri: Cut into julienne strips, that is, small lengthwise strips ⅛-inch thick.

Sasagaki: Cut into slivers, like sharpening a pencil with a knife.

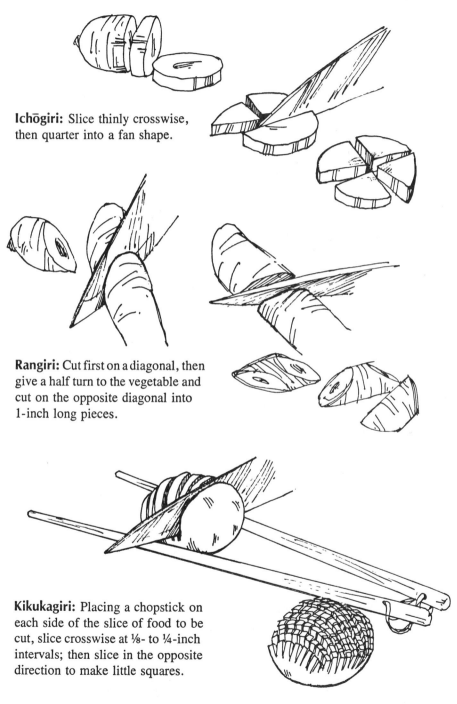

Ichōgiri: Slice thinly crosswise, then quarter into a fan shape.

Rangiri: Cut first on a diagonal, then give a half turn to the vegetable and cut on the opposite diagonal into 1-inch long pieces.

Kikukagiri: Placing a chopstick on each side of the slice of food to be cut, slice crosswise at ⅛- to ¼-inch intervals; then slice in the opposite direction to make little squares.

8

Cooking Equipment

Knives

Chopsticks: used as eating utensils and, when tied together at the top, used for cooking.

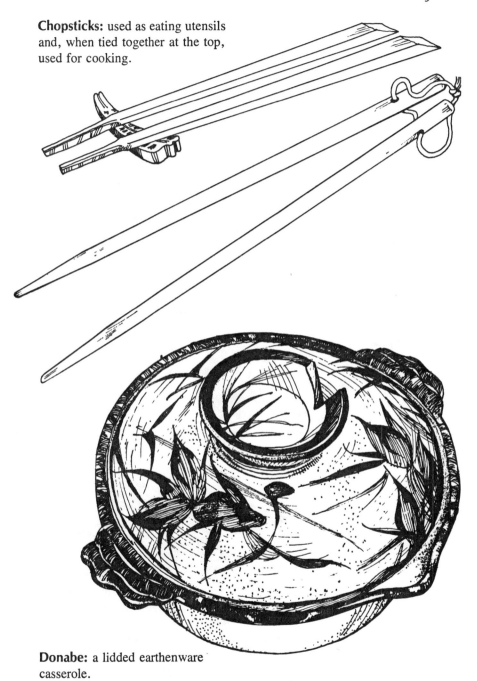

Donabe: a lidded earthenware casserole.

Donburi: a large ceramic bowl for rice or noodles.

Set of bowls: tiny, medium, and large.

Hibachi: a charcoal grill.

Jubako: the New Year's layer box.

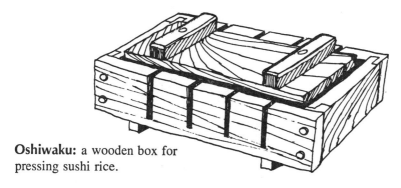

Oshiwaku: a wooden box for pressing sushi rice.

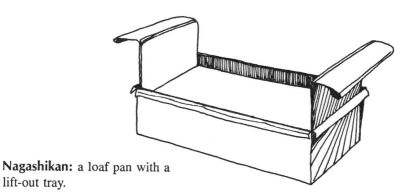

Nagashikan: a loaf pan with a lift-out tray.

Sukiyaki-nabe: a shallow round cast-iron pan for dishes like sukiyaki.

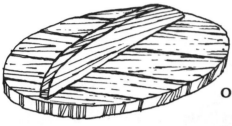

Otoshibuta: an inner wooden lid.

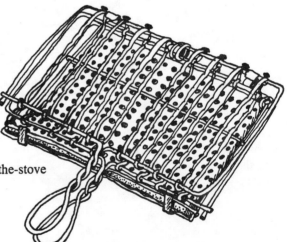

Sakanayaki: a top-of-the-stove grill.

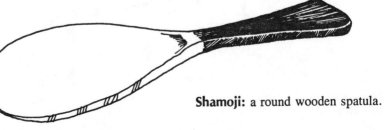

Shamoji: a round wooden spatula.

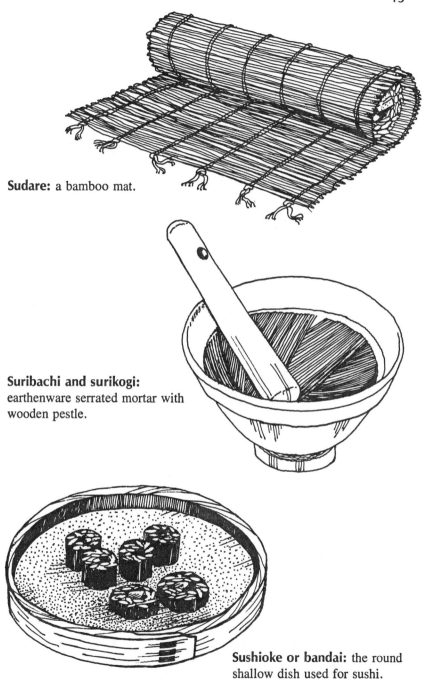

Sudare: a bamboo mat.

Suribachi and surikogi:
earthenware serrated mortar with
wooden pestle.

Sushioke or bandai: the round
shallow dish used for sushi.

Takegushi: small bamboo skewers.

Tamago-yaki nabe: an omelette pan.

Tempura pan: a round iron pan for deep-fat frying, with a built-in draining rack.

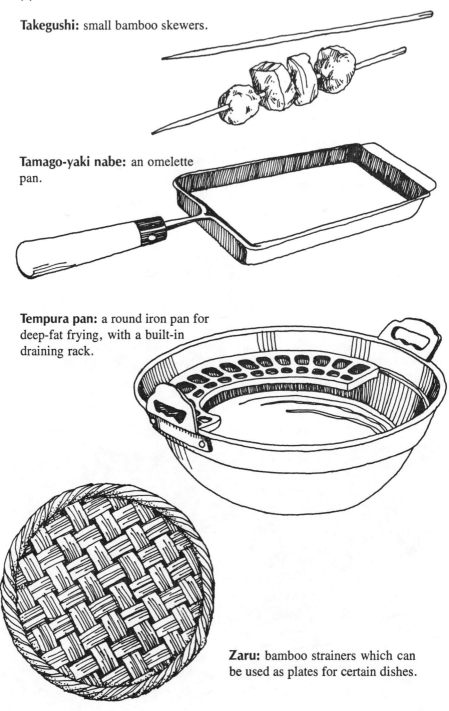

Zaru: bamboo strainers which can be used as plates for certain dishes.

Sake set: a flask with cups for drinking sake.

Serving platters

Ingredients

Hakusai: Chinese or celery cabbage.

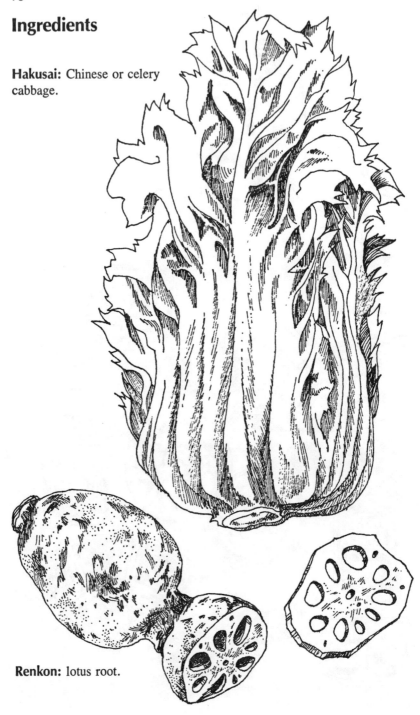

Renkon: lotus root.

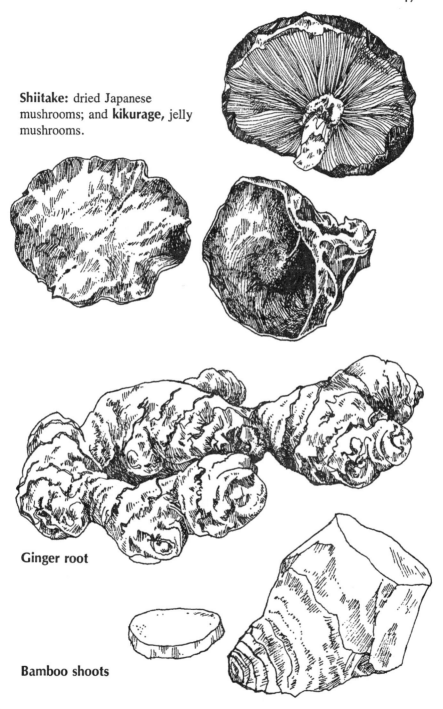

Shiitake: dried Japanese mushrooms; and **kikurage,** jelly mushrooms.

Ginger root

Bamboo shoots

Shungiku: edible chrysanthemum leaves.

Mitsuba: trefoil.

Shiso: beefsteak plant.

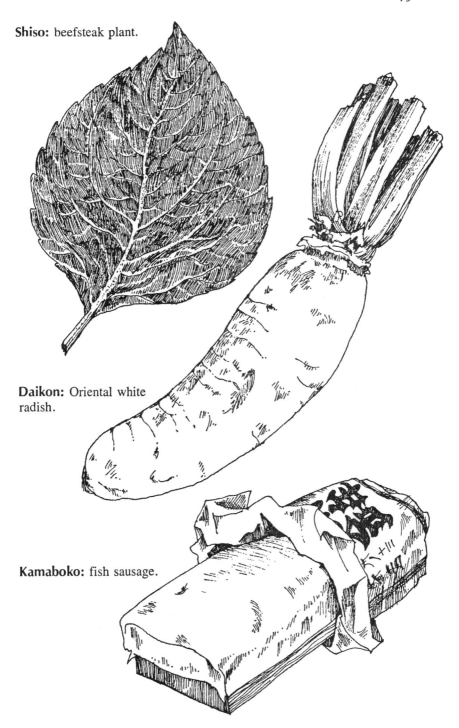

Daikon: Oriental white radish.

Kamaboko: fish sausage.

Menus

Breakfasts

Gohan (PLAIN BOILED RICE)
Kaki Dōfu Jiru (OYSTER AND BEAN CURD MISO SOUP)
Sakana No Misozuke-Yaki (FISH MARINATED IN BEAN PASTE)
Kyūrimomi (CUCUMBER SALAD)
Hakusai To Ninjin No Kaorizuke (CHINESE CABBAGE
    AND CARROT PICKLES)

Gohan (PLAIN BOILED RICE)
Wakame Jiru (MISO SOUP WITH LOBE-LEAF SEAWEED)
Wakasagi No Nanbanzuke (PICKLED SMELT)
Hōrensō No Ohitashi (SPINACH SALAD)

Luncheons

Hiyamugi (CHILLED NOODLES WITH EGGS)
Sawara No Teriyaki (GLAZED KING MACKEREL)
Green Asparagus No Kimijōyukake (GREEN ASPARAGUS SALAD)

Oyako Donburi (PARENTS AND CHILDREN RICE)
Tōfu To Shungiku No Misoshiru (MISO SOUP WITH *SHUNGIKU*)
Kyūri To Moyashi No Goma-ae (CUCUMBER AND SOY BEAN SPROUTS
    WITH SESAME SEEDS)

Dinners

Spring

Gohan (PLAIN BOILED RICE)
Tōfu To Wakame No Suimono (CLEAR SOUP WITH OKRA AND BEAN CURD)
Toriniku Dango No Terini (GLAZED CHICKEN BALLS)
Takenoko No Tamago-Toji (EGGS WITH BAMBOO SHOOTS)
Na-No-Hana No Gama-ae (RAPE BLOSSOMS WITH SESAME SEEDS)

Summer

Tempura (BATTER-FRIED SHRIMP AND VEGETABLES)
Toriniku No Oroshi-ae (CHICKEN AND VEGETABLE SALAD)
Okura To Hari Shōga No Suimono (CLEAR SOUP WITH OKRA
   AND GINGER)
Gohan (PLAIN BOILED RICE)
Sokuseki Misozuke (INSTANT-PICKLED VEGETABLES WITH BEAN PASTE)

Autumn

Hirame No Kohaku-age To Ebi No Iga-age (NOODLE-COATED SHRIMP
   WITH FRIED SOLE)
Nasu No Misoni (EGGPLANT WITH BEAN PASTE)
Gohan (PLAIN BOILED RICE)
Noppei-jiru (VEGETABLE AND FRIED BEAN CURD SOUP)

Winter

Karei No Karaage (DEEP-FRIED CRISPY FLOUNDER)
Kūya-mushi (BEAN CURD, CHICKEN AND VEGETABLE CUSTARD)
Gohan (PLAIN BOILED RICE)
Furofuki Daikon (STEAMED WHITE RADISH)
Toriniku To Shiraganegi No Suimono (CLEAR CHICKEN SOUP)

Any Time

Gyūniku No Teriyaki (GLAZED BEEF)
Saya-Ingen No Goma-ae (GREEN BEANS WITH WHITE SESAME SEEDS)
Gohan (PLAIN BOILED RICE)
Shimetama No Sumashi (CLEAR SOUP WITH EGG THREADS)
Karashi Renkon (STUFFED LOTUS ROOT)

Special

Sekihan (PINK RICE WITH RED BEANS)
Musubikisu No Suimono (CLEAR SOUP WITH SMELT)
Kodai No Shioyaki (SALT-BROILED PORGY)
Kōyadōfu To Shiitake No Takiawase (DRIED BEAN CURD WITH
    VEGETABLES)
Kōhaku-Namasu (WHITE RADISH AND CARROT SALAD)

Appetizers

The Japanese kitchen is most versatile with its appetizers whether they are to be served as a first course or as an accompaniment to drinks. Meat, poultry, shellfish and vegetables are all used. Easy to make and requiring little in the way of hard-to-find ingredients, they are a welcome addition to anyone's kitchen repertoire. They also provide a useful opportunity for anyone unfamiliar with Japanese food to experiment, perhaps trying them out as cocktail foods followed by a Western meal.

In Japan, appetizers are traditionally served with *sake;* their flavors are chosen to complement the taste of the drink. *Sashimi* (raw fish) presented in the Fish and Shellfish chapter, may also be served as an appetizer although it is usually a main dish.

Tairagai No Sanshō Yaki
BROILED SCALLOPS WITH JAPANESE PEPPER

4 large scallops	1½ tablespoons *sake*
2 tablespoons soy sauce	*Kona sanshō* (ground Japanese
1 teaspoon *mirin*	pepper)

Wash and dry the scallops and halve them horizontally.

Combine the soy sauce, *mirin* and *sake* in a small saucepan, bring to a boil uncovered over moderate heat, remove from the heat and cool. Add the scallops and marinate for 5 minutes. Lift out the scallops, pat dry and thread onto a steel skewer.

Grill over fairly high heat, 4 or 5 inches from the heat. Using a pastry brush, paint the scallops with the soy mixture 2 or 3 times while cooking, about 5 minutes in all, turning frequently. The scallops can also be broiled.

Place the cooked scallops in 4 small individual bowls, or on one larger platter. Sprinkle with the Japanese pepper. In Japan each serving would be garnished with a whole pepper leaf and one finely chopped leaf.

This is an appetizer dish and these are often placed in the center of the table and guests help themselves with chopsticks directly from the platter. SERVES 4.

Gyūniku No Tsukudani
SPICED BEEF

10 ounces lean beef, such as	2 tablespoons *mirin*
rump, round or chuck	2 tablespoons *sake*
2-inch cube fresh ginger root	1 teaspoon sugar
⅓ cup water	½ teaspoon msg
3 tablespoons soy sauce	

Cut the beef into thin slices, then chop coarsely. Peel the ginger root, then slice very thinly.

In a saucepan combine ⅓ cup water, the soy sauce, *mirin, sake,* sugar and msg and bring to a boil. Add the ginger and cook for a minute or two so that the stock is flavored with the ginger. Add the beef, and simmer on moderate heat, uncovered. Stir from time to time and cook about 15 minutes or until the liquid has evaporated and the meat is tender. The meat should not be dry but quite moist. Serve at room temperature or slightly chilled. SERVES 4.

This dish is also a great favorite for lunch boxes and may be served as a main dish.

Torikimo No Kushiyaki
GRILLED CHICKEN LIVERS

10 ounces chicken livers
4 scallions, trimmed, using only the white part
4 tablespoons soy sauce
2 tablespoons *mirin*

1 tablespoon *sake*
1 tablespoon sugar
Kona sanshō (ground Japanese pepper)

Wash the chicken livers in 2 or 3 changes of cold water, drain, and quarter the livers if large; if small halve them. Cut each scallion into 4 slices. Thread the pieces of liver, alternating with the scallions, on 8 small (about 5-inch) metal skewers. Set aside.

In a small saucepan combine the soy sauce, *mirin, sake* and sugar and bring to a boil. Remove from the heat immediately and set aside to use as a glazing sauce.

Heat a grill and grill the skewers over high heat, about 6 inches from the heat, for 2 minutes on each side. Remove and pour some of the sauce over the skewers and grill again for ½ minute. Repeat until all the sauce is used up. Sprinkle with Japanese pepper. Serve hot and eat from the skewers, or take off the skewers and eat with chopsticks. Or the livers may be broiled. SERVES 4.

Toriniku No Kushiage

SKEWERED CHICKEN

10 ounces skinned and boned chicken breast	Flour
	1 egg
4 large scallions, trimmed, using only white part	½ cup water
	¾ cup sifted cake flour
Salt	Vegetable oil

Cut the chicken into 24 slices, each about 1 inch long. Cut the scallions into 16 slices, each about 1 inch long. On each of 8 bamboo skewers alternately thread 3 pieces of chicken and 2 pieces of scallion. Sprinkle with salt, then with flour to coat lightly.

Break the egg into a bowl and stir with chopsticks until well blended but not foamy. Add ½ cup water to the egg, mixing well. Sift the cake flour into the egg and mix lightly into a batter.

Heat 2 to 3 inches of oil in a *tempura* pan or a saucepan to 345°F. on a frying thermometer, or until bubbles form on wooden chopsticks stirred in the oil. Dip the skewers in the batter, coating the chicken and scallion pieces thoroughly, then drop into the oil and cook for 4 or 5 minutes, or until very lightly browned, turning once. Drain on the rack of the *tempura* pan or on paper towels.

Serve with *kona sanshō* (Japanese pepper) and salt, or mustard and soy sauce, or *ponzu* (citrus vinegar) as dipping sauces. Eat by hand, holding the end of the skewer. SERVES 4.

Asparagus No Moromizoe
ASPARAGUS WITH MALTED BEAN PASTE

12 medium-sized stalks green
   asparagus, about ½ pound
Salt
1 tablespoon *usukuchi shōyu*
   (light soy sauce)

2 tablespoons *moromi miso* (soy
   bean paste with malted rice)

Wash the asparagus and cut off the hard ends. Cook in boiling salted water, uncovered, for 8 minutes, or until tender. Lift out onto a *zaru* (bamboo plate) or onto a chopping board and fan vigorously to cool it to lukewarm for 2 or 3 minutes. This keeps the asparagus an attractive bright green in color. Check that there is no hard part left, and trim the asparagus if necessary. Pour the soy sauce over the asparagus mixing lightly with chopsticks. Arrange the stalks on 4 platters or plates and put ½ tablespoon of the malted bean paste on top of the asparagus in the center. To eat spread the bean paste with chopsticks over the full length of the asparagus and eat with chopsticks. SERVES 4.

   This is a spring dish and can be served either as a vegetable dish or as an appetizer.

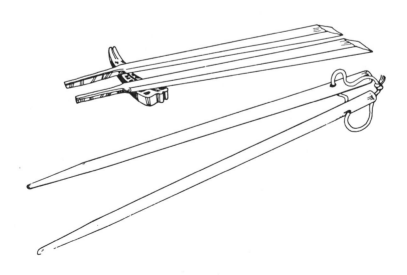

Denraku

BEAN CURD WITH BEAN PASTE

2 *momen tōfu,* each weighing about ½ pound
3 tablespoons white *miso* (bean paste)
5 tablespoons sugar

2½ tablespoons *mirin*
1 tablespoon *sake*
3 tablespoons red *miso* (bean paste)
Poppy seeds

Rinse the bean curd in cold water, then wrap in a kitchen cloth, place on a flat surface, cover with a weight such as a plate or light board and leave for 20 minutes. Unwrap and cut each bean curd into 4 lengthwise slices, then cut each slice in half, crosswise, to make 16 in all. Place the bean curd pieces in a shallow bowl and put into a steamer over boiling water, tightly cover, turn heat to low and steam for 10 minutes.

In the top of a double boiler over hot water, or in a small saucepan over very low heat, mix together the white bean paste, 3 tablespoons of the sugar, 1 tablespoon of the *mirin* and ½ tablespoon of the *sake.* Stir until the mixture is smooth and heated through. Do not let it boil.

In the top of another double boiler over hot water, or in a small saucepan over very low heat, mix together the red bean paste, the remaining 2 tablespoons of sugar, 1½ tablespoons of *mirin* and ½ tablespoon of *sake,* stirring constantly until the mixture is smooth and heated through. Do not let it boil.

Remove the bean curd pieces from the steamer and run bamboo skewers lengthwise through them, 2 to a skewer. Spread half of the skewered *tōfu* with the red bean paste mix, the other half of them with the white bean paste mix. Sprinkle the red bean paste with poppy seeds. In Japan the white would be garnished with a leaf of *sansho* (Japanese pepper). Put 1 red and 1 white bean curd on each of 8 plates. Eat from the skewers. SERVES 8.

Kinugoshi tōfu (silky bean curd) may also be used for this dish.

Shiitake No Tsumeage
DEEP-FRIED STUFFED MUSHROOMS

As fresh Japanese mushrooms are not available, use local mushrooms.

12 medium-sized mushrooms
¼ pound peeled, cleaned raw
   shrimp
Salt
Katakuriko starch *or* cornstarch
⅓ cup all-purpose flour
½ cup water

Vegetable oil
⅓ cup *dashi* (soup stock)
2 tablespoons *mirin*
3 tablespoons soy sauce
⅓ cup grated *daikon* (white
   radish)

Rinse the mushrooms, remove the stems and pat dry. Chop the shrimp to a paste with the back of a knife, and season with salt. Sprinkle the inside of the mushrooms with the starch and stuff with the shrimp mixture.

In a bowl mix together the flour and ¼ cup of *katakuriko* starch and stir in ½ cup water, mixing lightly with chopsticks.

In a *tempura* pan or saucepan, heat 1½ to 2 inches of oil to between 345° and 350°F. on a frying thermometer. Coat the stuffed mushrooms with the batter and fry, a few at a time, until lightly golden, about 2 minutes, turning them once or twice. Drain on the rack of the *tempura* pan or on paper towels.

In a small saucepan combine the soup stock, *mirin* and soy sauce, bring to a boil over moderate heat, and pour into a small bowl.

Lightly squeeze out the grated radish. Arrange the mushrooms with a mound of radish on a platter. Dip the mushrooms into the sauce and eat with the radish as an appetizer. SERVES 4.

Karashi Renkon
STUFFED LOTUS ROOT

1 medium *renkon* (lotus root), 6 to 7 inches long (about 9 ounces)
2 cups boiling water
2 teaspoons rice vinegar
1⅔ cups *dashi* (soup stock)
¼ teaspoon salt
¼ teaspoon soy·sauce
½ tablespoon *mirin*
3 tablespoons dry mustard, preferably Japanese
3 tablespoons white *miso* (bean paste)
1 teaspoon sugar
1 egg yolk
2 or 3 dashes msg
½ egg
½ cup sifted flour
Vegetable oil

Peel the lotus root and drop into a saucepan with the 2 cups of boiling water and the vinegar and boil for 5 minutes. Drain. In the saucepan combine the soup stock, salt, soy sauce and *mirin;* add the drained lotus root which should be covered by the liquid, and cook for about 5 minutes, or until tender. Lift out of the cooking liquid onto a plate and allow to cool.

Mix the mustard with 2 to 3 tablespoons of hot water to make a thick paste. Add the bean paste, sugar, egg yolk and msg and mix well. Using chopsticks and fingers, push the mustard mixture into the holes that run the length of the vegetable in a flower pattern. Sprinkle the stuffed lotus root with a little flour.

Stir the ½ egg, then mix with enough cold water to make ⅓ cup. Add the ½ cup of sifted flour, mixing lightly with chopsticks. Coat the lotus root with this batter.

In a *tempura* pan or saucepan heat enough oil to cover the lotus root to 300°F. on a frying thermometer, or until bubbles form on wooden chopsticks stirred in the oil. Put the prepared lotus root into the hot oil and fry about 6 minutes, turning it 2 or 3 times, until it is lightly golden. Lift out, drain on paper towels and cut into ½-inch slices. Arrange the slices on 4 small plates and serve as an appetizer. SERVES 4 TO 6.

VARIATION: *Karashi Shiitake* (Stuffed Mushrooms). Stuff mushroom caps with the mustard mixture, dip in batter and deep fry for 2 or 3 minutes.

Ebi No Shibaage
NOODLE-COATED SHRIMP

4 medium-sized fresh shrimp
Salt
½ teaspoon *sake*
Cornstarch
1 egg yolk, lightly beaten
1 ounce *sōmen* (thin wheat noodles)

4 strips *nori* (dried laver seaweed) ½ inch wide by 4 inches long
Vegetable oil

Peel the shrimp, leaving the tails on. Cut the end of the tails straight across as this end part has water in it. Using a toothpick, remove the intestinal vein. Cut a small lengthwise slit on the inside of the shrimp at the head end so that the shrimp can be straightened out. Sprinkle with salt and the *sake*.

Dip the shrimp in cornstarch, shaking to remove the excess. Coat the shrimp thoroughly with the egg yolk. Break the noodles into thirds and roll each shrimp in the noodles with the little pieces lengthwise, so that the shrimp look like little bundles of twigs. Put a strip of seaweed around the middle of each bundle and stick it in place with a little egg yolk.

In a *tempura* pan, or a saucepan, pour about 3 inches of oil and bring to moderate heat, 350°F. on a frying thermometer. Drop the prepared shrimp into the hot oil and cook for 1 or 2 minutes, or until the noodles are golden. Drain on the rack of the *tempura* pan or on paper towels. Serve on small plates. SERVES 4.

Soups

Soup plays an important and versatile role in the Japanese kitchen. Clear soup, with its infinite variety, is usually served at the beginning of a meal. Then there are the fermented bean paste soups, *miso shiru,* which may be served at the beginning or end of a meal and always with the traditional breakfast. And the thick soups with meat, poultry or fish with vegetables are almost a meal in themselves, needing only the addition of rice and pickles or a salad.

Dashi, the stock on which most Japanese soups are based, differs completely from Western chicken or beef stock. It is based on *kombu* (sometimes called tangle), which is a seaweed of the kelp family, and flaked *katsuobushi,* dried bonito. It is simple to make, but like everything else in this kitchen, it demands attention to detail. If the seaweed is left in until the water boils, the stock will be bitter, and if the bonito is cooked too long the stock will be fishy.

The clear soups achieve their variety through a range of garnishes which not only lend subtle flavor to the soup, but also please the eye. They should, if possible, be served in lacquered soup bowls with lids or in the handsome plastic imitations available. Usually red or black inside, these bowls show the garnish in the limpid gold broth to its best advantage, adding the dimension of beauty for which Japanese food is famous. It is polite usage to provide this type of lidded soup bowl for guests; it keeps the soup warm since the entire meal, on special occasions, is served on individual trays at the same time. At home, families often dispense with this refinement and use any small, cup-size (8-ounce) china bowls.

The *miso* soups are more robust in flavor, the fermented bean paste having a very characteristic taste. The taste is not difficult for the Western palate to appreciate, however. In fact, whether present in soup or other dishes, it is one of the flavors that most enchants me.

Chopsticks are used to eat soups. Solids are lifted out with the chopsticks and when all the solids are eaten, one drinks the liquid from the bowl. Spoons are never used.

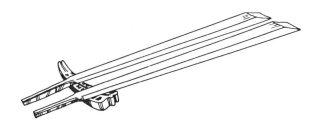

Dashi
JAPANESE SOUP STOCK

5¼ cups cold water
4-inch square *kombu* (dried kelp)

½ cup flaked *katsuobushi* (dried bonito)

Pour the water into a medium-sized saucepan. Clean the *kombu* with a damp cloth and cut into a ½-inch fringe. Drop the *kombu* into the saucepan, let the water come to just under a boil over moderate heat, uncovered. Lift out and reserve the *kombu*. Bring the water again to a boil, stir in the *katsuobushi,* remove from the heat and let it stand for 2 or 3 minutes. Strain through a double thickness of damp cheesecloth or a kitchen cloth and set the *katsuobushi* aside. The stock is now ready to be used. MAKES 4 CUPS.

Both the *kombu* and the *katsuobushi* may be used to make second soup stock for *miso* (bean paste) soup or for cooking vegetables. The stock will keep, refrigerated, for a day or two.

To make second soup stock, follow *dashi* directions exactly, using both the seaweed and the dried bonito flakes a second time, but reducing the amount of water to 3 to 3½ cups. Strain the stock through a double thickness of cheesecloth and discard the solids.

Butajiru
THICK PORK SOUP

10 to 12 ounces boneless pork loin, coarsely chopped

2 burdock roots, about 7 ounces, scraped and dropped into cold water

3 small *boniato* (white sweet potatoes), about 7 ounces, peeled

1 medium carrot, scraped

1 large potato, peeled and dropped into cold water

3-inch slice *daikon* (Japanese white radish), peeled, *or* 2 small white turnips, peeled

1-inch cube fresh ginger root, peeled and thinly sliced

7 tablespoons white *miso* (bean paste)

5 tablespoons red *miso* (bean paste)

2 scallions, using white and green parts, cut into ½-inch slices

Put the pork loin into a colander and pour boiling water over it. Drain and rinse in cold water.

Cut the burdock roots, sweet potatoes, carrot and potato *rangiri*, that is cut on a diagonal, turn half round and cut on the opposite diagonal into about 1-inch slices. Cut the radish or turnips into ½-inch slices, stack the slices and cut in half. Put the pork into a large saucepan with 7 cups cold water, cover, bring to a boil and skim. Add the vegetables and ginger to the pork, bring to a boil, lower the heat and simmer, covered, for 10 minutes. Mix the bean pastes until smooth with a little stock from the kettle, stir into the soup and cook slowly, at just under a simmer, for 2 hours. Just before the soup is done, add the scallions. Pour into 6 or 8 soup bowls and have *sanshō* powder (Japanese pepper) or *shichimi-tōgarashi* (seven-flavor spice) on the table to be used as liked. SERVES 6 TO 8.

Noppei-jiru
VEGETABLE AND FRIED BEAN CURD SOUP 1923905

4 *shiitake* (dried Japanese mushrooms)
Sugar
½ medium carrot, using thick end
½ pound *daikon* (Japanese white radish)
5 small taro
½ *gobō* (burdock root), scraped and dropped into cold water
1 *namaage* (type of fried bean curd) *or* 2 pieces *aburaage* (fried bean curd)

¼ pound *warabi* (cooked, packaged fernbrake, bracken), optional
6 ounces *shirataki* (devil's tongue noodles)
3 cups *dashi* (soup stock)
1 teaspoon salt
1 tablespoon soy sauce
Dash msg
1 teaspoon arrowroot
1 tablespoon chopped flat Italian parsley

Soak the mushrooms for 30 minutes in warm water with a pinch of sugar, squeeze out, remove hard stems and cut into quarters. Thinly slice the scraped or peeled carrot and white radish, stack the slices and cut into quarters. Peel the taro and slice thinly. Slice the burdock root and put back in the cold water as it discolors very quickly. Rinse the fried bean curd in hot water. If using *namaage* cut into ½-inch cubes. If using *aburaage* halve and cut into ½-inch slices. If using fernbrake, rinse it and cut into 1-inch slices.

Drop all the vegetables into a saucepan of boiling water and boil for 2 minutes. Drain and set aside. Drop the noodles into boiling water for 2 minutes, drain and chop into 1-inch pieces.

Pour the stock into a saucepan, add all the vegetables, the bean curd and noodles and simmer, covered, until tender, 10 to 15 minutes. Season with the salt, soy sauce and msg. Mix the arrowroot with a teaspoon of cold water, stir into the soup and cook until it is lightly thickened. Add the parsley. Pour the soup into 4 bowls. SERVES 4.

Kenchinjiru
VEGETABLE SOUP

1 tightly packed cup raw spinach
½ medium carrot, scraped
5 small taro, peeled and thinly
  sliced
1 *momen tōfu* (bean curd)
  weighing about 8 ounces

2 tablespoons vegetable oil
3 cups *dashi* (soup stock)
4 tablespoons *miso* (bean paste)

Wash the spinach and drop into a large saucepan of boiling salted water and boil for 1 minute. Drain and rinse 3 times in cold water, squeeze out the moisture, form into a roll, and slice into 1-inch pieces. Set aside.

Cut the carrot *rangiri,* that is cut on a diagonal, turn half round and cut on the opposite diagonal into about 1-inch slices. Cook the carrot and the taro in boiling water for 5 minutes. Drain. Rinse the bean curd and dry with a kitchen cloth, then crush in the cloth.

Heat the oil in a saucepan and add the bean curd, sauté over high heat for a minute or two, then add the carrot and taro and stir to mix. Add the soup stock, reduce the heat, cover and simmer for 20 minutes. Mix the bean paste until smooth with a little stock and stir it into the soup; cook only long enough to heat through but do not let it boil. Divide the spinach among 4 soup bowls and pour in the hot soup. SERVES 4.

If taro is not available, use potatoes.

Kakitama-Jiru
EGG DROP SOUP

2⅓ cups *dashi* (soup stock)
¾ teaspoon salt
1 teaspoon soy sauce
1 tablespoon *katakuriko or*
  cornstarch mixed with 2
  tablespoons cold water
1 egg, beaten and stirred with 1
  tablespoon cold soup stock

Small piece fresh ginger root
Lime peel
Nori (dried laver seaweed),
  optional
Mitsuba leaves (trefoil), optional

In a saucepan bring the stock to a boil, covered. Season with salt and soy sauce and stir in the *katakuriko* mixture over medium heat and cook, stirring, until the soup is lightly thickened and smooth. Lower the heat to keep the soup at a bare simmer then pour egg mixture through a flat skimmer or a sieve, moving it in a circle over the soup. Cook for a few seconds longer to set the egg which will be in threads. Remove from the heat. Pour the soup into 4 bowls. Grate the giner and squeeze about 4 drops of juice into each soup bowl. Garnish with the lime peel cut into 4 V-shapes to represent pine needles. If preferred toast a small sheet of dried laver on both sides for a few seconds over a gas flame or electric burner, crumble it and sprinkle it over the soup, or garnish with a trefoil leaf. SERVES 4.

Okura To Hari Shōga No Suimono
CLEAR SOUP WITH OKRA AND GINGER

2 small okra	½ teaspoon salt
Boiling salted water	¼ teaspoon *usukuchi shōyu*
½-inch cube ginger	(light soy)
1-inch square *kombu* (kelp)	

Drop the okra into boiling salted water and cook, uncovered, for 5 minutes. Drop the okra into cold water to cool. This gives it a very bright green color. Trim the ends and slice into 6 pieces. Set aside. Peel the ginger, slice it with the grain, then cut it into very thin strips. Cover with cold water for a few minutes. Drain and set aside.

In a saucepan bring 2 cups water to a boil. Clean the *kombu* (kelp) with a damp cloth, then holding it with chopsticks or tongs, swish it back and forth in the boiling water 5 or 6 times. This makes a very light, delicate stock. Add the salt and light soy sauce. Divide the okra and ginger among 4 soup bowls and pour in the hot stock. SERVES 4.

This is a very pretty soup especially if it is served in black lacquer bowls.

Tōfu To Okura No Suimono
CLEAR SOUP WITH OKRA AND BEAN CURD

4 small okra
Boiling salted water
2 cups *dashi* (soup stock)
½ teaspoon salt

¼ teaspoon *usukuchi shōyu* (light soy)
1 *kinugoshi tōfu* (silky bean curd) weighing about 6 ounces

Drop the okra into boiling salted water and cook, uncovered, for 5 minutes. Drain. Trim the ends and chop finely. Put into a bowl and stir briskly round with chopsticks for a minute or two to release the sticky content. Set aside.

Heat the soup stock with the salt and the light soy. Cut the bean curd into quarters and add to the soup stock. Remove from the heat and let stand for a few minutes to heat the bean curd through. Carefully lift the bean curd into 4 soup bowls. Top with the okra. Reheat the soup and pour into the bowls, taking care not to disturb the okra. SERVES 4.

Tōfu To Wakame No Suimono
CLEAR SOUP WITH BEAN CURD AND LOBE-LEAF SEAWEED

4 8-inch fronds (½ cup soaked) *wakame* (lobe-leaf seaweed)
1 *kinugoshi tōfu* (silky bean curd), weighing 8 to 10 ounces

3 cups *dashi* (soup stock)
Salt
1 teaspoon *usukuchi shōyu* (light soy sauce)

Soak the seaweed in cold water for about 10 minutes. Drain, squeeze lightly, cut away any hard ribs and chop coarsely. Set aside. Rinse the bean curd, slice it in half horizontally, then cut into ½-inch cubes. Pour the soup stock into a saucepan, season to taste with salt, add the soy sauce, bean curd and seaweed and bring to a boil. Lower the heat and cook just long enough to heat the bean curd and seaweed through. Pour into 4 soup bowls. SERVES 4.

Shimetama No Sumashi

CLEAR SOUP WITH EGG THREADS

3 eggs
Boiling water
8 leaves *shungiku* (see glossary)
  or raw spinach, blanched
1 ounce *harusame* (bean gelatin
  noodles)

3 cups *dashi* (soup stock)
¾ teaspoon salt
¾ teaspoon soy sauce
2 to 3 dashes msg
4 small strips lime peel

Break the eggs into a bowl and stir with chopsticks until they are well mixed but not foamy. Pour the eggs, gradually and gently, over the surface of 2 cups of boiling water in a saucepan. As soon as the eggs are set, strain through a sieve lined with a double thickness of dampened cheesecloth. When the egg threads are cool enough to handle, squeeze out the excess moisture. Lay the cheesecloth on top of a *sudare* (bamboo mat). Form the eggs into a roll on top of the cheesecloth and roll up, squeezing gently to firm the shape. This is the *shimetama* of the title, literally squeezed eggs. Unroll and cut into 4 slices. Place a slice of egg in each of 4 soup bowls and top with the *shungiku* or spinach.

Soak the noodles in hot water until they are softened, a matter of minutes. Drain and transfer to a saucepan with the stock, salt, soy sauce and msg and bring to a boil. Pour the hot soup into the bowls over the eggs and garnish with the lime peel. SERVES 4.

Sōmen No Hiyashisuimono
CLEAR SOUP WITH NOODLES

1 ounce *sōmen* (thin wheat noodles)
Boiling water
3 cups *dashi* (soup stock)
Salt
1 teaspoon *usukuchi shōyu* (light soy sauce)
6 large green beans

Put the noodles into a medium-sized saucepan of boiling water and cook, uncovered, for 5 minutes. Bring to a boil again, add 1 cup cold water, bring back to a boil, drain. Rinse in cold water, drain, and set aside.

In a saucepan bring to a boil the soup stock, 1 teaspoon of salt, or to taste, and the light soy sauce. Set aside to cool.

Drop the green beans into boiling salted water and cook, uncovered, for 5 minutes. Drain, rinse in cold water and cool. Trim the ends and cut each of the beans into 3 diagonal slices.

Divide the noodles among 4 soup bowls, add the beans and soup stock. This is a summer soup which looks very cool and attractive. SERVES 4.

Toriniku To Shiraganegi No Suimono
CLEAR CHICKEN SOUP

¼-pound skined and boned chicken breast, cut into 8 diagonal slices
1 teaspoon *sake*
Salt
1 teaspoon *katakuriko* or cornstarch
1½ scallions, trimmed, using white part, cut lengthwise into fine strips
3½ cups *dashi* (soup stock)
1 teaspoon soy sauce
1 teaspoon salt
⅛ teaspoon msg
4 slivers lime peel

Place the chicken in a small bowl with the *sake* and salt to taste. Sprinkle with the *katakuriko* and set aside. Drop the scallions in cold water to crisp for a few minutes, drain and squeeze out in a kitchen cloth. Set aside. Pour the stock into a saucepan, bring to a boil, add the chicken pieces and cook, uncovered, for 2 minutes. Add the soy sauce and msg and 1 teaspoon salt. Pour into 4 soup bowls. Garnish with the scallion strips and the lime peel which may be cut into V-shapes to represent pine needles. SERVES 4.

Toriniku No Tsumirejiru
CLEAR SOUP WITH CHICKEN

3-inch square *kombu* (kelp)
¼ pound finely ground chicken
1 tablespoon flour
2 teaspoons *miso* (bean paste)
1 *kikurage* (jelly mushroom), soaked in warm water about 10 minutes
2 medium-sized fresh mushrooms, thinly sliced

1 teaspoon salt
1 teaspoon *usukuchi shōyu* (light soy sauce)
2 to 3 dashes msg
1 scallion, using white and green parts, sliced diagonally
½-inch cube fresh ginger root, grated

Clean the seaweed (kelp) with a damp cloth and cut into a ½-inch fringe. Place in a saucepan with 4 cups cold water and bring to a boil, uncovered, over moderate heat. Just before the water boils, remove the seaweed and set the stock aside.

Grind or pound the chicken in a *suribachi* (mortar) until light and fluffy. Add the flour and bean paste, pounding to mix well. Squeeze out the jelly mushroom, slice it finely and add to the chicken mixture. Form the mixture into 12 small balls and simmer in the stock, with the fresh mushrooms, for 2 minutes. Add the salt, light soy sauce, msg and scallion to the stock and heat through. Pour into 4 soup bowls, placing 3 chicken balls in each. Squeeze a little juice from the grated ginger into each bowl. SERVES 4.

Saba No Semba Jiru
CLEAR MACKEREL SOUP

This is an old recipe. It comes from Semba, a business quarter in the heart of Osaka, known for many old stores.

1 fillet of mackerel, about 6 ounces
Salt
1½-inch slice *daikon* (white radish), about 3 ounces, peeled
4-by-2-inch piece *kombu* (kelp)
Soy sauce (optional)
Lime peel cut into 4 V's

Slice the mackerel fillet diagonally into quarters. Sprinkle with salt on both sides and let stand for 30 minutes. Rinse, drop into boiling water for 30 seconds, lift out, rinse in cold water, drain and set aside.

Cut the peeled radish as thinly as possible as one would peel an apple, roll up and slice thinly. Or slice thinly, stack the slices and cut into julienne strips. Drop into boiling water and simmer, uncovered, for 3 minutes. Drain.

Clean the seaweed (kelp) with a damp cloth and cut it into a ½-inch fringe. Place in the bottom of a medium-sized saucepan, add ½ teaspoon salt, mackerel, radish and 3 cups water. Cover and bring to a boil over medium heat, removing the seaweed just before the water boils. Skim, reduce the heat and cook for about 5 minutes, uncovered. Taste the soup and add a little soy sauce, if necessary. Pour into 4 bowls and garnish with the lime. Serve hot. This soup has a very fresh, natural flavor. SERVES 4.

Shiromizakana No Suimono
CLEAR FISH SOUP

¼ pound red snapper, or any white fish, cleaned and cut into 8 diagonal slices
Salt
2 cups raw spinach, tightly packed
3¼ cups *dashi* (soup stock)
¾ teaspoon *usukuchi shōyu* (light soy sauce)
⅛ teaspoon msg
4 slivers lime peel

Drop the fish into a saucepan of boiling salted water, bring back to a boil and simmer, uncovered for 2 minutes; add 1 teaspoon salt and simmer the fish, uncovered, for another 2 minutes. Drain and place 2 pieces in each of 4 soup bowls. Drop the spinach into a large saucepan of boiling salted water and simmer for 2 minutes. Drain, rinse in cold water, drain and squeeze lightly. Chop the spinach coarsely and divide among the soup bowls. Heat the stock with the light soy sauce and msg and salt to taste. Pour the stock into the bowls. Garnish with the lime peel which may be cut into V-shapes to represent pine needles. SERVES 4.

Hamaguri No Sumashi-Jiru
CLEAR CLAM SOUP

8 Little Neck or Cherrystone
   clams
Salt
1 scallion, trimmed
Lime peel
4-inch square *kombu* (kelp)

3¼ cups water
1 tablespoon *sake*
⅛ teaspoon *usukuchi shōyu*
   (light soy sauce)

Soak the clams in 2 cups cold water and 1 tablespoon salt overnight to get rid of any sand. Scrub thoroughly, rinse and drain.

Cut the scallion into 1½-inch lengthwise strips, drop into cold water to crisp, then squeeze out in a kitchen towel and set aside. Cut the lime peel into 4 V-shapes to represent pine needles. Set aside.

Clean the seaweed (kelp) with a damp cloth and put into a medium-sized saucepan with 3¼ cups water, bring to a boil over moderate heat, removing the seaweed just before the water boils. Add the clams and when they begin to open add the *sake,* reduce the heat and skim. Simmer for 3 or 4 minutes, then add ¾ teaspoon salt and the light soy sauce. Place 2 clams in their shells in each of 4 soup bowls, pour on the broth and garnish with the scallions and lime peel. SERVES 4.

This is a popular dish for New Year's Day and for wedding feasts If the clams when opened still have the shells joined at the hinge it is regarded as a symbol of a happy marriage, woman and man united.

Musubikisu No Suimono
CLEAR SOUP WITH SMELT

4 medium-sized smelt, weighing
   together about 10 to 12 ounces,
   scaled and cleaned
Boiling salted water
1-inch piece cucumber
3 cups *dashi* (soup stock)

¾ teaspoon salt
¾ teaspoon *usukuchi shōyu*
   (light soy sauce)
Dash msg
Lime peel

Cut the heads off the smelt and discard them. Split the fish open and remove the backbone, any small bones and the fins, taking care not to break the skin. Rinse and drain. Cut the fish along the line of the backbone about three quarters up its length, starting at the tail end and leaving the fish in one piece for the remaining quarter of its length. Tie the two pieces in a loose knot. Drop the fish into boiling salted water, bring back to a boil and simmer, uncovered, for 2 minutes. Lift out the fish and place one in each of 4 soup bowls.

Peel the piece of cucumber in alternate strips. Scrape out the seeds with a vegetable peeler and cut into 8 crosswise slices. Drop into boiling water for a few seconds. Lift out and drop immediately into cold water. Drain; add 2 slices to each soup bowl.

In a saucepan combine the soup stock, salt, light soy sauce and msg and bring to a boil. Cut the lime peel into 4 V-shapes to represent pine needles and place one on top of each smelt. Pour the soup into the bowls. SERVES 4.

Cooked sliced okra may be used instead of the cucumber, in which case drop 4 small okra into boiling salted water and cook 5 minutes. Drain, trim and slice.

This is a congratulatory dish for a couple. It is very graceful to serve it at a wedding anniversary dinner.

Satsuma-Jiru

MISO SOUP WITH MIXED VEGETABLES

This rich, thick soup takes its name from the region of Satsuma, now called Kyushu. The sweet potato, a main ingredient in the soup, was first cultivated in Peru in 2500 B.C. It was taken to other parts of the world by the Portuguese and Spanish, reaching Kyushu in the 17th century. The soup is very comforting on a cold winter day.

8 ounces chicken, boned, skinned and cut into bite-sized pieces

1-inch slice *daikon* (Japanese white radish), peeled

½ medium-sized carrot, peeled

½ medium-sized *boniato* (white sweet potato), peeled

4 inches *gobō* (burdock root), scraped and cut into slivers and dropped into cold water

3¼ cups second soup stock *or* water

2 tablespoons red *miso* (bean paste

1 tablespoon white *miso* (bean paste)

1 scallion, using white and green parts, coarsely chopped

Drop the chicken pieces into boiling water, blanch for 10 seconds, drain and set aside. Slice the radish very thinly, stack the slices and cut them into quarters. This is called cutting *ichōgiri* which means to look like a ginkgo leaf, that is, fan-shaped. Cut the carrot and sweet potato the same way. Cut the burdock root into slivers (*sasagaki*).

Pour the soup stock into a saucepan and add the chicken; simmer, covered, for 10 minutes, then add the radish, carrot, sweet potato and burdock root and cook until the vegetables are tender, about 15 minutes. Mix the bean pastes until smooth with a little stock and add to the soup with the scallion. Cook just long enough to heat through, but do not let it boil. Divide the soup among 4 soup bowls. SERVES 4.

Cooked boneless pork loin may be used instead of chicken; both potato and winter squash may be added as well as a piece of *aburaage* (fried bean curd), halved and cut into crosswise slices.

Have white pepper, chili pepper and *shichimi-tōgarashi* (seven-flavor spice) on the table.

Tōfu To Shungiku No Misoshiru
MISO SOUP WITH SHUNGIKU

4 cups loosely packed *shungiku* (see glossary) *or* raw spinach
Boiling salted water
2⅓ cups *dashi* (soup stock)
2 tablespoons red *miso* (bean paste)

1½ tablespoons white *miso* (bean paste)
8-ounce *momen tōfu* (bean curd) or *kinugoshi tōfu* (silky bean curd), cut into 1-inch slices

Drop the *shungiku* or spinach into boiling salted water and blanch for 1 minute, rinse twice in cold water and drain, squeezing out any moisture. Form into a roll and cut into ½-inch slices.

In a saucepan combine the soup stock with the red and white bean pastes mixed with a little stock until smooth. Add the *shungiku* and the bean curd. Heat through gently without letting the mixture come to a boil. Pour into soup bowls. SERVES 4.

Wakame Jiru
MISO SOUP WITH LOBE-LEAF SEAWEED

8 8-inch fronds *wakame* (lobe-leaf seaweed), 1 cup soaked
3 cups *dashi* (soup stock)
2½ tablespoons white *miso* (bean paste)
1½ tablespoons red *miso* (bean paste)

1 teaspoon soy sauce
1 scallion, using white and green parts, chopped
2 tablespoons flaked *katsuobushi* (dried bonito)

Soak the seaweed in cold water for about 10 minutes, drain, squeeze lightly, cut away any hard ribs and chop coarsely. Set aside. Heat the soup stock and add the bean pastes mixed until smooth with a little stock. Add the seaweed, soy sauce and scallion, stir to mix and heat through without letting the soup boil. Pour into 4 soup bowls and sprinkle with the bonito flakes. SERVES 4.

Kaki Dōfu Jiru

OYSTER AND BEAN CURD *MISO* SOUP

3½ cups *dashi* (soup stock)
1 tablespoon red *miso* (bean paste)
4 tablespoons white *miso* (bean paste)
1 piece *aburaage* (fried bean curd)
1 *momen tōfu* (bean curd), about 8 ounces

16 oysters (8 ounces, about, bulk shelled)
½ cup *seri* (Japanese parsley) *or* flat Italian parsley
Small piece fresh ginger root
Sanshō powder (Japanese pepper)

In a large saucepan heat the soup stock and add the red and white bean pastes mixed until smooth with a little soup stock. Rinse the fried bean curd in hot water, halve lengthwise and cut into ⅓-inch strips. Add to the soup. Rinse the bean curd, cut it into 1-inch cubes and add to the soup with the oysters, rinsed in cold salted water and drained. Cook just until the oysters plump, about ½ minute. Remove from the heat. Coarsely chop the parsley and add. Pour the soup into 4 soup bowls. Grate the ginger root and squeeze a few drops of ginger juice into each bowl, or sprinkle with Japanese pepper. SERVES 4.

Rice, Noodles and Sushi

RICE

Gohan translates as "honorable food"; certainly nothing is more important in the Japanese kitchen than rice since it is eaten morning, noon and night, in between or at any meal. It is not cooked with every grain separate, like the long-grain rice of India, since it would be impossible to eat with chopsticks. It is more like Chinese rice in consistency: not gummy, but holding together nicely.

Japanese rice is short-grain and in the U.S. is grown extensively in California. It is sold in all Japanese shops and in many supermarkets. The instructions for cooking it are precise and if followed faithfully promise good results. *Shinmai* or new rice, which is recently harvested rice marketed in late summer and autumn, is greatly esteemed by the Japanese. It behaves just a little differently from old rice, needing less water and a slightly shorter cooking time. However, reliable judgment comes with a little practice so that, old or new, perfect rice is easily attainable. Other ingredients such as *sake* are often added, and where rice is used as the main ingredient in a complex dish, precise instructions are given.

A Japanese electric rice cooker, available in U.S. Japanese stores, is a worthwhile investment since it takes the guesswork out of cooking rice. It will also keep the rice warm for hours, making it possible to cook it in advance.

Gohan

PLAIN BOILED RICE

1½ cups rice
1½ cups (plus 1 or 2 tablespoons)
   water

Thoroughly wash the rice in several changes of water until the water runs clear, then drain in a sieve for at least 30 minutes. Put into a heavy saucepan with a tightly fitting lid. Add the water. Cover and bring to a boil over high heat. Reduce the heat to moderate and cook for 5 to 6 minutes. Reduce the heat to very low and cook for 10 to 13 minutes. Raise the heat to high for 10 seconds, then let the rice stand, off the heat, for 10 minutes. Stir with a *shamoji* (wooden spatula) and serve. If the rice is not to be served immediately, cover with a kitchen cloth, then the saucepan lid, until ready to use. SERVES 4.

For 2 cups of raw rice use 2½ cups of water.

Endō Gohan

RICE WITH GREEN PEAS

2 cups rice
¼ cup *mochigome* (sweet rice)
½ teaspoon salt

2 teaspoons *mirin*
¾ cup freshly shelled raw green
   peas

Mix the rice and the sweet rice and wash thoroughly in several changes of water until the water runs clear. Drain in a sieve for at least 1 hour. Transfer the rice to a heavy saucepan with a tightly fitting lid, add 2½ cups water, the salt and *mirin* and bring to a boil, covered, over moderate heat. Add the peas and mix them lightly into the rice with a *shamoji* (wooden spatula). Smooth the top, cover and cook for 4 minutes over moderate heat then reduce the heat to very low and cook for 7 minutes longer. Turn the heat to high for about 10 seconds, then let the rice stand, off the heat, for 10 minutes. Stir with the wooden spatula and serve in bowls as the rice course of a meal. SERVES 4 TO 6.

Oyako Donburi
PARENTS AND CHILDREN RICE

This is a charming culinary joke; parents and children refer to the garnishes on the rice which are chicken and egg. The companion dish Gyutama Donburi *with a beef and egg garnish is known as Strangers and Children.*

1½ cups rice
5 ounces skinned and boned
   chicken breast
4 *shiitake* (dried Japanese
   mushrooms)
Sugar
2 scallions, trimmed, using white
   and green parts

3 tablespoons soy sauce
3 tablespoons *mirin*
¼ cup flaked *katsuobushi* (dried
   bonito)
4 eggs

Cook the rice according to the recipe for *Gohan* (Plain Boiled Rice).

Cut the chicken breast diagonally into thin slices. Soak the mushrooms in warm water with a pinch of sugar for 30 minutes. Drain, remove the stems and squeeze out lightly. Cut into ½-inch slices. Cut the scallions into very fine 1-inch strips.

In a small saucepan combine 1⅓ cups water, the soy sauce, *mirin* and bonito and bring to a boil over moderate heat. Strain through cheesecloth into a bowl. Discard the bonito. Rinse out the saucepan and pour in ¼ of the stock. Add ¼ of the chicken and 1 mushroom and simmer for 2 or 3 minutes, or just long enough to cook the chicken, skimming if necessary. Add ¼ of the scallion and cook for 1 minute longer.

Break an egg into a bowl and stir with chopsticks until it is thoroughly blended but not foamy. Pour the egg into the saucepan, holding the chopsticks about 2 inches apart at the front of the bowl to slow the flow of the egg, in a thin stream to cover the whole surface of the pan. Cover and cook until the egg is set, about 30 seconds. Repeat with the remaining ingredients, using one quarter each time.

Stir the rice with a *shamoji* (wooden spatula) and serve into 4 *donburi* (large bowls). Ladle the chicken and egg mixture over the rice and pour on the soup. *Mitsuba* (trefoil) can be used instead of scallions in which case use 10 sprigs, cutting the stems into thirds and the leaves in half; add just before serving. If preferred this can be cooked all at once in a single saucepan and divided among 4 bowls of rice. It is a marvelous impromptu dish, especially when coping with unexpected friends. SERVES 4.

Kamameshi
GARNISHED RICE

1 small whole chicken breast, skinned and boned
1½ teaspoons soy sauce
12 medium-sized shrimp, shelled and deveined with tails left on
4 tablespoons plus 1 teaspoon *sake*
4 fresh mushrooms, halved

10 sprigs *mitsuba* (trefoil), cut into 1-inch lengths, *or* 1 small scallion, cut into fine 1-inch strips
2 cups rice
2 cups *dashi* (soup stock)
Salt to taste

Cut each half chicken breast in half lengthwise, then cut into ½-inch slices on the diagonal. Pour 1 teaspoon soy sauce over the shrimp and mix. Pour the teaspoon of *sake* over the mushrooms and mix. If using scallion instead of trefoil, put to crisp in a bowl of water.

Rinse the rice thoroughly and drain in a sieve for at least 1 hour. Put the rice in a large earthenware casserole with the stock, the 4 table-spoons of *sake,* salt to taste, and remaining ½ teaspoon of soy sauce. Add the chicken, shrimp and mushrooms to the rice, mix lightly, cover and bring to a boil over medium heat, lower the heat and cook for 15 minutes. Let stand off the heat for 5 minutes. Add the trefoil, or squeezed-out scallions, cover quickly and let stand for another 4 minutes. Serve in large bowls. SERVES 4.

This dish can be cooked in 4 individual *donabe* (earthenware bowls), or casseroles, in which case cook the rice for 8 instead of 15 minutes. In Japan this is a favorite station lunch, to be eaten on the train. One gets the casserole as a bonus.

Kuri Gohan

RICE WITH CHESTNUTS

2 cups rice
¼ cup *mochigome* (sweet rice)
12 large or 16 medium-sized
  chestnuts
4-inch square *kombu* (kelp)
2½ cups water

1 tablespoon *sake*
½ tablespoon salt
2 tablespoons *mirin*
⅛ teaspoon black sesame seeds,
  toasted

Mix the rice and sweet rice and wash thoroughly. Drain in a sieve for at least 1 hour.

Using a small sharp knife remove the peel from the flat end of the chestnuts and put them into a heavy skillet over moderate heat, turning them constantly with chopsticks until the shells are browned and begin to crack. As soon as they are cool enough to handle, remove the peel with a knife. It should come away quite easily. Cut the chestnuts into 2 or 3 pieces according to their size. Canned whole chestnuts may also be used.

Clean the seaweed (kelp) with a damp cloth and cut into a ½-inch fringe. Put into a saucepan with the rice, 2½ cups water, *sake,* salt and the chestnuts. Stir to mix. Cover and bring almost to a boil over high heat.

Remove the seaweed and stir in the *mirin.* Reduce the heat to moderate and cook, covered, for 5 minutes, then reduce the heat to low and cook for 15 minutes longer. Turn heat high for 10 seconds, remove from the heat and let the rice stand for 15 minutes. Mix lightly with a *shamoji* (wooden spatula), cover with a kitchen cloth and the saucepan lid until ready to use. Serve in large bowls. Top with a pinch of black sesame seeds. SERVES 6.

Takenoko Gohan
RICE WITH BAMBOO SHOOTS

2 cups rice
3 ounces boned and skinned
   chicken breast
2 whole canned bamboo shoots,
   about 5 ounces

1½ pieces *aburaage* (fried bean
   curd)
1½ tablespoons *sake*
3 tablespoons soy sauce
4-inch square *kombu* (kelp)

Thoroughly wash the rice and let it drain in a sieve for at least 30 minutes.

Coarsely chop the chicken breast and put into a bowl. Slice the bamboo shoots thinly lengthwise, stack and cut into ¼-by-¾-inch slices. Add to the chicken breast. Rinse the friend bean curd in hot water, drain, and cut into pieces the same size as the bamboo shoots. Add to the bowl and mix. Pour the *sake* and soy sauce over the chicken mixture and let it stand for 10 minutes, stirring once or twice.

Put the rice into a saucepan, add 2 cups plus 2 tablespoons water, and add the chicken mixture. Clean the seaweed with a damp cloth, cut into a ½-inch fringe and bury in the rice. Bring the rice to a boil, covered, over high heat. Just before it comes to a boil, remove the seaweed and set aside. Cook rice mixture over medium heat for 5 or 6 minutes, then over very low heat for 15 minutes. Turn the heat high for 10 seconds and let the rice stand, off the heat, for 10 minutes.

Toast the reserved seaweed for a few seconds over a gas flame or electric burner and crush in a piece of cheesecloth.

Serve the rice in large bowls or rice bowls and garnish with the seaweed. SERVES 4.

This is a spring dish when fresh bamboo shoots are in season, but can be eaten at any time using canned ones.

Onigiri

RICE BALLS

Onigiri *(rice balls), also called* omusubi, *are a great favorite for* bento, *the picnic boxes that are a feature of both picnics and train travel in Japan.*

3 ounces fresh salmon fillet with
 skin
Salt
2 cups rice
1 sheet *nori* (dried laver seaweed)

Umeboshi (pickled plums)
⅓ cup flaked *katsuobushi* (dried
 bonito)
Soy sauce

Sprinkle the salmon on both sides with salt and leave for half a day in a cool place or for one day in the refrigerator. Rinse quickly in cold water and pat dry. Grill, or broil under medium heat, skin side down for 5 minutes, then turn and broil the skin side for 3 minutes. Remove the skin and any bones and break with chopsticks into pieces about ½ inch square.

Cook the rice according to the recipe for *Gohan* (Plain Boiled Rice).

Toast the seaweed for a few seconds over a gas flame or electric burner, then cut with scissors into 2-inch squares. Remove the pits from 4 small pickled plums, or cut a large plum into quarters. Divide the bonito into two heaps and crumble with the fingers. Put into separate bowls, mixing one with a teaspoon of soy sauce.

To make the rice balls check that the rice is cool enough to handle though it should still be warm. Wet the hands and sprinkle with a little salt. Take some rice, about 1 heaping tablespoon, flatten it in the palm of the hand and put a plum or piece of plum in the center. Form it into a ball, about 2½ inches in diameter, pressing it firmly into shape. Continue with the rest of the plums, wetting the hands and sprinkling them with a little salt from time to time. Stuff 4 more balls with the salmon. Press the seaweed squares on the tops and bottoms of the rice balls, then press again to fit the squares around the balls. Arrange on a tray, salmon at one end, plum at the other.

Make more rice balls using the bonito mixed with soy sauce as the stuffing. Roll these in the plain bonito and place on the tray. The balls can also be made into cylindrical shapes with a triangular piece of seaweed pressed onto each side. Any leftover rice can be mixed with any leftover salmon, finely shredded, making pretty pink and white balls.

Eat the rice balls with the fingers or chopsticks at room temperature, allowing 2 or 3 per serving according to appetite. MAKES 12 OR MORE.

There are many fillings: Salted roes, such as cod or salmon, or *uni,* sea urchins which can be bought as a prepared paste, can be used and *Gyūniku No Tsukudani* (Beef with Ginger) or *Kombu No Tsukudani* (Cooked Kelp), which can also be bought ready-prepared, are both good. There is a lot of freedom.

In Japan salt-cured salmon is available ready-prepared.

Gyūdon
RICE WITH BEEF

2 cups rice
6 ounces flank or skirt steak
6 ounces *shirataki* (devil's tongue noodles)
Boiling water
4 scallions, trimmed, using white and green parts

1 *yakidōfu* (broiled bean curd)
1 cup *dashi* (soup stock)
5 tablespoons soy sauce
5 tablespoons *mirin*
2 or 3 dashes msg

Cook the rice according to the recipe for *Gohan* (Plain Boiled Rice).

Cut the meat crosswise into thin pieces. Drop the noodles into boiling water and cook for 1 minute. Drain and cut into 1½-inch pieces. Slice the scallions diagonally. Halve the bean curd, then cut into ⅓-inch pieces.

In a saucepan combine the soup stock, soy sauce, *mirin* and msg. Bring to a boil, add the beef, noodles and scallions and bring back to a boil. Skim. Add the bean curd and cook for 2 or 3 minutes over moderate heat.

Stir the rice with a *shamoji* (wooden spatula) and divide among 4 large bowls. Top with the beef mixture and sauce. SERVES 4.

Gyūtama Donburi
RICE WITH BEEF AND EGGS

This is sometimes referred to humorously as strangers and children, an extension of the culinary joke of parents and children, Oyako Donburi, *which is rice with chicken and eggs.*

1½ cups rice
½ pound flank or skirt steak
5 *shiitake* (dried Japanese mushrooms)
12 thin strips *kamaboko* (fish sausage), about 1 ounce
10 sprigs *mitsuba* (trefoil) *or* ½ bunch watercress *or* spinach

3 tablespoons soy sauce
3 tablespoons *mirin*
¼ cup flaked *katsuobushi* (dried bonito)
4 eggs

Cook the rice according to the recipe for *Gohan* (Plain Boiled Rice).

Thinly slice the beef, then cut it into ½-inch pieces. Soak the mushrooms in warm water with a pinch of sugar for 30 minutes. Drain, remove the stems and squeeze out lightly. Cut into thin slices. If *mitsuba* is available, stack the sprigs and cut the stems into 3 pieces. If using cress or spinach, gather it together and cut across at 2-inch intervals. Set these ingredients aside with the fish sausage.

In a saucepan combine 1⅓ cups water, the soy sauce, *mirin* and bonito and bring to a boil over moderate heat. Strain through cheese-cloth into a bowl and discard the bonito. Rinse out the saucepan, pour in the strained stock and bring to a boil. Add the fish sausage, beef and mushrooms and simmer, skimming if necessary, for 3 minutes. Add the *mitsuba,* cress or spinach.

Break the eggs into a bowl and stir with chopsticks until they are well blended but not foamy. Pour the eggs into the saucepan, holding the chopsticks about 2 inches apart at the front of the bowl to slow the flow of the egg, in a thin stream to cover the whole surface of the pan. Cover and cook until the egg is set, about 30 seconds.

Stir the rice with a *shamoji* (wooden spatula) and serve into 4 *donburi* (large china bowls). Ladle the beef and egg mixture over the rice and pour on the soup. Each serving can be cooked separately if preferred. Makes an ideal lunch dish. SERVES 4.

Sekihan

PINK RICE WITH RED BEANS

This is a congratulatory dish and might be served at a birthday or similar happy occasion.

¼ cup red *azuki* (adzuki) beans   1 teaspoon black sesame seeds
3 cups sweet rice   1 teaspoon salt

Wash and pick over the beans and put on to cook with ¾ cup water over low heat. Bring to a boil and drain. Add 3 cups cold water and simmer, covered, over low heat 20 to 30 minutes. Drain, reserving the water. Cool.

Wash and drain the rice then put to soak in the reserved water from the beans for at least 6 hours, or overnight. The bean water will give the rice an attractive pink color. Drain the rice in a sieve for at least 30 minutes. Reserve the soaking water. Mix the rice and beans together.

Line a steamer with a kitchen cloth, bring the water in the steamer to a boil. Add the rice and beans, pat smooth then poke 5 holes in the rice with your fingers. Steam over high heat for 40 to 50 minutes, or until rice and beans are done. Sprinkle the rice mixture 3 or 4 times during the cooking period with the reserved soaking water, using your fingers. It is not necessary to use up all the water.

In a small skillet toast the sesame seeds until they begin to jump. Transfer them to a small bowl and mix with the salt.

Serve the rice in bowls or on plates and sprinkle with the sesame seed mixture. This can be made into rice balls, can be reheated if necessary, or eaten cold. SERVES 6 TO 8.

Soboro Gohan

RICE WITH EGGS, CHICKEN AND SNOW PEAS

1½ cups rice
1¾ cups water
3 tablespoons soy sauce
Salt
4 eggs
2 teaspoons sugar
2 tablespoons plus 2 teaspoons
    mirin

1 tablespoon *sake*
½ teaspoon ginger juice
7 ounces ground chicken
10 snow peas, about 1 ounce
¼ cup *dashi* (soup stock)

Thoroughly wash the rice and drain in a sieve for at least 1 hour. Put into a heavy saucepan with a tightly fitting lid, 1¾ cups water, 1 tablespoon of the soy sauce and ½ teaspoon salt. Bring to a boil over high heat, reduce the heat to moderate and cook 5 to 6 minutes, then reduce to low and cook 10 to 13 minutes longer. Turn heat to high for 10 seconds, then let the rice stand off the heat for 10 minutes.

Break the eggs into a bowl and stir with chopsticks until they are well blended but not foamy. Add ¼ teaspoon salt, 1 teaspoon of the sugar and the 2 teaspoons of *mirin*. Pour into a saucepan and set over moderate heat. As soon as the eggs begin to set on the bottom, remove from the heat and stir quickly 3 or 4 times round the pan with 5 or 6 chopsticks held in a bunch in one hand. Return the pan to the heat and repeat the operation 12 or 13 times. This process makes the eggs *soboro,* which means tiny curds. The whole process is very quick. Set the eggs aside.

In another saucepan combine the remaining 2 tablespoons of soy sauce, 2 tablespoons of the *mirin,* the *sake* and the ginger juice made by squeezing out grated fresh ginger root. Add the chicken in 3 or 4 lots and cook over moderate heat, stirring with chopsticks from time to time, until all the liquid has evaporated, about 5 minutes. Set aside.

Drop the snow peas into boiling salted water and boil for 2 minutes. Drain. Add the soup stock, 1 teaspoon sugar and ¼ teaspoon salt to the saucepan. Add the snow peas and cook, uncovered, over brisk heat until the liquid has evaporated. (The amount of snow peas may be doubled, in which case use ⅓ cup soup stock.) Green beans may be used instead of the snow peas: cut into ½-inch slices on the diagonal and cook as for the peas.

Turn the rice out into a large, shallow bowl. Spread half the surface with the egg mixture, the other half with the chicken mixture, then make a line down the center with the snow peas or the green beans. Serve in bowls. SERVES 4.

VARIATION: For *Sanshoku Soboro* (Three-Color *Soboro*) drop ¼ pound peeled and deveined shrimp into boiling water and cook for 2 minutes. Transfer to a *suribachi* and grind until smooth. Add 2 teaspoons *sake,* 1 teaspoon *mirin,* 1 teaspoon sugar, ¼ teaspoon salt and about 6 drops of soy sauce. Put into the top of a double boiler over simmering water and stir until the liquid has evaporated. Place this shrimp *soboro* over one third of the rice, the chicken and egg *soboro* over the remaining two thirds. Make a line of snow peas or green beans down the side of the dish. A little red or pink pickled ginger makes a pretty garnish.

Good for picnics and lunch boxes.

Kaki-zōsui
RICE AND OYSTERS IN SOUP

This is a practical dish as it uses leftover rice. It can be eaten at any time: breakfast, lunch or dinner, or as a snack between meals.

1 cup cooked rice	5 or 6 oysters, rinsed in salted
½ scallion, trimmed, using white	water and drained
and green parts	¼ teaspoon salt
1⅓ cups *dashi* (soup stock)	¼ teaspoon soy sauce

Put the rice in a sieve or fine colander, rinse quickly under cold water and leave to drain. Cut the scallion into 1-inch pieces, then slice them finely lengthwise. Put into a bowl of cold water to crisp for a few minutes, drain and squeeze dry in a kitchen cloth.

In a saucepan bring the stock to a boil, add the rice and simmer for 3 or 4 minutes. Add the oysters, salt, soy sauce and scallions and cook just long enough to plump the oysters, about 1 minute. Serve in a large soup bowl and eat with chopsticks and a soup spoon. SERVES 1.

Tendon

RICE WITH DEEP-FRIED SHRIMP AND GREEN BEANS

1½ cups rice	Vegetable oil
1 egg	½ cup *dashi* (soup stock)
⅓ cup cake flour	¼ cup soy sauce
8 jumbo shrimp	¼ cup *mirin*
4 large or 8 small green beans	3 or 4 dashes msg

Cook the rice according to the recipe for *Gohan* (Plain Boiled Rice).

Break the egg into a bowl and stir with chopsticks until it is well blended but not foamy. Measure 2 tablespoons of the egg into another bowl. (Reserve the remaining egg for another use.) Add 2 tablespoons water to the 2 tablespoons of egg and stir. Sift the cake flour and add to the egg mixture, stirring lightly to mix.

Peel and devein the shrimp, leaving the last segment of shell and the tail on. Make a small, shallow slit on the inside of the shrimp at the head end to prevent its curling when it is fried. Straighten the shrimp by bending the tails back slightly, taking care not to break them. Cut the ends off the tails as this part of the tail has water in it and will splutter in the hot oil.

Trim the beans and cut into 2 or 3 diagonal slices.

Heat 2 or 3 inches oil in a *tempura* pan or a saucepan to between 345°F. and 350°F. on a frying thermometer, or until bubbles form on wooden chopsticks stirred in the oil.

Dip the shrimp in the batter and fry for 2 minutes; turn and fry for 1 minute longer or until golden. Drain on the rack of the *tempura* pan or on paper towels. Make 4 bundles of the beans, dip in the batter and fry as for the shrimp. If preferred, fry the beans without batter.

Make a *tentsuyu* sauce: In a small saucepan combine the soup stock, soy sauce, *mirin* and msg. Stir to mix and heat through.

Divide the cooked rice among 4 *donburi* (earthenware bowls), or large china bowls. Arrange the shrimp and green beans on top of the rice and pour the sauce over them. SERVES 4.

Toriniku No Kijiyaki Donburi
CHICKEN LOOKING LIKE PHEASANT WITH RICE

1½ cups rice
1 whole large chicken breast,
   skinned and boned
3 tablespoons *sake*
5 tablespoons soy sauce

2 to 3 dashes msg
4 large scallions, trimmed, using
   white and green parts
Kona sanshō (ground Japanese
   pepper)

Cook the rice according to the recipe for *Gohan* (Plain Boiled Rice).

Thinly slice the chicken on the diagonal and put into a bowl. Sprinkle with 2 tablespoons of the *sake* and 3 tablespoons of the soy sauce, turning to mix. Let stand 5 minutes. Lift the chicken pieces out of the mixture and grill or broil ½ minute on each side. Add the msg to the soy and *sake* mixture, toss the chicken pieces in it and grill or broil again for ½ minute on each side. Repeat the process two or three times, or until the chicken is lightly browned, but do not add any more msg to the marinade. Reserve the marinade.

Cut scallions in halves crosswise, and grill or broil until browned, turning frequently, about 1 minute. Dip in the marinade and cook for a minute or two longer. Cut into 1-inch pieces.

Divide the cooked rice among 4 *donburi* (earthenware bowls), or large china bowls. Arrange the chicken pieces and scallions on top and sprinkle to taste with Japanese pepper. Pour the remaining marinade into a small saucepan, add the remaining tablespoon of *sake* and the remaining 2 tablespoons of soy sauce. Heat and pour over the chicken and rice. SERVES 4.

NOODLES

Japan has a wide variety of noodles, readily available in stores specializing in Japanese foods. Packaged noodles made from wheat flour can be bought dried. Among these are thick noodles called *udon;* thin ones, *sōmen;* broad, flat ones, *kishimen;* as well as buckwheat noodles, *soba.* They can also be bought fresh as *nama udon,* either cooked or uncooked, in the refrigerator section.

More exotic are *harusame* or bean gelatin noodles, commonly called cellophane noodles. The Japanese name translates into "spring rain." They are in fact reminiscent of spring rain which falls with the sun shining through it. *Shirataki* is made from the root of an aroid; it is called devil's tongue or snake palm in English, and "shining waterfall" in Japanese.

The noodle dishes, though they can be eaten at any time, are superb for lunch. A steaming bowl of noodles can be very comforting on a bleak winter day, and chilled noodle dishes are cooling and refreshing in hot weather. They take very little time and effort to prepare. The ready-cooked noodles are heated briefly in hot water, requiring no cooking at all. And once the philosophy of the Japanese kitchen is understood, toppings for noodle dishes may be freely improvised.

Cooked Dried Noodles

To cook *udon* (thick wheat-flour noodles) or *kishimen* (broad, flat wheat-flour noodles) put the noodles into a large saucepan of boiling water and bring back to a boil over moderate heat. Add 1 cup cold water and bring back to a boil. Repeat the process twice more, adding 3 cups cold water in all. Test the noodles and if necessary boil for 2 or 3 minutes longer until they are tender. Do not overcook or they will become mushy. Drain the noodles, rinse them under hot running water and drain again in a colander. The noodles are now ready to serve. If cooked ahead of time, they may be reheated. Simply pour boiling water over them, let stand for a minute, drain and serve. Other uncooked fresh noodles are cooked in the same way.

To cook *sōmen* (thin wheat-flour noodles), *hiyamugi* (varicolored thin wheat-flour noodles) and *soba* (buckwheat noodles) add 1 cup cold water twice instead of 3 times. For summer dishes in which the noodles are eaten chilled, rinse them in cold instead of hot water.

For *nama udon* (fresh, cooked thick wheat-flour noodles) put the noodles into a saucepan and pour boiling water over them. Let stand for a few minutes, just long enough to heat them through. Separate the noodles gently with chopsticks while in the water. Drain and serve.

Miso Udon
NOODLES WITH BEAN PASTE

1 pound chicken with bone, any part
4 fresh mushrooms *or* 4 *shiitake* (dried Japanese mushrooms)
2 scallions, trimmed, using white and green parts

4 7-ounce packages *nama udon* (fresh, cooked thick wheat-flour noodles)
8 tablespoons *miso* (bean paste)

Chop the chicken, bone and all, into approximately 1-inch pieces. Put the chicken into a large saucepan with 5 cups water, cover and bring to a boil over high heat. Skim, reduce heat and simmer, covered, until the chicken is tender, about 30 minutes.

If using fresh mushrooms, wipe the caps, trim the stems and cut into quarters. If using dried Japanese mushrooms, soak for 30 minutes in warm water with a pinch of sugar, drain, remove the stems and cut the mushrooms into quarters. Cut the scallions into ¼-inch slices. Heat the noodles according to the recipe Cooked Dried Noodles. Set aside.

When the chicken is tender, add the bean paste mixed until smooth with a little of the chicken stock to the saucepan. Stir to mix and add the noodles, mushrooms and scallions and cook at a bare simmer for about 3 minutes. Serve in *donburi* (earthenware) bowls. This is a winter dish. SERVES 4.

Uncooked fresh noodles or dried noodles may also be used. See recipe Cooked Dried Noodles.

Hiyamugi
CHILLED NOODLES WITH EGGS

This is a perfect summer luncheon dish. The noodles are white with a sprinkling of pink and green ones. In Japan it is said that seeing these fresh pretty colors makes one feel cooler.

1 cup *dashi* (soup stock)
⅓ cup soy sauce
⅓ cup *mirin*
2 or 3 dashes msg
10 ounces *hiyamugi* (thin
   wheat-flour noodles)
1 scallion, trimmed, using white
   and green parts

½ medium-sized cucumber
1 medium-sized tomato, peeled
2 hard-boiled eggs, sliced in half
   lengthwise
Shichimi-tōgarashi
   (seven-flavor spice), or
   tōgarashi-ko (ground hot red
   pepper)

In a saucepan combine the soup stock, soy sauce, *mirin* and msg, bring to a boil, remove from the heat and cool. Chill slightly, then pour the sauce into 4 medium-sized bowls, preferably glass. Set aside.

Cook the noodles according to the recipe Cooked Dried Noodles and place in a large bowl, preferably cut glass. Cover the noodles with cold water and add a few ice cubes so that the noodles will be thoroughly chilled.

Chop the scallion, put in cold water to crisp for a few minutes, drain, squeeze dry in a cloth and put into a small dish.

Peel the cucumber if it is waxed; if not, peel it in alternate lengthwise strips, then slice fairly thinly on the diagonal. Cut the tomato into 4 slices and poke out the seeds with chopsticks. Arrange the cucumber around the edge of the drained chilled noodles with the tomato slices at even intervals between them. Arrange the eggs, cut side up, in the center of the bowl in a flower pattern. Add a few more ice cubes if desired. Place noodle dish in the center of the table with a bowl of the sauce at each place.

To eat add a little scallion to the sauce in the serving bowls, season to taste with either of the peppers, serve cucumber, tomato, egg and some of the noodles into the bowl and eat with chopsticks. If preferred the noodles and garnish can be served in individual bowls with the sauce on the side in another bowl.

Hiyashi Sōmen
CHILLED NOODLES WITH SHRIMP

8 ounces *sōmen* (thin wheat noodles)
8 medium-sized unpeeled raw shrimp, preferably with heads left on
Salt
1 small cucumber
1 cup *dashi* (soup stock)

¼ cup soy sauce
2½ tablespoons *mirin*
½ cup *daikon* (white radish) grated with 1 seeded dried red pepper
2 small scallions, trimmed, using white and green parts

Cook the noodles according to the recipe Cooked Dried Noodles; drain and set aside.

Drop the shrimp into boiling salted water and cook for 2 minutes. Drain and set aside.

Trim the ends from the cucumber and scrape out the seeds with a vegetable peeler. If the cucumber is waxed, peel it. Cut the cucumber into ¼-inch slices, drop into boiling water and cook for 1 minute. Drain and set aside.

In a small saucepan combine the soup stock, soy sauce and *mirin*, bring to a boil, remove from the heat, cool and pour into 4 small bowls.

Put the grated radish and hot pepper* into a small bowl. Chop the scallions and put into another small bowl.

To assemble the dish put the noodles into a deep serving bowl, preferably cut glass, pour in cold water barely to cover the noodles, and add a few ice cubes. Arrange the shrimp on top of the noodles in a decorative pattern and surround with the cucumber slices. Place the noodles in the center of the table with the bowls of radish and scallion; a bowl of sauce should be at each place. To eat, put some of the scallion and radish into the sauce, then dip some of the drained noodles and cucumber slices into it. Peel the shrimp and dip into the sauce. SERVES 4. This is a summer dish, pleasant for luncheon on a hot day.

*The easiest way to grate the hot pepper and radish together is to peel the radish, poke a hole in the center with chopsticks and stuff the pepper into the hole. Then grate the radish. This is called *momijioroshi,* described as autumn leaves. The color is reminiscent of leaves turning in fall, apt, as are all the poetic phrases in Japanese cooking.

Odamakimushi

NOODLES WITH EGGS, SHRIMP, FISH SAUSAGE AND CHICKEN

4 large raw unpeeled shrimp
¼ pound skinned and boned
  chicken, any part
4 teaspoons *usukuchi shōyu*
  (light soy sauce)
4 *shiitake* (dried Japanese
  mushrooms)
Pinch sugar
10 sprigs *mitsuba* (trefoil) *or* 1
  scallion
4 ⅓-inch slices fish sausage,
  preferably *naruto-maki*

3 7-ounce packages *nama udon*
  (fresh, cooked thick
  wheat-flour noodles)
3 eggs
3 cups *dashi* (soup stock), about
1 teaspoon salt
1 teaspoon *mirin*
⅛ teaspoon msg
Lime peel, optional

Peel and devein the shrimp, but leave the tails on. Cut the chicken into diagonal bite-sized pieces. Put into a bowl with 1 teaspoon of the light soy sauce, mix and set aside. Soak the mushrooms for about 30 minutes in warm water with the sugar, squeeze out and remove the hard stems. Cut the trefoil into 1-inch pieces, or if using the scallion, cut into 1½-inch pieces crosswise, then slice them finely lengthwise.

Sprinkle the cooked noodles with 1 teaspoon of the light soy sauce and separate gently with the fingers. Divide the noodles among 4 *donburi* (earthenware) bowls or 4 large china bowls. Arrange the shrimp, chicken, mushrooms, trefoil or scallion and the fish sausage in an attractive pattern on top of the noodles.

Stir the eggs with chopsticks until they are well blended but not foamy. Measure the eggs, pour them into a bowl and add 4½ times the quantity of soup stock, the salt, *mirin,* msg and the remaining 2 teaspoons of light soy sauce. Stir to mix and strain through cheesecloth. Pour an equal amount into each bowl of noodles.

Place the bowls in a steamer over boiling water and partially cover each bowl. A saucer will do. Steam for 15 to 20 minutes. Garnish with lime peel. Eat with chopsticks and a soup spoon. This is a winter luncheon dish, complete as a meal in itself. SERVES 4.

Naruto-maki fish sausage is preferred because its pink and white is attractive with the other garnishes.

VARIATION: 10 ounces dried *udon* (thick wheat-flour noodles) cooked according to the recipe Cooked Dried Noodles may be used instead of *nama udon*.

Kitsune Udon
NOODLES WITH FRIED BEAN CURD

4 pieces *aburaage* (fried bean curd)
Hot water
¾ cup *dashi* (soup stock)
3 tablespoons sugar
2 tablespoons soy sauce
4-inch square *kombu* (kelp)
⅓ cup flaked *katsuobushi* (dried bonito)

⅓ cup *usukuchi shōyu* (light soy sauce)
2 tablespoons *mirin*
12 ounces *udon* (thick wheat-flour noodles)
1½ scallions, trimmed, using white and green parts
Shichimi-tōgarashi (seven-flavor spice)

Cut the bean curd pieces into triangles and simmer in hot water for 5 minutes. Drain. Return to the saucepan with the soup stock and sugar and cook over low heat for 5 minutes longer. Add the soy sauce and cover with an *otoshibuta* (inner wooden lid), or use a smaller saucepan lid or a plate. Cook over low heat until the liquid is reduced to one third. Set aside.

Clean the seaweed (kelp) with a damp cloth and cut into a ½-inch fringe. Put into a saucepan with 4 cups water, the bonito, light soy sauce and *mirin* and bring to just below a boil over moderate heat. Strain and set aside.

Cook the noodles according to the recipe Cooked Dried Noodles and divide among 4 large bowls. *Donburi* (earthenware) bowls are most often used. Top the noodles with the reserved bean curd triangles and any liquid. Slice the whole scallion in 1-inch diagonal pieces and add to the noodles. Finely chop the ½ scallion. Reheat the sauce and pour it over the noodles, garnish with the chopped scallion and sprinkle with a little *shichimi-tōgarashi*. SERVES 4.

VARIATION: For *Kitsune Soba* (Buckwheat Noodles with Fried Bean Curd) substitute *soba* (buckwheat noodles) for the *udon*.

Tsukimi Udon
NOODLES WITH POACHED EGGS

Translated literally this is "looking-like-the-moon noodles." This dish does indeed look like the moon on a cloudy night: the noodles represent the clouds and the poached egg, with its white filming the yolk, resembles the moon.

4-inch square *kombu* (kelp)
½ cup flaked *katsuobushi* (dried bonito)
½ cup *usukuchi shōyu* (light soy sauce)
2 tablespoons *mirin*
2½ cups tightly packed spinach
10 ounces *udon* (thick wheat-flour noodles) *or* 4 7-ounce packages *nama udon* (fresh, cooked thick wheat-flour noodles)

4 eggs
Nori (dried laver seaweed)
Shichimi-tōgarashi (seven-flavor spice)

Clean the seaweed (kelp) with a damp cloth and cut into a ½-inch fringe. Put into a large saucepan, add 4½ cups water and bring to a boil, uncovered, over moderate heat. Just before the water boils, remove and discard the seaweed. Add the bonito and simmer for 2 or 3 minutes. Add the light soy sauce and the *mirin,* bring back to a boil and remove from the heat. Strain through a sieve lined with a double layer of cheesecloth. Set aside.

Wash and drain the spinach and drop into a large saucepan of boiling salted water. Simmer for 2 or 3 minutes, drain, rinse 3 times in cold water and drain. Squeeze out the excess moisture and form into a roll. Cut into 4 equal slices. Set aside.

Heat the noodles according to the recipe Cooked Dried Noodles and divide among 4 large, warmed bowls, preferably with covers. Reheat the soup, pour it over the noodles and put a slice of spinach on top to the side. Break an egg into each bowl, cover with the lid (or use a plate or saucer) so that the egg poaches lightly. Serve garnished with a 1-inch square of *nori* lightly toasted over a gas flame or electric burner to crisp. Pass *shichimi-tōgarashi* at the table. SERVES 4.

Torinanban
SPICED CHICKEN WITH BUCKWHEAT NOODLES

¾ pound skinned and boned chicken breast
½ cup plus 1 tablespoon soy sauce
1 tablespoon *sake*
2½ cups tightly packed spinach
Salt
6 scallions, trimmed, using white and green parts

3 cups *dashi* (soup stock)
¼ cup *mirin*
10 ounces *soba* (buckwheat noodles)
Shichimi-tōgarashi (seven-flavor spice) *or* 1 tablespoon grated fresh ginger root

Slice the chicken breast diagonally into bite-sized pieces, sprinkle with the tablespoon of soy sauce, then the *sake;* mix and set aside.

Wash and drain the spinach and drop into a large saucepan of boiling salted water. Simmer for 2 or 3 minutes, drain, rinse 3 times in cold water and drain again. Squeeze out the excess moisture and form into a roll. Cut into 4 equal slices. Set aside.

Slice 4 of the scallions diagonally into pieces about 2 inches long. Finely chop the remaining 2 scallions, put into a small bowl and set aside.

In a saucepan combine the soup stock, the ½ cup soy sauce and the *mirin* and bring to a boil. Add the chicken and simmer gently for 2 or 3 minutes. Add the diagonally sliced scallions and cook for 1 minute longer.

Cook the noodles according to the recipe Cooked Dried Noodles. Divide the noodles among 4 warmed *donburi* (earthenware) bowls or large china bowls. Arrange the chicken pieces and scallions on top of the noodles with a slice of spinach at the side. Pour the hot soup over them. Serve with the seven-flavor spice or grated ginger and the chopped scallions. This is a luncheon dish. SERVES 4.

VARIATION: Use either *udon, name udon* or *kishimen* noodles cooked according to the recipe Cooked Dried Noodles.

Zaru Soba

BUCKWHEAT NOODLES ON BAMBOO PLATES

3 tablespoons *mirin*
5 tablespoons soy sauce
1 tablespoon sugar
4-inch square *kombu* (kelp)
½ cup flaked *katsuobushi* (dried bonito)
1 scallion, trimmed, using white and green parts

10 ounces *soba* (buckwheat noodles)
1 tablespoon *wasabi* (green horseradish powder)
2 sheets *nori* (dried laver seaweed)

In a small saucepan bring the *mirin* to a boil over low heat. Add 1¼ cups cold water, the soy sauce and sugar. Clean the kelp with a damp cloth, cut into a ½-inch fringe and add to the sauce with the bonito. Cook, uncovered, over low heat until the mixture is about to boil. Lift out and discard the kelp. Simmer the mixture gently for 5 minutes longer, then strain through a double thickness of cheesecloth into a bowl. Put the bowl of sauce into a larger bowl of cold water to chill it quickly. It should be a little cooler than room temperature so add a few ice cubes to the water if necessary. Pour the sauce into 4 soup bowls.

Finely chop the scallion and divide among 4 tiny bowls. Put one at each place setting with a soup bowl.

Cook the noodles according to the recipe Cooked Dried Noodles and chill in cold water. Drain and divide among 4 *zaru* (bamboo plates).

Mix the horseradish to a paste with a little water and place a small mound of it on each plate beside the noodles.

Toast the sheets of seaweed for a few seconds over a gas flame or electric burner then crumble in a piece of cheesecloth, or with the fingers, and sprinkle over the noodles.

To eat the noodles add the horseradish to the chilled sauce. This is very hot, so the amount of horseradish used is a matter of taste. Add the scallions to the sauce. Dip the noodles into the sauce before eating. This is a summer dish, wonderfully refreshing on a hot day.
SERVES 4.

VARIATION: Other noodles may be used. For *Zaru Udon,* for example, use *udon* (thick wheat-flour noodles) cooked according to the recipe Cooked Dried Noodles. The noodles may, of course, be served on china plates instead of *zaru.*

Tojikishimen
BROAD NOODLES WITH EGG AND CHICKEN

3 cups *dashi* (soup stock)
¼ cup soy sauce
2½ tablespoons *mirin*
¼ teaspoon salt or to taste
⅛ teaspoon msg
½ pound skinned and boned chicken breast
1½ tablespoons *katakuriko or* cornstarch
3 eggs, stirred

10 sprigs *mitsuba* (trefoil) *or* 10 spinach leaves
10 ounces *kishimen* (broad, flat noodles)
1 scallion, trimmed, using white and green parts, finely chopped
Shichimi-tōgarashi (seven-flavor spice)

In a saucepan combine the soup stock, soy sauce, *mirin,* salt and msg and bring to a simmer over moderate heat. Cut the chicken into bite-sized diagonal slices, add to the stock and cook over low heat until tender, about 3 minutes. Mix the *katakuriko* or cornstarch with 1½ tablespoons water and stir into the stock until it is lightly thickened. Holding a pair of chopsticks against the side of the bowl, pour the stirred eggs in a thin stream over the chicken and stock to cover the whole surface of the pan. Chop the trefoil stalks into thirds and the leaves in half and add to the saucepan. If using spinach, cook the leaves for 2 minutes in boiling water, squeeze out and chop coarsely. Add to the saucepan.

Cook the noodles according to the recipe Cooked Dried Noodles. Divide the noodles among 4 warmed *donburi* (earthenware) bowls. Top with the chicken, egg and stock mixture, and sprinkle with the scallion and *shichimi-tōgarashi.* Eat with chopsticks. SERVES 4.

Nikuan Udon
PORK NOODLES

1-inch slice from thick part of
  medium-sized carrot
2 scallions, trimmed, using green
  and white parts
2 tablespoons vegetable oil
¾ pound lean ground pork
3 tablespoons soy sauce

4 tablespoons *mirin*
1 tablespoon *katakuriko or* potato
  starch
3 7-ounce packages *nama udon*
  (fresh, cooked thick
  wheat-flour noodles)

Scrape the carrot and cut it into julienne strips. Slice the scallions diagonally into ½-inch pieces. Heat the oil in a skillet, add the pork and cook over high heat, stirring constantly with chopsticks, for 2 minutes. Add the carrot and continue to stir fry for 2 minutes longer. Reduce the heat to moderate and add the soy sauce, *mirin* and scallions and continue cooking for a minute or two. Mix the potato starch with 1 tablespoon water and stir into the meat mixture. Cook until lightly thickened.

Heat the noodles according to the recipe Cooked Dried Noodles. Divide among 4 large bowls and top with the pork mixture. SERVES 4.

SUSHI

One of the glories of the Japanese kitchen is *sushi,* an array of dishes based on vinegar-flavored rice. Frequent garnishes include slices of raw fish or shellfish, omelette strips or vegetables. The rice can also be stuffed into little bags of fried bean curd, pressed with various toppings and cut into bite-sized squares, rolled in sheets of laver seaweed and sliced, or made into a rice salad. *Sushi* is a great favorite for picnics, as a main course, a first course, or as an accompaniment to drinks. Some of the *sushi* dishes require a certain amount of work, but since they are prepared ahead of time and are served at room temperature, they are ideal for parties. Perhaps the most important rule in making *sushi* is to keep the hands moistened with vinegared water to prevent the rice sticking to the fingers when pressing it into shape.

Japanese cooks sometimes vary the standard *sushi* recipe by adding a tablespoon or so of *sake* or *mirin* to the rice before cooking it or by increasing the amounts of sugar and vinegar in the dressing to suit personal, or regional, tastes after the rice is cooked. There is even a special vinegar, *sushi su,* flavored with sugar, salt and msg and available in Japanese markets.

Sushi
RICE WITH VINEGAR DRESSING

2 cups rice	1 tablespoon sugar
3-inch square *kombu* (kelp)	2 teaspoons salt
2¼ cups water	½ teaspoon msg
¼ cup rice vinegar	

Thoroughly wash the rice in several changes of water until the water runs clear, and drain in a sieve for at least 1 hour. Put into a heavy saucepan with a tightly fitting lid. Clean the seaweed with a damp cloth and cut with kitchen shears into a ½-inch fringe. Bury the seaweed in the rice. Add the water, cover and bring to a boil over high heat, removing the seaweed just before the water boils. Otherwise it will flavor the rice too strongly. Reduce the heat to moderate and cook for 5 to 6 minutes, then reduce the heat to very low and cook for 15 minutes. Raise the heat to high for 10 seconds, then let the rice stand off the heat for 10 minutes.

In a small saucepan combine the rice vinegar, sugar, salt and msg. Heat through, stirring to mix. Turn the rice out into a large, shallow dish, preferably wooden. In Japan a *bandai* (sushioke), a large round wooden dish, would be used. Pour the vinegar mixture little by little over the rice, mixing it with a *shamoji* (wooden spatula) or a fork, and fanning it vigorously to make it glisten. It is a good idea to have a helper do the fanning, though it can be managed alone. The fanning cools the rice quickly and this is what makes it glisten.

Cover the rice with a cloth until ready to use. It can be left standing at room temperature for several hours before using if necessary.

Nigiri-Zushi

HANDMADE SUSHI

This is the sushi *of the* sushiya, *small restaurants that specialize in this dish. Here, the most commonly served form of* sushi *consists of little patties of vinegared rice topped by slices of raw fish or shellfish. If the rice and fish are prepared ahead of time, it is important to assemble the actual dish only at the last minute. This procedure is necessary because the rice may stand at room temperature but the fish should be kept covered in a cool place, refrigerated if necessary, until serving time.*

The larger the number of guests, the wider can be the assortment of fish. But it is perfectly possible to settle for one kind, sole for example, if it is more convenient.

2 cups rice	8 medium-sized raw shrimp,
¾ pound cleaned fish or	about ¼ pound
shellfish: tuna, striped bass,	Salt
sea bass, porgy, red snapper,	1 teaspoon rice vinegar
squid, cuttlefish, octopus,	1 tablespoon *wasabi* (green
clams, sea urchins, salmon	horseradish powder)
caviar, abalone, scallops	Soy sauce

Cook the rice and season it with vinegar mixture according to the recipe for *Sushi* (Rice with Vinegar Dressing).

Cut the fish into ¼-inch-thick diagonal slices about 1 by 2 inches. There should be about 24 slices. Remove the intestinal vein from the shrimp with a toothpick, but do not peel. Using small bamboo skewers, or toothpicks, skewer the shrimp full length on the underside to keep them from curling when they are cooked. Drop the shrimp into rapidly boiling salted water with the vinegar and boil over high heat for 1½ minutes. Drain, remove the toothpicks, peel the shrimp and cut along the underside three-quarters through, taking care not to cut too deeply. Gently open and flatten out the shrimp. In a small bowl mix the *wasabi* powder to a paste with a little cold water and set aside.

Wet hands in water to which a little rice vinegar has been added and form about 2 tablespoons of the *sushi* rice into an oblong patty about 1 by 2 inches. Spread a dab of horseradish paste down the center of a piece of fish and place the fish, horseradish side down, on top of the rice. Continue until all the fish is used. Place the shrimp on top of patties of rice in the same way, but without any horseradish. Arrange the *sushi* on a large platter and place in the center of the table with some *wasabi* paste and a tiny bowl of soy sauce at each place setting, or arrange on individual platters. To eat, dip one end of the *sushi* in the soy sauce, using either chopsticks or fingers. *Sake* or green tea are the best accompaniments but dry white wine is also appropriate. SERVES 4 AS A MAIN COURSE, FROM 8 TO 16 AS AN APPETIZER.

Norimakizushi
VINEGARED RICE ROLLED IN SEAWEED

A great favorite with children, especially for birthdays, it is also one of the dishes made to celebrate Hina Matsuri, *the Dolls' Festival on March 3. Sometimes called Girls' Day, this old festival dates from the 8th-century Heian Court when girls were given elaborately dressed dolls.* Norimakizushi *is also a favorite with adults as the main course of a light lunch, as an accompaniment to drinks or as an appetizer. Served at room temperature, it can be made ahead of time for special occasions.*

2 cups rice
4 *shiitake* (Japanese dried mushrooms)
Sugar
2 tablespoons plus 1 teaspoon soy sauce
10 9-inch pieces *kanpyō* (dried gourd strips)
Salt
⅔ cups *dashi* (soup stock)
3 tablespoons *mirin*
2 tablespoons *usukuchi shōyu* (light soy sauce)
¼ pound fillet of sole
2 eggs, stirred
Vegetable oil
1 tablespoon *sake*
Red food coloring
1½ cups tightly packed spinach
4 sheets *nori* (dried laver seaweed)
Pickled red ginger

Cook the rice and season it with the vinegar mixture according to the recipe for *Sushi* (Rice with Vinegar Dressing).

Rinse the mushrooms and soak in water to cover for 30 minutes with a pinch of sugar. Squeeze out lightly and cut away the hard stems. Put into a saucepan with the water in which they soaked and cook over moderate heat, uncovered, until the liquid is reduced by ¼, about 4 minutes. Add 1 tablespoon sugar and simmer for 5 minutes longer, turning the mushrooms from time to time. Add the 2 table-spoons of soy sauce, reduce the heat to low and cook, turning once or twice, for 3 minutes longer or until the liquid has evaporated. Cool, squeeze out any moisture, and cut into ⅓-inch diagonal slices. Put on a large plate.

Sprinkle the gourd strips with salt and wash, rubbing lightly. Soak in warm water for about 2 minutes, place in a small saucepan with water to cover, bring it to a boil and simmer for about 2 minutes.

Drain. Return the strips to the saucepan with the soup stock, bring to a boil over high heat, then add 1 tablespoon each of sugar and *mirin* and cover with an *otoshibuta* or with a smaller saucepan lid that will fit on top of the contents of the pan. Or use a plate. Cook for 10 minutes over low heat, then add the light soy sauce and simmer for 5 minutes longer. When cool enough to handle squeeze out and put on the plate beside the mushrooms.

Put half the fish into a *suribachi* (mortar) with 1 tablespoon each of sugar, *mirin* and water and ¼ teaspoon salt; pound to a paste, then add the eggs, little by little, mixing well. Lightly oil the sides and bottom of an 8-inch covered skillet as well as the inside of the lid. Heat the skillet, pour in the egg mixture, reduce the heat to very low and cook for about 3 minutes. Using the lid, turn the omelette, add a little more oil to the pan and lightly brown the other side. Lift out, cut into ⅓-inch strips and add to the plate beside the mushrooms.

Rinse out and dry the skillet and half fill with water. Bring to a boil, add the other half of the fish and simmer until the fish loses its translucent look, about 2 minutes. Lift out and drain on a piece of cheesecloth, squeezing out the moisture and breaking up the fish. Pour the water out of the skillet, add the fish, the *sake,* 1 teaspoon of sugar, the remaining tablespoon of *mirin* and salt to taste. Add just enough red food coloring to make the fish a light and pretty pink. Cook, stirring with 5 or 6 chopsticks held in a bunch, over low heat until the mixture is dry and grainy. This is *soboro* which can also be made with shrimp or bought ready made in jars in Japanese markets. Put with the other ingredients on the plate.

Wash the spinach and drop it into a large saucepan of boiling salted water, bring back to a boil and cook for 1 minute. Drain and squeeze dry. A *sudare* (bamboo mat) is useful for this. Form into a roll and sprinkle with the teaspoon of soy sauce; let stand for a few minutes, then squeeze out again. Add to the plate. Divide each of the ingredients into 4 portions.

Toast the seaweed sheets on both sides for a few seconds over a gas flame or electric burner. Lay a bamboo mat on a wooden chopping board and place a sheet of seaweed on it. Wet the hands with rice vinegar and pat ¼ of the rice evenly over the seaweed leaving a ½-inch border along the bottom. Starting from the top, about 1½ inches from the edge, arrange ¼ of the spinach on top of the rice in a horizontal row. Next to the spinach make a row of omelette strips, then gourd strips, then *soboro,* then mushrooms. Roll up the seaweed, using the bamboo mat to help, pressing lightly but firmly to make a neat cylinder. Let it rest a minute or two in the mat, then unroll and set aside. Tap the ends of the roll on the chopping board to firm them up. Repeat with the remaining ingredients to make 4 rolls. Using a sharp knife wiped with a cloth wrung out in cold vinegared water, cut the rolls into ¾-inch slices, about 9 to a roll. Arrange on individual platters, garnish with thin slices of ginger and eat with chopsticks or by hand. SERVES 4 TO 6.

Hirame No Nigiri-Zushi
SOLE WITH VINEGARED RICE

Wasabi (green horseradish   Soy sauce
   powder)
¼ pound fillet of sole
Vinegared rice (see recipe for
   Sushi; you will need about half
   of it for this dish)

Mix a little green horseradish powder, about ½ teaspoon, with water to make a smooth paste.
   Cut the fish into 8 diagonal slices. Wet the hands. Take a slice of fish and put a dab of horseradish on top of it, then top with about a tablespoon of vinegared rice, making it into an oblong patty. Continue with the remaining slices of fish. Arrange on a plate and serve with a little soy sauce poured into a small saucer. Eat with chopsticks or by hand, dipping in the soy sauce as liked. SERVES 1 AS A MAIN COURSE, 4 AS AN APPETIZER.
   In Japan a variety of fish would be served, including tuna, striped bass, red snapper, cuttlefish, octopus, clams, sea urchins, salmon caviar, abalone, shrimp, scallops, etc.

Inarizushi
FRIED BEAN CURD STUFFED WITH VINEGARED RICE

These little bags of fried bean curd stuffed with sushi *(vinegared rice) are a great favorite for children's picnics and birthday parties, as well as being a fine accompaniment for drinks. They can be prepared ahead of time and are easy to make.*

1 cup rice
10 slices *aburaage* (fried bean curd)
⅔ cup *dashi* (soup stock)
5 tablespoons *mirin*
2 tablespoons sugar
4 tablespoons *usukuchi shōyu* (light soy sauce)
Pickled red ginger, thinly sliced
Pickled cucumber, preferably *kyūri narazuke* (Nara-style cucumber pickles)

Cook the rice and season it with the vinegar mixture according to the recipe for *Sushi* (Rice with Vinegar Dressing), halving the quantities. Or make the full recipe with 2 cups of rice, use half and reserve the other half for another type of *sushi*. It is difficult to cook less than 1 cup of rice successfully, and it is easier to cook 2 cups than 1.

Rinse the bean curd slices in hot water to remove the oil. Squeeze lightly, pat dry and cut in half, crosswise, giving 20 little bags. In a saucepan combine the soup stock, *mirin* and sugar and bring to a boil. Add the bean curd bags and simmer, uncovered, over moderate heat until the liquid is reduced to half, about 5 minutes. Add the light soy sauce and continue cooking until all the liquid is absorbed. Take care not to let the bean curd burn. Transfer the bean curd pieces to a colander and when they are cool enough to handle, gently press out any excess liquid. Stuff each bag with rice to make a little package, pushing the rice down firmly with the fingers. Turn the ends of the bags over and lay with the turned side down to keep the package closed.

On small oblong platters arrange 5 of the stuffed bags for each person. Garnish the right-hand front side of the dish with red ginger or cucumber pickles or both. Eat with chopsticks or by hand at room temperature. SERVES 4.

Chirashi-Zushi
MANY GARNISHED VINEGARED RICE

2 cups rice
1½ tablespoons *mirin*
6 feet *kanpyō* (dried gourd strips)
Salt
Boiling water
4 *shiitake* (dried Japanese
  mushrooms)
1-inch slice *renkon* (lotus root)
½ tablespoon rice vinegar

12 medium-sized snow-pea pods
2 eggs
Vegetable oil
⅔ cup *dashi* (soup stock)
4 tablespoons sugar
2 tablespoons soy sauce
4 slices pickled ginger root
1 sheet *nori* (dried laver seaweed)

Cook the rice and season it with the vinegar mixture according to the recipe for *Sushi* (Rice with Vinegar Dressing). Add the *mirin* to the rice when it is put on to cook.

Sprinkle the dried gourd strips with salt and wash in cold water, rubbing lightly. Rinse thoroughly and squeeze out. Put into a saucepan of boiling water and cook for a minute or two. Drain, fold up and cut into ½-inch pieces. Place on a platter.

Soak the mushrooms in warm water with a pinch of sugar for 30 minutes. Drain, squeeze out, remove the stems and cut the mushrooms into thin slices. Add to the platter with the dried gourd strips.

Peel the lotus root, slice it thinly. Put into a saucepan with 1 cup cold water and the rice vinegar. Simmer until tender, about 5 minutes, drain and add to the platter.

Drop the snow-pea pods into a small saucepan of boiling salted water and boil for 2 minutes. Drain, slice thinly and add to the platter.

Break the eggs into a bowl, add a pinch of salt, and stir with chopsticks until the eggs are well blended but not foamy. Heat a 7- to 8-inch skillet and pour in just enough oil to film the surface. Pour in a quarter of the eggs, tilting the pan so that it covers its whole surface. When the bottom of the omelette is lightly browned, turn it and cook for a few seconds longer to brown the other side. Lift out onto a chopping board. Repeat with the remaining egg mixture and lay the three omelettes on top of the first. Cut the omelettes in half, stack, and cut into thin crosswise strips. Add to the platter.

In a small measured saucepan heat ⅓ cup of the soup stock with 3 tablespoons of the sugar and ½ teaspoon salt. Add the snow-pea pods and cook for 1 minute. Lift out, drain and put on the platter. Add the lotus root slices to the saucepan, simmer for 2 minutes, lift out, drain and add to the platter. Add the remaining ⅓ cup soup stock to the saucepan with the soy sauce and the remaining tablespoon of sugar. The sugar may be omitted if a less sweet dish is preferred. It is a matter of taste. Add the dried gourd strips and simmer for 5 minutes. Lift out, drain and put on the platter. Add the mushrooms and cook over moderate heat until all the liquid has evaporated, about 5 minutes. Lift out onto the platter. Cut the slices of pickled ginger root into julienne strips. Add to the platter.

Toast the seaweed on both sides for a few seconds over a gas flame or electric burner. Crush in a piece of cheesecloth or crumble with the fingers and place in a small bowl.

Divide the rice among 4 large bowls. Top with the ingredients on the platter in a decorative way and put a small heap of the crushed seaweed in the center of each bowl. SERVES 4.

PRESSED *SUSHI* (VINEGARED RICE)

An *oshiwaku,* or oblong wooden box with removable top and bottom, is used to press the vinegared rice (*sushi*) and its garnishes into a firm cake that can be sliced into individual servings. Available in most Japanese stores, the boxes come in various sizes. If you do not have the size indicated in a recipe, simply distribute the garnish according to the size of the box in hand. If an *oshiwaku* is not available, a spring-form cake pan is probably the best substitute; the cook can nibble on the uneven pieces from the edges if the pan is round.

Sushi may be kept refrigerated overnight. Traditionally it would be wrapped in a dried bamboo leaf, but kitchen aluminum foil will do. If using right away, let the *sushi* stand for 20 minutes before slicing to firm up the rice; otherwise it may crumble when cut. When ready to serve, wipe a very sharp knife with a damp cloth and cut the rice into individual portions.

Kanizushi
PRESSED VINEGARED RICE WITH CRAB

2 cups rice
½ pound cooked crab meat,
    fresh, frozen or canned
2 tablespoons lemon juice
2 eggs
1 teaspoon sugar

¼ teaspoon salt
Vegetable oil
20 freshly cooked green peas,
    about 1 tablespoon
Pickled red ginger, thinly sliced

Cook the rice and season it with the vinegar mixture according to the recipe for *Sushi* (Rice with Vinegar Dressing).

Pick over the crab meat to remove any shell or cartilage; sprinkle with the lemon juice and a little salt. Separate the claw meat from the rest and set it aside. Stir the remaining crab meat into the rice, mixing gently.

Break eggs into a bowl and stir with chopsticks until well blended but not foamy. Stir in the sugar and ¼ teaspoon salt. Heat an 8-inch skillet and add just enough oil to film the bottom lightly. Pour in ¼ of the egg mixture, tilting the pan so that the egg covers the whole surface. When the egg is set and lightly browned, turn the omelette to brown the other side. Place the omelette on a cutting board. Make three more omelettes in the same way, placing them on top of the first. Roll the omelettes up and cut into very thin slices making a pile of golden threads.

Pack a dampened *oshiwaku* about 3 by 6 inches with the *sushi* rice, pressing down firmly with the lid. There will be enough rice for 4 boxes. Arrange ¼ of the eggs, crab claw meat and peas on top of the rice and again press down firmly with the lid. The success of the recipe lies in firm pressing. Remove the bottom of the box and press out the rectangle of decorated rice, using the lid, which fits inside the box, to do so. Wash the box thoroughly in vinegared water after each use; otherwise the rice will stick. Repeat, using up all the ingredients. Let stand for 20 minutes to firm up the rice which otherwise may crumble when cut.

To serve, slice in half lengthwise with a very sharp knife wiped with a damp cloth, then cut into 1-inch slices crosswise, giving slices 1 by 1½ inches. Arrange on 4 plates. Garnish with pickled ginger and eat with chopsticks or by hand. This is a very attractive dish, a favorite for picnics and a pleasant accompaniment to drinks or, in larger servings, for a light lunch. SERVES 4 TO 8.

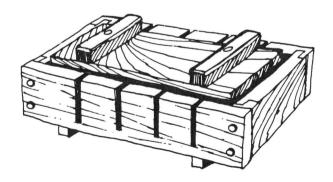

Hakozushi

PRESSED VINEGARED RICE WITH SHRIMP AND SALMON

This sushi *is made Osaka-style, using more sugar than Tokyo-style* sushi.

2½ cups rice
2 tablespoons *sake*
4-inch square *kombu* (kelp)
5 tablespoons plus 1 teaspoon
   rice vinegar
4 tablespoons sugar
Salt
1 teaspoon msg

8 sprigs *na-no-hana* (rape
   blossoms)
8 medium-sized raw shrimp
4 ounces smoked salmon *or* fillet
   of red snapper *or* sole. Use
   very fresh fish.
¼ lemon, thinly sliced

Thoroughly wash the rice and drain in a sieve for at least 30 minutes. Put into a heavy saucepan with a tightly fitting lid and add 2½ cups water and the *sake*. Clean the seaweed with a damp cloth and cut into a ½-inch fringe. Bury in the rice. Let stand for 15 minutes. Bring to a boil, covered, on high heat, removing the seaweed just before the water boils. Reduce the heat to moderate and cook for 5 to 6 minutes, then reduce the heat to low and cook for 10 minutes. Turn the heat to high for 10 seconds, then let the rice stand off the heat for 10 minutes.

In a small saucepan combine the 5 tablespoons rice vinegar with the sugar, 1 tablespoon of salt and the msg. Heat through, stirring to mix. Turn the rice out into a large shallow dish, preferably wooden. In Japan a *bandai* (*sushioke*), a large round wooden dish, would be used. Pour the vinegar mixture over the rice, mixing it with a *shamoji* (wooden spatula) and fanning it vigorously at the same time to make it glisten.

Rinse the rape blossoms and cut away most of the stems, leaving just the leafy tops with the yellow blossoms. Drop into boiling salted water and cook, uncovered, over high heat for 2 minutes. Rinse in cold water, drain and sprinkle with a little salt and msg.

Remove the intestinal vein from the shrimp with a toothpick, but do not peel. Using small bamboo skewers, skewer the shrimp full length on the underside to keep them from curling when they are cooked. Drop the shrimp into boiling salted water with the teaspoon of rice vinegar and boil over high heat for 1½ minutes. Drain, remove the skewers, peel the shrimp and cut along the back to open them out flat, taking care not to cut them through.

Cut the salmon or other fish into thin slices on the diagonal and set aside with the lemon slices.

Arrange 4 shrimp at even intervals on the bottom of a dampened *oshiwaku*. Arrange the sprigs of rape in a row above the shrimp. With damp hands press a quarter of the rice into the box, then press down firmly with the lid. Turn the box over, removing the lid so that the side with the shrimp is uppermost, and the plain side is down uncovered. Press down with the lid to remove the box. Set the pressed rice aside and repeat with the remaining rice, shrimp and rape sprigs. (Rinse and dry the box in vinegared water between each use, otherwise the rice will stick.) Wet the hands from time to time so that the rice will not stick to them.

Using the same technique arrange half the smoked salmon or other fish pieces on the bottom of the box and top with half the lemon slices in a row. Add the rice and press out; repeat with the rest of the rice. Let stand 20 minutes for rice to firm before slicing into small rectangles, each with a shrimp or a piece of salmon on top. If the *sushi* is to be served later, store tightly wrapped in the refrigerator. Let come to room temperature before serving. Place 2 slices, each with a different topping, on small plates and eat with chopsticks or fingers. SERVES 4 TO 8.

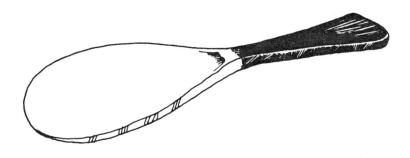

Fish and Shellfish, Sashimi and Tempura

FISH AND SHELLFISH

Japan has access to an astonishing variety of fish and shellfish in the waters surrounding the country. Here, a special marine environment exists, similar to that off the Chilean coast, where fish and shellfish are spectacular. These special conditions stimulate the growth of plankton, prime food for marine life, and result in a particularly rich sea harvest.

Since the islands which make up Japan offer little room for grazing or growing—consisting mainly of rugged mountains and narrow coastal plains—food from the sea has always been valued and appreciated. The Japanese are a seafaring people who crossed the ocean to reach their islands in the first place, and they have never lost their affection for the sea. Nowhere is this more evident than in the kitchen.

Nijimasu No Karaage
DEEP-FRIED RAINBOW TROUT

4 rainbow trout, each weighing 5
  to 6 ounces, cleaned with head
  and tail left on
1 tablespoon *sake*
Salt
1 medium cucumber
¼ cup grated *daikon* (white
  radish)

4 fresh hot green peppers
Pickled red ginger
Katakuriko starch *or* cornstarch
Vegetable oil
3 tablespoons rice vinegar
1 tablespoon sugar
½ teaspoon salt
1 teaspoon fresh ginger juice

Rinse the trout thoroughly. Pat dry and make 2 equally spaced shallow diagonal cuts on each side of the fish. Sprinkle with the *sake,* then lightly sprinkle with salt and set aside.

Cut a slice from each end of the cucumber and rub the cut surfaces with the ends. Discard the slices. Roll the cucumber in salt for a minute or two. This removes the bitter taste. Rinse and pat dry. If waxed, peel. If not, peel in alternate strips, scrape out the seeds and grate on a fine grater. Squeeze out the moisture and set aside. Squeeze out the radish and set aside. Cut the stems off the peppers and scrape out the seeds with chopsticks. Slice the ginger very thin.

Drain the trout and dry with paper towels. Coat the fish lightly inside and out with the *katakuriko* starch or the cornstarch.

Heat 3 inches of oil in a *tempura* pan or saucepan to 350°F. on a frying thermometer or until bubbles form on wooden chopsticks stirred in the oil. Add the peppers and fry for 30 seconds. Lift out and drain on the rack of the *tempura* pan or on paper towels. Add the trout and cook, one at a time unless the pan will hold more, for 4 or 5 minutes, turning once or twice. Serve on 4 oblong platters garnished with the peppers and pickled ginger.

In a bowl combine the rice vinegar, sugar, salt and ginger juice, grated cucumber and radish. Stir until the sugar is dissolved and pour over the fish. SERVES 4.

Hirame No Ageni

SOLE WITH BEAN CURD AND MUSHROOMS

8 ounces fillet of sole
Flour
1 *momen tōfu* (bean curd)
   weighing about ½ pound
8 fresh mushrooms

1⅛ cups *dashi* (soup stock)
4 tablespoons soy sauce
1 tablespoon sugar
1½ tablespoons *mirin*
Vegetable oil

Halve the fish fillet lengthwise, then cut diagonally into bite-sized pieces. Coat with flour. Roll the bean curd in a *sudare* (bamboo mat) or a kitchen cloth and set a plate on top of it. Let it stand for about 8 minutes to press out excess moisture. Pat dry and cut into 1-inch cubes. Coat with flour. Trim the mushrooms and coat with flour. Set aside.

In a small saucepan combine the soup stock, soy sauce, sugar and *mirin* and set aside.

Heat 2 to 3 inches of oil in a *tempura* pan or a saucepan to 350°F. on a frying thermometer (slow to moderate). Add the pieces of sole, one at a time, to keep them separate; then add the mushrooms and the bean curd and fry until lightly browned, turning once, about 2 to 3 minutes. Do this in more than one batch so as not to crowd the pan. Drain on the rack of the *tempura* pan, or on paper towels.

Bring the soup stock mixture to a boil, add the fish, mushrooms and bean curd. Bring back to a boil, then remove from the heat. Serve in medium bowls with the sauce poured over. SERVES 4.

In Japan fresh *shiitake* mushrooms would be used. Dried *shiitake* can be used instead of fresh local mushrooms, in which case soak them for 30 minutes in warm water with a pinch of sugar, squeeze out, and cut off the hard stems.

Tsumamono-age
PEPPERS STUFFED WITH FISH

6 small green bell peppers
¾ pound fillet of sole or any
  white fish
1½ tablespoons *sake*
3 tablespoons *katakuriko or*
  cornstarch
½ teaspoon salt
⅛ teaspoon msg

1 tablespoon finely chopped
  parsley
Vegetable oil for deep frying
1½ teaspoons rice vinegar
4½ teaspoons soy sauce
3 teaspoons dry mustard,
  preferably Japanese

Rinse the peppers, cut out stem and remove the seeds and fibers, leaving the peppers intact. Rinse to remove any remaining seeds and set to drain. Rinse the fish, pat dry and grind in a *suribachi* or in a blender. Add the *sake,* 2½ tablespoons of the cornstarch, salt, msg and parsley and mix well. Put ½ teaspoon cornstarch into each pepper and shake to coat the inside thoroughly. Shake out the excess. Stuff the peppers with the fish mixture, pushing it in firmly with the fingers and taking care not to break the peppers.

Heat the oil to 300°F. on a frying thermometer, a little lower than moderate, in a saucepan large enough to hold all the peppers comfortably. There should be enough oil to cover the peppers. Fry the peppers until tender, about 8 to 10 minutes, turning 2 or 3 times during the cooking. Drain on paper towels. When cool enough to handle, cut the peppers into 4 to 6 slices according to size and arrange on 4 serving platters. Mix the vinegar with the soy sauce and put into 4 small bowls or saucers. Mix the mustard with hot water in a small dish and add to the platter with the peppers. Eat at room temperature, dipping the peppers into the sauce and adding a dab of mustard.
SERVES 4.

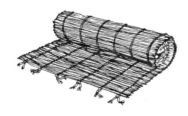

Sake No Kenchin-Mushi

SALMON STEAMED WITH BEAN CURD

¾ pound fresh salmon fillet with
skin on
Salt
5 teaspoons *mirin*
2 *kikurage* (jelly mushroom)
1 *momen tōfu* (bean curd),
weighing about ½ pound
1 egg
20 small peeled and cleaned
cooked shrimp, about 2
ounces
1 tablespoon green peas
2 teaspoons *usukuchi shōyu*
(light soy sauce)

½ teaspoon salt
1½ cups *dashi* (soup stock)
1 tablespoon *usukuchi shōyu*
(light soy sauce)
1 tablespoon *mirin*
1 teaspoon *katakuriko or* potato
starch *or* cornstarch *or*
arrowroot
1-inch cube fresh ginger root, cut
into julienne strips

Slice the salmon into 4 diagonal pieces. Sprinkle with salt, then with
2 teaspoons of the *mirin,* on both sides and set aside.

Soak the jelly mushrooms for 10 to 15 minutes in warm water.
Squeeze out and cut into julienne strips. Rinse the bean curd and wrap
loosely in a kitchen cloth or piece of cheesecloth, place a plate on top
of it and let it stand for about 5 minutes to get rid of excess moisture.
Transfer to a bowl and mash with a whisk or fork. Break the egg into a
small bowl, stir with chopsticks until well blended but not foamy and
add to the bean curd. Add the mushroom strips, the shrimp, peas, 2
teaspoons light soy sauce, ½ teaspoon salt, and remaining 3 teaspoons *mirin.* Mix well.

Rinse off the salmon and pat dry. Put a slice of salmon in the center
of a piece of cheesecloth. Spread ¼ of the bean curd mixture on top
and fold up into a neat package. Repeat with the rest of salmon and
bean curd mixture to make 4 packages.

Place the packages in a steamer, bean curd side up, over boiling
water, lower the heat to moderate and steam for 12 to 13 minutes.

In a small saucepan combine the soup stock, salt to taste, 1
tablespoon light soy, *mirin* and *katakuriko* mixed with 1 teaspoon

cold water and simmer over low heat until the mixture is lightly thickened and smooth.

Unwrap the salmon and place in individual bowls, bean curd side down, skin side up. Place a little heap of ginger in the center of each salmon slice and pour on the hot sauce. Serve hot. SERVES 4.

Sake No Isobeyaki
GRILLED MARINATED SALMON

This salmon (sake) *dish is garnished with* nori *(dried laver seaweed), a combination reminiscent of a scene at the beach (* isobe *). The poetic element, ever-present in Japanese food, conveys a desire to please the mind as well as the palate.*

½ pound fresh salmon fillet with skin on	¼ sheet *nori* (dried laver seaweed)
4 tablespoons *mirin*	4 pickled ginger sprouts, optional
4 tablespoons soy sauce	

Cut the salmon fillet into 4 diagonal slices. In a bowl combine the *mirin* and soy sauce; add the salmon and marinate for 30 minutes.

Lift out the salmon pieces and pour the marinade into a saucepan. Reduce to half over moderate heat. Dip the salmon in the marinade and grill over moderate heat for 2 minutes. Turn, paint with the marinade using a pastry brush, grill for 1 minute, paint again with marinade and cook for 1 minute, then turn. Repeat grilling and basting. The salmon may also be broiled instead of grilled.

Place the cooked salmon on 4 small oblong platters. Toast the seaweed for a few seconds on both sides over a gas flame or electric burner, crumble and put on top of the salmon. Garnish each platter with a pickled ginger sprout (optional). SERVES 4.

Sake No Teriyaki

GLAZED SALMON

2 6-ounce salmon steaks with
  skin on
2 tablespoons vegetable oil
2 tablespoons soy sauce

1 tablespoon *mirin*
Pickled ginger or pickled
  cucumber

Cut the salmon steaks in half. Heat the oil in a skillet large enough to hold the salmon pieces comfortably and sauté over fairly high heat until the fish is browned all over, about 3 or 4 minutes. Mix the soy sauce with the *mirin*, pour over the fish, reduce the heat and cook, turning frequently, until the fish is glazed, 1 or 2 minutes.

Serve on 4 small platters, garnished with either pickled ginger or pickled cucumber. SERVES 4.

Saba No Nanban-ni

MACKEREL WITH HOT RED PEPPERS

1¾ pounds mackerel fillets
Flour
Vegetable oil
1 cup *dashi* (soup stock)
3 tablespoons soy sauce

1 tablespoon sugar
1½ tablespoons rice vinegar
1 dried hot red pepper, seeded
  and chopped

Cut each of the mackerel fillets into 4 slices and dust lightly with flour. Heat 2 to 3 inches of oil in a *tempura* pan or a saucepan to 350°F. on a frying thermometer, or until bubbles form on wooden chopsticks stirred in the oil. Fry the mackerel pieces for 2 minutes, turning once, and drain on the rack of the *tempura* pan or on paper towels.

In a saucepan large enough to hold the mackerel pieces in a single layer combine the soup stock, soy sauce, sugar and vinegar and bring to a boil. Add the mackerel and the hot pepper and simmer, uncovered, over moderate for 5 minutes. Serve in medium-sized bowls with the sauce poured over the fish. SERVES 4.

Sawara No Teriyaki
GLAZED KING MACKEREL

½-pound king mackerel fillet
3 tablespoons *mirin*

2 tablespoons soy sauce
½ tablespoon *sake*

Cut the fish into 8 slices. In a bowl combine the *mirin*, soy sauce and *sake*. Add the fish and marinate for 15 minutes. Lift out the fish and set aside. Pour the marinade into a small saucepan, bring to a boil and reduce to about a quarter of the original volume.

Thread the fish pieces on 2 or 3 metal skewers and grill the fish over high heat about 6 inches from the source of heat until lightly browned; or broil. When the fish pieces are almost cooked, use a pastry brush and paint with the marinade 3 or 4 times to glaze, still over high heat. Turn frequently. Let the fish cool before removing the skewers and arrange on plates. Serve at room temperature. SERVES 8.

This dish may also be served as a New Year dish.

Saba No Shioyaki
GRILLED MACKEREL FILLETS

2 small mackerel fillets with skin
  on
Salt

½ cup grated *daikon* (white
  radish)
2 teaspoons soy sauce

Cut the fillets in half crosswise and sprinkle lightly with salt on both sides. Leave for about 3 minutes, then rinse in cold water and pat dry with paper towels. Sprinkle very lightly with salt on both sides again and cut a shallow cross in the skin of each piece, taking care to cut only through the skin. This will prevent the fish from curling when it is being cooked.

Grill the fish over moderate heat until lightly browned on both sides, about 10 minutes in all. Or broil about 3 inches from the source of heat.

Put the fish on 4 medium-sized plates, skin side up. Lightly squeeze out the radish, form into mounds and add to the plates with the fish. Pour the soy sauce over the radish. Eat with chopsticks, putting a little radish on each bite. SERVES 4.

Saba No Ginshiyaki
MACKEREL IN ALUMINUM FOIL

2 mackerel fillets, about ¾
   pound in all
2 tablespoons *mirin*
3 tablespoons soy sauce
½ teaspoon sugar
8 medium-sized fresh
   mushrooms

Vegetable oil
4 chestnuts canned in syrup
16 cooked ginkgo nuts, canned or
   bottled
½ lemon, cut into 4 wedges

Halve the mackerel fillets. Mix the *mirin* and 2 tablespoons of the soy sauce and pour over the fish. Marinate for 20 minutes, turning once or twice. Mix the remaining tablespoon of the soy sauce with the sugar and pour over the mushrooms.

Cut 8 12-by-10-inch pieces of aluminum foil. Use 2 sheets of foil, one on top of the other, for each serving. Brush the top sheet with oil, leaving an unoiled margin of about 1 inch. Arrange a piece of mackerel in the center of the foil, skin side up, top with 2 mushrooms, 1 chestnut and 4 ginkgo nuts. Fold the top piece of foil over to make a neat package, then wrap the second piece of foil over the first, twisting the ends. Repeat with the rest of the ingredients. Place the packages on a baking sheet and bake in a preheated 350°F. oven for 7 or 8 minutes.

Place the foil packages on 4 individual platters and garnish each with a lemon wedge. Unwrap the packages, squeeze lemon juice over the fish and eat with chopsticks. SERVES 4.

In Japan fresh local mushrooms (*nama-shiitake*), which are a pretty brown color, would be used, enhancing the appearance of the dish. Instead of fresh local mushrooms, *shiitake* (Japanese dried mushrooms), soaked 30 minutes in warm water with a pinch of sugar, squeezed out and the tough stems removed, may be used to get the color contrast.

Saba No Misoni
MACKEREL WITH RED BEAN PASTE

4 mackerel fillets, about 12
  ounces in all
1-inch cube fresh ginger root
1 cup *dashi* (soup stock)
2 tablespoons sugar

¼ cup *sake*
5 tablespoons red *miso* (bean
  paste)
1 scallion, trimmed, using white
  part only

Cut the fish into 1-inch diagonal slices. Peel the ginger and cut it into julienne strips.

In a saucepan large enough to hold the fish in a single layer combine the soup stock, sugar and *sake* and bring to a boil, stirring to dissolve the sugar. Add the ginger and the fish and cover with an *otoshibuta* (an inner wooden lid), or use a smaller saucepan lid or cover with a plate. Simmer for about 5 minutes over moderate heat, or until the fish is done. Mix the red bean paste with a little of the soup stock to make a smooth paste and add to the saucepan, mixing gently. Bring to a boil, reduce the heat to low and simmer for 12 minutes.

Thinly slice the scallion and crisp for a few minutes in cold water. Drain and squeeze out in a cloth.

Arrange the fish on plates with the sauce poured over it. The sauce should be moderately thick. If it is too thick, thin with a little soup stock. Garnish with the scallion. SERVES 4.

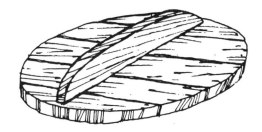

Saba No Oroshini

MACKEREL WITH GRATED WHITE RADISH

4 small mackerel fillets, about 12
  ounces in all
Flour
Vegetable oil
1 cup finely grated *daikon* (white
  radish)

1 scallion, trimmed, using white
  and green parts
1⅓ cups *dashi* (soup stock)
5 tablespoons soy sauce
3 tablespoons *mirin*
1 tablespoon sugar

Cut the mackerel fillets into 1-inch diagonal slices and flour lightly.
Let stand for a minute or two. Heat 2 to 3 inches of oil in a *tempura*
pan or saucepan to 350°F. on a frying thermometer, or until bubbles
form on wooden chopsticks stirred in the oil. Fry the mackerel pieces
for 2 to 3 minutes or until lightly browned. Drain on the rack of the
tempura pan or on paper towels.

Lightly squeeze out the grated radish. Cut the scallion into 4
diagonal slices.

In a small saucepan combine the soup stock, soy sauce, *mirin* and
sugar and bring to a boil. Add the mackerel, radish and scallion and
bring back to a boil, uncovered. Remove from heat and serve in
medium-sized bowls with the sauce poured over the fish. Eat with
chopsticks. SERVES 4.

Wakasagi No Nanbanzuke

PICKLED SMELT

12 small smelt, about 10 ounces,
  with heads and tails left on
Salt
Flour
Vegetable oil

½ cup rice vinegar
4 tablespoons sugar
Dash msg
2 dried hot red peppers

Clean and scale the smelt, or have the fish store do it. Sprinkle with
salt and set aside for 20 minutes. Pat dry with paper towels and
sprinkle with flour.

In a *tempura* pan heat about 2½ inches vegetable oil to 350°F. on a frying thermometer, or until bubbles form on wooden chopsticks stirred in the oil. Add the smelt, a few at a time, and fry for 5 or 6 minutes, or until golden brown all over. Transfer to a shallow dish.

In a saucepan combine the vinegar, sugar and msg. Heat to warm, stirring. Seed and chop or crumble the peppers and add to the vinegar mixture. Pour the mixture over the smelt and refrigerate for 2 or 3 days, turning the fish from time to time. Serve at room temperature as a main course or an appetizer. To eat, pick up the whole fish with chopsticks. SERVES 4.

Wakasagi No Ageni

GLAZED SMELT

12 small smelt, cleaned and scaled with heads and tails left on
Salt
Katakuriko or cornstarch
Vegetable oil

2 tablespoons sugar
2 tablespoons *sake*
3 tablespoons soy sauce
1-inch cube fresh ginger root, grated

Sprinkle the fish lightly with salt and let stand for a few minutes. Pat dry and coat with *katakuriko* or cornstarch. Heat 2 to 3 inches of oil in a *tempura* pan or a saucepan to 350°F. on a frying thermometer, or until bubbles form on wooden chopsticks stirred in the oil. Fry the smelt in batches for 10 minutes, turning the fish once or twice.

In a skillet large enough to hold all the fish comfortably combine the sugar, *sake* and soy sauce; mix, bring to a boil, add the smelt and glaze in the mixture over fairly high heat for a minute or two. Turn so that the fish are glazed on all sides.

Arrange the smelt on 4 individual platters and garnish with the grated ginger. SERVES 4.

Karei No Karaage
DEEP-FRIED CRISPY FLOUNDER

4 flounder, weighing about ½
  pound each, cleaned, with
  heads, tails and fins left on
Flour
1 scallion, trimmed, using white
  and green parts
1-inch slice *daikon* (white
  radish), about 3 ounces

1 dried hot red pepper
1 tablespoon *ponzu* (citrus
  vinegar)
1 tablespoon soy sauce
1½ to 2 tablespoons *dashi* (soup
  stock)
Vegetable oil

Wash and dry the fish and score diagonally in both directions at 1-inch intervals to form a diamond pattern. Do this on both sides. Dust fish all over with flour and set aside for 2 or 3 minutes.

Cut the scallion into 1-inch slices, then cut these finely lengthwise. Put into a bowl of cold water to crisp for a few minutes, drain and dry in a cloth. Set aside for garnish.

Peel the radish, poke a hole in the center with a chopstick. Seed the pepper and stuff into the hole. Finely grate the radish, squeezing out the excess moisture. Set aside with the scallions.

To make the dipping sauce, mix together the vinegar, soy sauce and soup stock and pour into 4 small bowls. Put one at each place setting.

In a tempura pan or a saucepan heat 2 to 3 inches of oil to 350°F. on a frying thermometer and fry the fish, as many at a time as the pan will comfortably hold, turning once, until they are golden, 7 to 8 minutes. Lift out and drain on the rack of the *tempura* pan or on paper towels.

Place folded paper napkins on 4 medium-sized platters and place the fish on them, dark-skinned side up and head facing left. Garnish the front of the platter with a pile each of radish and scallion.

To eat, mix the garnishes into the sauce, cut the fish into convenient pieces with chopsticks and dip into the sauce. SERVES 4.

Fillet of sole, halved, can be used for this, as can horse mackerel fillets and whole small whiting or smelt or other small white fish.

Karei No Sawani
SIMMERED FLOUNDER

1 flounder, about 1 pound, cleaned and scaled
Boiling water
5 small scallions, trimmed, using white and green parts
⅔ cup plus ⅓ cup *dashi* (soup stock)

5 tablespoons *sake*
1½ tablespoons *mirin*
1½ tablespoons *usukuchi shōyu* (light soy sauce)
¼ teaspoon salt
½ teaspoon fresh ginger juice (from grated ginger)

Cut the flounder into 4 crosswise slices. Score the skin of each piece with an H cut on the diagonal. Pour 2 cups boiling water gently over the fish, then rinse in cold water. Finely chop the scallions.

In a saucepan large enough to hold the fish comfortably, combine the ⅔ cup soup stock, *sake, mirin,* light soy sauce and salt; stir to mix, bring to a boil uncovered over high heat, add the fish and cover with an *otoshibuta* (inner wooden lid), or use a smaller saucepan lid or a plate. Simmer over moderate heat for 6 minutes. Add the scallions, remove the *otoshibuta* and cover with the saucepan's own lid. Cook for 2 minutes. Add the ⅓ cup soup stock and the ginger juice and remove from the heat. Place the fish slices on 4 individual dishes and pour the sauce over them. Serve hot. SERVES 4.

Karei No Nitsuke

BOILED FLOUNDER

4 flounder, weighing about ½
    pound each, cleaned, with
    heads, tails and fins left on
¼ cup *sake*

4 tablespoons *mirin*
5 tablespoons soy sauce
¼ tablespoon sugar
8 fresh hot green peppers

Wash and dry the fish and score diagonally across in both directions at 1-inch intervals to form a diamond pattern. Do this on both sides.

In a saucepan large enough to hold the fish comfortably combine ⅔ cup water, the *sake, mirin,* 4 tablespoons of the soy sauce and the sugar; bring to a boil. Add the flounder, dark-skinned side up, bring back to a boil, skim, then cover with an *otoshibuta* (an inner wooden lid), or use a smaller saucepan lid or cover with a plate. Cover with lid of the saucepan and simmer 10 minutes over moderate heat, shaking the pan from time to time so the fish does not stick.

Cut the stems off the peppers and slit them lengthwise, taking care not to cut them through. Scrape out the seeds. Put into a saucepan with the remaining tablespoon of soy sauce, bring to a boil, and remove from the heat.

Arrange the fish on 4 oblong platters, dark-skinned side up and head facing left. Garnish with the peppers, placing them at the right-hand front of the dish. Pour 1 tablespoon liquid from the pan in which the fish were cooked over each serving. Eat with chopsticks, using the chopsticks to cut the fish into convenient pieces. SERVES 4.

Ginshiyaki
FOIL-WRAPPED FISH, SHRIMP AND VEGETABLES

½ pound fillet of striped bass
8 medium-sized raw unpeeled
  shrimp
Salt
1 tablespoon *sake*
Vegetable oil

8 medium-sized fresh
  mushrooms
4 chestnuts canned in syrup
12 cooked ginkgo nuts, canned or
  bottled
4 lemon wedges

Cut the fish into 4 slices. Remove the head, legs and intestinal vein of the shrimp, but do not peel. Put the fish and shrimp into separate bowls and sprinkle each lightly with salt and ½ teaspoon of *sake*. Let stand for 10 minutes, turning once or twice.

Cut 8 12-by-8-inch sheets of aluminum foil and arrange them in pairs, one sheet on top of the other. Brush each top sheet with oil, leaving an unoiled margin of about 1 inch. Arrange a slice of fish, 2 shrimp, 2 mushrooms, a chestnut and 3 ginkgo nuts in the center of the foil. Fold up the top piece to make a neat package, then wrap the second piece of foil over the package, twisting the ends. Repeat with the remaining pieces of foil and the rest of the ingredients.

Arrange the packages on a baking sheet and bake in a preheated moderate (350°F.) oven for 7 to 8 minutes. Serve on separate plates, still in the foil. Garnish with lemon wedges. SERVES 4.

Sole, turbot, halibut or any white fish may be used instead of striped bass; or chicken breast, skinned, boned and cut into bite-sized pieces may be added.

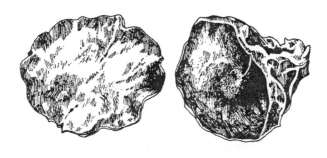

Sakana No Misozuke-Yaki
FISH MARINATED IN BEAN PASTE

4 small butterfish, cleaned and   1 cup *miso* (bean paste)
   scaled   3 tablespoons *sake*
Salt   Red pickled ginger

Wash and dry the fish and sprinkle lightly on both sides with salt. Mix the bean paste with the *sake* until smooth. Spread half the bean paste mixture over the bottom of a glass or enamel dish or baking pan large enough to hold the fish in one layer. Cover the bean paste mixture with a piece of cheesecloth cut to fit the dish. Place the fish on top of the cheesecloth and cover with another piece of cheesecloth. Spread top cheesecloth with the remaining bean paste mixture. Cover the dish tightly with aluminum foil or plastic wrap and refrigerate for 2 days at least or up to 5 days for a more pronounced flavor.

    When ready to use the fish, remove the cheesecloth, scrape off the bean paste and store it in a covered container in the refrigerator for use another time. Do not wash the fish. If there is any paste on the fish, wipe it off with a cloth. Broil the fish until done, about 4 minutes on each side. The bean paste will have flavored the fish. Garnish to taste with pickled ginger. SERVES 4.

NOTE: To reuse bean paste, see recipe for *Sokuseki Misozuke* (Instant Pickled Vegetables with Bean Paste).
    King mackerel, red snapper, porgy or bluefish may also be used.

Kodai No Shioyaki
SALT-BROILED PORGY

1 porgy or red snapper, weighing   Salt
   about 10 ounces, scaled and   Red pickled ginger
   cleaned with head and tail left
   on

Wash the fish, pat dry with paper towels and sprinkle generously with salt inside and out. Set aside for 30 to 40 minutes. Rinse off the salt and pat dry. With a long thin skewer make holes all over the fish on both sides, then skewer the fish, entering just under eye then taking skewer through middle and out at the tail. Put a second skewer through the fish, starting close to the first but about an inch below. Tie the mouth of the fish shut with a piece of kitchen string. Sprinkle the tail and fins with salt to prevent them browning too quickly. Season the fish with salt.

Lightly oil the rack of a grill or broiler. Preheat grill or broiler, then cook the fish about 5 minutes on each side, or until golden brown.

Carefully slip the skewers out of the fish and place it on an oblong platter with the head to the left. Remove the string from the mouth. Garnish with a little pickled ginger at the right-hand side front of the platter. Because the skewers have forced the fish into a curve, it will appear to be swimming. For outdoor cooking an *hibachi* is ideal for this sort of dish. SERVES 1.

Kaki No Koganeyaki

GOLDEN-BROWN FRIED OYSTERS

¼ pound spinach, about 2 cups tightly packed
16 large fresh oysters removed from shells
Salt

½ tablespoon *sake*
Flour
2 eggs
1 tablespoon vegetable oil

Thoroughly wash the spinach, drain and drop into a saucepan of boiling water. Bring back to a boil and boil for 2 minutes. Drain, rinse 3 times in cold water, squeeze out, form into a roll and cut into ½-inch slices.

Wash the oysters in salted water and drain. Put into a bowl and mix with the *sake* and a pinch of salt and let stand for a few minutes. Lift out and pat dry with paper towels. Roll in flour, shaking to remove the excess. Break the eggs into a bowl and stir with chopsticks until well blended but not foamy.

Heat the oil in a large, heavy skillet. Dip the oysters in the egg and fry for 1 or 2 minutes until golden brown on both sides. Drain on paper towels.

Arrange the oysters on platters and garnish with the spinach. SERVES 4.

Kaki No Iso-age
DEEP-FRIED OYSTERS

16 large oysters removed from
the shells
Salt
3 tablespoons *sake*
Flour to coat oysters
12 medium-sized green beans
1-inch slice *daikon* (white
radish)

2 dried hot red peppers
1 egg
¼ teaspoon sugar
⅔ cup sifted cake flour
1 sheet *nori* (dried laver seaweed)
Vegetable oil
4 tablespoons soy sauce

Rinse the oysters in cold salted water, drain and place in a bowl with 1 tablespoon of the *sake* and a little salt and marinate for about 5 minutes. Then drain and lightly coat with flour; set aside to dry.

Wash and trim the green beans and cut in half crosswise. Arrange in little bundles of 4.

Peel the radish, poke a hole in the center with a chopstick. Seed the peppers and stuff into the radish. Finely grate the radish and set aside.

Break the egg into a bowl and stir with chopsticks to blend thoroughly but without making it foamy. Add ⅓ cup water, ¼ teaspoon salt, the sugar and the remaining 2 tablespoons of the *sake*. Add the flour and mix lightly into a batter.

Cut the seaweed into 4 squares, then cut the squares into 16 strips and wrap a strip round each oyster. Or, toast the seaweed on both sides for a few seconds over a gas flame or electric burner, crush and add to the batter. It is a matter of choice.

In a saucepan or *tempura* pan heat 2 to 3 inches of oil to moderate (350°F. on a frying thermometer). Dip the beans into the batter and fry for 2 minutes. Drain on the rack of the *tempura* pan or on paper towels. Skim the oil. Dip the oysters into the batter and add to the pan, a few at a time. Fry until light gold, about 2 minutes. Drain on the rack of the *tempura* pan or on paper towels.

Pour 1 tablespoon of soy sauce into each of 4 small saucers. In the center put a little pile of grated radish. Serve the oysters and beans on *zaru* (bamboo plates) lined with paper napkins. Serve quickly while the oysters and beans are hot. The *sake* makes this batter very light and crisp. SERVES 4.

Hamaguri No Karashisumiso-ae
CLAMS IN BEAN PASTE, MUSTARD AND VINEGAR SAUCE

½ pound Little Necks or
  Cherrystone clams
Salt
Boiling water
Rice vinegar
2 8-inch fronds *wakame*
  (lobe-leaf seaweed)
6 scallions, trimmed, using white
  and green parts

6 tablespoons red *miso* (bean
  paste)
2 tablespoons sugar
1 tablespoon *sake*
2 tablespoons rice vinegar
1 teaspoon dry mustard,
  preferably Japanese
2 teaspoons fresh ginger root, cut
  into julienne strips

Rinse the clams in cold salted water, drain and drop into a saucepan of boiling water and cook for 1 minute. Drain, chop coarsely, and sprinkle with a little rice vinegar.

Soak the seaweed for 10 to 15 minutes, squeeze out, cut away the hard ribs and chop coarsely. Pour boiling water over the seaweed, drain and cool.

Drop the scallions into boiling water and cook for 2 or 3 minutes. Drain and lay the scallions on a wooden board. Press the scallions along their full length with the back of a knife to remove the liquid, then chop coarsely or cut into ½-inch pieces.

In a small saucepan combine the bean paste, sugar, *sake* and 2 tablespoons of rice vinegar. Mix together until smooth over low heat without letting the sauce boil. Mix the mustard with a teaspoon of hot water and stir into the sauce. Cool.

Combine the scallions, seaweed and clams with the sauce, mixing lightly. Serve in small, deep bowls garnished with the ginger. This is a very traditional dish and all the flavors come through independently, so carefully balanced that no one flavor predominates. SERVES 4.

Kaki No Sumiso-Kake

OYSTERS IN VINEGARED BEAN PASTE SAUCE

20 shucked oysters, about ¾ pint
Salt
1 tablespoon *sake*
8 scallions, trimmed, using white and green parts
1 scant teaspoon dry mustard, preferably Japanese

4 tablespoons *miso* (bean paste)
2 teaspoons sugar
2 tablespoons *mirin*
2 tablespoons rice vinegar

Rinse and drain the oysters. In a saucepan combine the *sake* with 1 cup salted water and bring to a boil. Add the oysters and cook just long enough to plump them, about 30 seconds. Drain the oysters and discard the liquid.

Drop the scallions into boiling water for 30 seconds, drain and pat dry. Cut into 1-inch pieces.

Mix the mustard into a paste with a little hot water and mix, in a bowl, with the bean paste, sugar, *mirin* and vinegar, stirring until well blended.

Divide the oysters among 4 small bowls and garnish with the scallions. Pour the sauce over the oysters. Eat with chopsticks. SERVES 4.

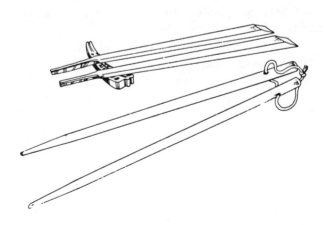

Yaki Hamaguri
GRILLED OR BROILED CLAMS

8 large Cherrystone or Little   Salt
Neck clams in the shell

Soak clams overnight in cold salted water, scrub thoroughly, rinse
and drain. Roll the clams in salt and arrange on a grill that goes on top
of the stove, or on the rack of a broiler. Cook over moderate heat for a
minute or two, or until the clams open. The clams will be done by
about the time the salt underneath is dry.

Place the clams on small plates on a bed of salt and decorate with
pine needles if any are available. Lift out clam with chopsticks to eat;
drink the liquid out of the shell. Serves 4.

VARIATION: *Hamaguri No Sakamushi* (Clams Steamed with *Sake*):
Prepare clams in same way as above and put into a saucepan with 2
tablespoons *sake*. Cover and cook over moderate heat for 5 minutes.
Lift clams carefully out of the saucepan and arrange on 4 small plates
on a bed of salt. Decorate as before with a pine needle sprig if
available. No liquid will be left in the pan but the clams will be
flavored with the *sake*. SERVES 4.

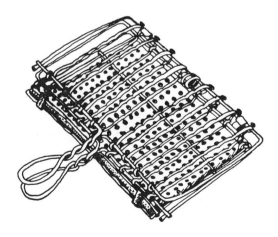

SASHIMI

Sashimi, sliced raw fish, is one of the glories of the Japanese kitchen, as respected as oysters or clams on the half shell and the Latin-American *seviches* (marinated raw fish and shellfish) are in the Western world. The secret lies in the absolute freshness of the fish, which for this reason will never taste "fishy."

Sashimi can be made of just one fish or several varieties and can be served either as a main course or as a light and refreshing first course. Suitable fish include sole, porgy, mackerel, flounder, red snapper, bass, squid, octopus, tuna or fresh sardines, all of which vary both in taste and texture.

Ika No Sashimi
GARNISHED RAW SQUID OR CUTTLEFISH

1 squid or ¾ pound peeled
  cuttlefish
Nori (dried laver seaweed)
2 tablespoons soy sauce
½ tablespoon *wasabi* (green
  horseradish powder)

Cucumber and carrot strips for
  garnish

Have the fish store clean the squid or cuttlefish (different fish with names used interchangeably for this relative of the octopus whose flavor is slightly sweet and rather rich). Rinse the cleaned squid and pat dry. Cut it open so that there are 2 pieces, then halve each piece crosswise to make 4.

Cover 2 of the squid pieces with seaweed cut to fit. Top with the other 2 pieces to make "sandwiches." With a very sharp knife, cut each sandwich crosswise into very thin slices. Arrange on 4 oblong platters. Divide soy sauce among 4 tiny bowls; put a small mound of *wasabi* mixed with just enough cold water to make a stiff paste on each plate to mix with the soy to taste. Garnish the platters with the vegetable strips. SERVES 4. Or arrange all the squid, garnishes and flavorings on a large platter and serve as appetizers to 12 to 16.

Hirame No Kobujime
RAW SOLE WITH WHITE RADISH

Kombu (kelp)
½ pound fillet of sole
1½-inch slice *daikon* (white radish)

½ tablespoon *wasabi* (green horseradish powder)
Soy sauce

Cut 2 pieces of seaweed (kelp) large enough to cover the sole, top and bottom. Clean it with a damp cloth and place underneath and on top of the fish in a glass baking dish or baking pan. Weight with plates and refrigerate for 1 hour.

Peel the radish, then slice it in a thin circular strip like peeling an apple. Roll the thin spiral up and cut the roll into very thin strips. Or thinly slice the radish, stack, and cut into julienne strips. Put into a small bowl, cover with cold water and leave to crisp. Drain the radish, squeeze out lightly in a cloth and place in a neat pile on each of 4 plates. Pour some soy sauce into a small bowl.

Remove the sole from the refrigerator, discard the seaweed and using a very sharp knife cut the fish into the thinnest possible diagonal slices. Divide the fish among the 4 plates, placing it so that it partly covers the radish.

Mix the horseradish to a paste with a little water and put a small mound of it on each plate. Eat the *sashimi* with chopsticks, putting a tiny bit of horseradish on a slice of fish, folding the fish over and dipping it in the soy sauce. Eat the radish at the same time, also dipping it in the sauce. SERVES 4.

Carrot, cut into fine julienne strips, may be used instead of radish; the orange-yellow of the carrot makes an attractive contrast to the translucent white of the fish.

Maguro No Sashimi
SLICED RAW TUNA

2½ ounces fresh tuna fillet
2 teaspoons *wasabi* (green
   horseradish powder)

2 teaspoons soy sauce
¼ cup thinly sliced *daikon* (white
   radish)

Cut the fish, which should be a deep rose color, into ¼-inch-thick slices. Professional chefs slice the fish on a slight diagonal halfway through the slice, then reverse the angle of the knife for the rest of the slice.

Arrange the fish on a medium-sized platter. Mix the horseradish with water to make a smooth stiff paste and place beside the tuna slices. Pour the soy sauce into a small bowl. Using chopsticks place a little bit of horseradish on a slice of tuna, fold the fish over, then dip it in soy sauce and eat. Dip the radish in soy sauce and eat, alternating with the tuna. SERVES 4.

In Japan the dish would be garnished with *shungiku* (see glossary) and a stalk of *shiso* (beefsteak plant) seeds which would be stripped from the stalk and added to the soy sauce. Freshly grated green horseradish would, of course, be preferred.

Suzuki No Sashimi
GARNISHED RAW STRIPED BASS

1-inch slice *daikon* (white
   radish)
1½-inch slice cucumber
½ tablespoon *wasabi* (green
   horseradish powder)

Soy sauce
½ pound fillet of striped bass,
   cleaned of bones and skin

Peel the radish, then cut it in a thin circular strip like peeling an apple. Roll it up and cut the roll into very thin strips; if this is too difficult, thinly slice the radish, stack, and cut into julienne strips. Place in a bowl of cold water for about 20 minutes, drain, pat dry. Cut the cucumber into very thin strips. Crisp in cold water and divide among 4 plates with the radish.

Mix the horseradish to a smooth paste with a little water, form into a mound and put at the front of the plates with the cucumber and radish. Pour soy sauce into 4 tiny saucers or bowls.

Cut the fish into ⅙-inch diagonal slices and arrange on 4 plates. Eat with chopsticks. Put a little horseradish on slice of fish, fold the fish over, dip it in soy sauce and eat with the radish and cucumber. The white of the radish makes a subtle contrast with the translucent white of the fish. SERVES 4.

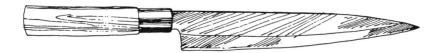

TEMPURA

Tempura, probably the best known of any Japanese food, belongs in the *agemono* (fried-thing) group. It is believed to have been introduced into Nagasaki by Portuguese priests in the 16th century.

There is some confusion over the origin of the name *tempura.* Some authorities believe it derives from the Portuguese *tempero,* seasoning, dressing, condiment, or from the Spanish verb *templar,* to heat lightly. I have never fully accepted this theory, not believing that the holy fathers went to Asia with spices and frying thermometers tucked into their habits.

It seems more likely that *tempura* comes from the Portuguese word *temporas* (also Spanish *temporas*), referring to the Ember Days, the Christian Church's four periods of fasting and prayer during the year. The connection is that most *tempura* consists of fish, shellfish and vegetables, traditional fast-day foods for Christians.

Batter-coated and deep-fried, *tempura* are a kind of small fritter, whose most important ingredient is shrimp. The batter is light and delicate, and the *tempura* are cooked, only until golden, at a lower temperature than most of our deep frying. A *tempura* pan is the ideal cooking equipment, but any deep frying pan or a heavy saucepan will do.

Tempura should be served as quickly as possible after cooking. It is also important to skim the oil frequently and always before adding a new batch of food to the pan.

Tempura

BATTER-FRIED SHRIMP AND VEGETABLES

8 large shrimp
12 large green beans
2-inch slice from top of a large
　carrot
1 small potato
2-inch square *nori* (dried laver
　seaweed)
2-inch slice *daikon* (white
　radish), about ⅓ cup
Grated fresh ginger root,
　optional

1 egg
1 cup cake flour *or* all-purpose
　flour
Vegetable oil
¼ cup *mirin*
¼ cup soy sauce
¼ cup flaked *katsuobushi* (dried
　bonito)
2 or 3 dashes msg

Peel and devein the shrimp leaving the last segment of shell and the tail on. Make a small, shallow slit on the inside of the shrimp at the head end to prevent its curling when it is fried. Straighten the shrimp by bending the tail back slightly, taking care not to break it. Cut off the point of the tail of the shrimp as it has some water in it which makes the shrimp splutter in the hot oil.

Trim the beans and cut into 2 or 3 diagonal slices. Scrape the carrot and cut into thin lengthwise strips. Peel the potato and cut into ⅛-inch lengthwise slices. Cut the seaweed into four 1-inch squares. Divide these ingredients into groups of 4 and cook each portion separately.

Peel the radish and grate it. Squeeze it out lightly, then place in mounds on 4 tiny individual dishes. Grate the ginger if it is to be used; place next to the grated radish on the individual dishes.

Break the egg into measuring cup and stir with chopsticks until it is well blended but not foamy. Add enough water to increase the liquid to ⅔ cup. Stir to mix and pour into a bowl. Sift the flour, and add to the egg mixture, stirring lightly.

Heat 2 or 3 inches oil in a *tempura* pan or a saucepan to between 345°F. and 350°F. on a frying thermometer, or until bubbles form on wooden chopsticks stirred in the oil. Another test of temperature is to drop a small piece of batter into the oil. If it rises immediately to the surface, the heat is right.

Dip the shrimp in the batter. Make little bundles of the beans and carrot and dip in the batter. Dip the potato slices in the batter. Coat one side only of the seaweed in the batter. Fry the ingredients until golden, turning once, about 2 minutes, being careful not to overcrowd the pan. Drain on the rack of the *tempura* pan or on a paper towel on a *zaru* (bamboo plate) or on paper towels. Continue until all the ingredients are cooked.

In a small saucepan bring the *mirin* to a boil. Add ¾ cup water, the soy sauce and the bonito flakes. Bring back to a boil, strain and add 2 or 3 dashes msg. Pour into 4 small bowls. This is *tentsuya* sauce.

Arrange the *tempura* on 4 plates. The effect is very pretty with the black seaweed, white potato, pink shrimp, orange carrot and green beans. To eat place a little of the grated ginger on top of the radish, if liked. Add the radish to the sauce and mix. Using chopsticks, dip each piece of *tempura* into the sauce. SERVES 4.

Squid or cuttlefish, any white fish, sweet potato, green bell peppers, eggplant, scallions or celery, cut into bite-sized pieces, may be used for *tempura*.

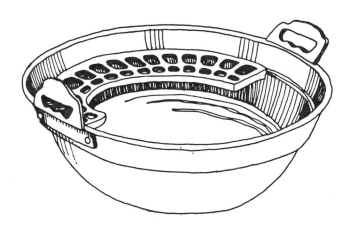

Hirame No Kohaku-age To Ebi No Iga-age
NOODLE-COATED SHRIMP WITH FRIED SOLE

This dish has a very romantic name. It signifies a wild chestnut (the noodle-coated shrimp), a chestnut leaf turning gold, and the maple leaf turning to flame (white radish grated with dried hot pepper) in autumn.

¾-pound fillet of sole
Cake flour
1 egg, separated
2 tablespoons *katakuriko or* cornstarch
8 medium-sized shrimp
1 ounce *harusame* (bean gelatin noodles)

1½-inch slice *daikon* (white radish)
2 or 3 dried hot red peppers
4 teaspoons soy sauce
Vegetable oil for deep frying

Cut the sole into 4 pieces and sprinkle with flour, shaking to remove excess. Beat the egg white until stiff, add the starch and mix well with chopsticks. Dip the fish into the egg white mixture. Stir the egg yolk with chopsticks, then spoon it over both sides of the fish pieces. Set aside.

Wash the shrimp, peel and devein, but leave the tail and the last segment of shell on. Cut the tail tip off as it contains water which makes the shrimp splutter when fried. Roll the shrimp in flour, dip in the remaining beaten egg white. Cut the noodles into 1-inch pieces using kitchen shears (they are quite tough), and coat the shrimp with the noodles pieces.

Peel the radish. Seed the peppers. Poke a hole in the center of the radish with chopsticks and stuff with the peppers. Grate the radish and lightly squeeze out the excess liquid. Set aside.

Heat 2 to 3 inches oil in a *tempura* pan or saucepan to 320°F. on a frying thermometer, rather lower than moderate heat. Add the fish and fry for 1 minute, turn and fry for a minute longer. Lift out and drain on the rack of the *tempura* pan or on paper towels. Fry the shrimp in the same way, lift out and drain.

Place the fish on 4 medium-sized plates with the shrimp in front. At the right-hand side in front place a small pile of grated radish and pour 1 teaspoon of soy sauce over each. SERVES 4.

Endō No Kakiage
DEEP-FRIED PEAS

1⅓ cups fresh green peas
1 egg
⅔ cup cake flour
Vegetable oil
¼ cup *mirin*
¼ cup soy sauce

¼ cup flaked *katsuobushi* (dried bonito)
1 or 2 dashes msg
7 ounces *daikon* (white radish), about a 3-inch slice

Rinse and drain the peas. Break the egg into a bowl and stir with chopsticks until well blended but not foamy. Pour into a measuring cup and add enough water to make ⅔ cup. Stir to mix and pour back into the bowl. Sift in the flour, mixing lightly. Add the peas.

Heat 2 to 3 inches oil in a *tempura* pan or saucepan to 325°F., a little lower than moderate. Add the pea mixture by scant table-spoons, easing the mixture out of the spoon with chopsticks so that it makes small fritters. Fry for about 2 minutes, turning once during cooking. Do not crowd the pan. Put the fritters to drain on the rack of the *tempura* pan or drain on paper towels.

To make the dipping sauce, pour the *mirin* into a small saucepan and bring to a boil. Add ¾ cup water, the soy sauce and the dried bonito flakes and bring back to a boil over low heat. Strain through cheesecloth and season with a dash or two of msg.

Peel and grate the radish and squeeze it lightly to get rid of excess moisture.

Pour the sauce into 4 small bowls and put at each place setting. Serve the fritters on medium-sized dishes. At the right-hand side in front place a small pile of radish. To eat, add the radish to the sauce. Using the chopsticks, dip the fritters into the sauce. Makes about 20 fritters. SERVES 4.

Satsuma-age

MACKEREL AND BEAN CURD CAKES

This dish is in the style of Satsuma, as it was called in the Edo era, in the southern part of Kyushu.

1 *momen tōfu* (bean curd) weighing about ½ pound
1 *gobō* (burdock root), about 12 inches long
10 or 11 ounces mackerel fillets, horse mackerel, pike or sardine fillets (Horse mackerel is bluefin tuna as found on the Atlantic coast up to Nova Scotia.)
1 tablespoon white *miso* (bean paste)
1 teaspoon sugar
1 teaspoon salt
1 teaspoon soy sauce
2 tablespoons *sake*
1 egg
2 teaspoons *katakuriko or* cornstarch
1 teaspoon finely chopped fresh ginger root
1 tablespoon black sesame seeds
Vegetable oil
Pickled red ginger root (optional)

Drop the bean curd into boiling water for 10 seconds, lift out and drain in a colander. Put into a piece of cheesecloth and squeeze out the moisture. Push through a sieve and set aside.

Scrape the burdock root under running water with the back of a knife, cut it into slivers and drop them into cold water, as it discolors very quickly.

Skin the fish. Using tweezers, remove any tiny bones there may be down the center of the fillet. Put into a *suribachi* (mortar) and pound to a smooth paste, beating with the pestle until the fish is light and fluffy. Add the bean curd and pound to mix well. Add the bean paste, sugar, salt, soy sauce and *sake*, mixing well. Break the egg into a bowl and stir with chopsticks until it is well blended but not foamy. Add the egg to the fish mixture, little by little, pounding constantly until the mixture has increased in bulk and is very light. Drain the sliced burdock root and add, stirring. Add the *katakuriko*, the ginger and the sesame seeds and mix with chopsticks. Divide into 8 slightly flattened oval cakes.

Heat 2 to 3 inches oil in a *tempura* pan or saucepan to 345°F. on a frying thermometer, or until bubbles form on wooden chopsticks stirred in the oil. Carefully slide in the fish cakes which will float to the surface in 1 or 2 minutes. Cook only for a minute or two longer, or until the cakes are golden. Do not overcrowd the pan—cook the cakes in batches. Drain on the rack of the *tempura* pan or on paper towels. Serve whole and eat at room temperature, garnished with pickled ginger. SERVES 4.

Ebi No Harusame-age
FRIED SHRIMP COATED WITH BEAN GELATIN NOODLES

8 medium-sized, or 4 large, shrimp
Salt
1 ounce *harusame* (bean gelatin noodles)

1 egg white
Katakuriko starch *or* cornstarch
Vegetable oil

Peel and devein the shrimp and cut into 1-inch pieces. Sprinkle lightly with salt.

Cut the noodles into pieces about ⅓-inch long with kitchen shears. (They are quite tough.) Makes about ¼ cup.

Stir the egg white with chopsticks until light.

Coat the shrimp pieces with *katakuriko* starch or cornstarch, dip in the egg white and roll in the noodles to coat thoroughly.

Heat 2 to 3 inches oil in a *tempura* pan or saucepan to 320°F. on a frying thermometer, or until bubbles form on wooden chopsticks stirred in the oil. Add the shrimp pieces and fry until the noodles have puffed up but are only slightly colored. Drain on the rack of the *tempura* pan or on paper towels and serve hot as an appetizer. SERVES 4.

One-Pot Dishes

The *nabemono* (one-pot dishes which are cooked at the table) were introduced during the *Meiji* period in the 19th century, when Japan modified its strict Buddhist vegetarianism. These attractive dishes are especially favored for family dining and entertaining guests. Cooking *nabemono* presents no difficulties for anyone owning a *donabe* (fireproof or ovenware earthenware casserole), a *sukiyaki* (round cast-iron pot), and an on-the-table heater or an electric skillet. Beautiful *donabe* are available in Japanese stores and are worth acquiring for the added grace they lend to the table.

The ingredients for the dishes are prepared ahead of time and set out attractively on one or more platters. Sauces and chopsticks are set at each place. The garnishes rest at the center of the table with the cooking pot. Thse dishes need little cooking time, so cooking begins only after the diners are seated.

The presentation varies. Sometimes, as with *shabu shabu* (Simmered Beef and Vegetables), each diner selects the piece of food to be cooked and holds it with chopsticks in the simmering stock to cook it. Or the ingredients can be added to the pot by the hostess, who will add fresh ingredients from time to time to replenish the pot.

The dishes are versatile, allowing for substitution of ingredients according to the diners' fancy: for example, chicken or pork for beef, watercress for spinach, and so on. Though the recipes here are given for four, they can be doubled successfully. For a large party, with guests seated at a series of tables for four, all that is needed is an adequate number of table heaters or electric skillets and casseroles. For outdoor dining, a charcoal-burning *hibachi* is fine.

Tarachiri Nabe

CODFISH STEW

4-inch square *kombu* (kelp)
¾-pound cod fillet with skin left
  on
Boiling water
4 leaves *hakusai* (Chinese
  cabbage)
4 large fresh mushrooms
5 scallions, trimmed, using white
  and green parts
1 *momen tōfu* (bean curd),
  weighing about ½ pound, *or*
  kinugoshi tōfu (silky bean
  curd)

5 ounces *shungiku* (see glossary)
  or spinach
7 ounces *daikon* (white radish),
  about 5 by 2 inches
2 dried hot red peppers
4 teaspoons soy sauce
4 teaspoons *ponzu* (citrus
  vinegar) *or* lemon or lime
  juice

Clean the seaweed with a damp cloth and cut into a ½-inch fringe. Cut the cod into pieces about 1 by 2 inches. Put into a colander and pour boiling water over them. Cut the cabbage into 2-inch diagonal slices. Rinse the mushrooms and cut into ¼-inch slice. Cut 4 of the scallions into 2-inch diagonal slices. Finely chop the remaining scallion and put to crisp in cold water for a few minutes, drain and squeeze out in a cloth. Put into a small bowl for use as garnish. Cut the bean curd into 8 slices. Wash and dry *shungiku* or spinach; remove tough stems. Arrange all the ingredients on a platter.

Peel the radish. Use a chopstick to poke a hole in the center. Seed the peppers and stuff into the hole. Grate the radish and put into a small bowl. Put the garnishes in the center of the table.

Have ready a 2-quart *donabe* (fireproof earthenware casserole) on a table heater (or an electric skillet) and add the seaweed. Pour in 4 cups water and bring to a boil over moderate heat. Remove seaweed before the water boils. Add the cod and any bones from the fish, then add the cabbage, mushrooms, bean curd, scallions and *shungiku* or spinach; skim as necessary and cook for 5 to 10 minutes or until fish and vegetables are both done.

Pour 1 teaspoon of the soy sauce into each of 4 bowls with 1 teaspoon of the citrus vinegar or lemon or lime juice and stir to mix. To eat add a little scallion and radish to the soy sauce mixture and use as a dipping sauce, lifting out fish and vegetables from the pot. Add more sauce as needed. This is a very popular winter dish. SERVES 4.

Oden

MIXED FISH CAKE AND VEGETABLE CASSEROLE

4-inch slice *daikon* (white
    radish)
½ large carrot
12 ginkgo nuts
1 *konnyaku* (devil's-tongue root
    cake)
Salt
Boiling water
2 small *chikuwa* (fish sausages)
2 *satsuma-age* (fried fish cakes)
2 medium potatoes
4 *ganmodoki* (fried bean curd
    balls)

1 *yakidōfu* (broiled bean curd),
    about 7 ounces drained weight
4 treasure bags, prepared but no
    cooked (see recipe for *Takara
    Bukuro,* page 194-5)
4½ cups *dashi* (soup stock)
2 teaspoons salt
⅓ cup *sake*
2 teaspoons sugar
2 tablespoons *usukuchi shōyu*
    (light soy sauce)
4 teaspoons dry mustard,
    preferably Japanese

Peel the white radish and cut into 4 slices, then peel a thin strip, about
¼-inch, round top and bottom edges to prevent it breaking up during
cooking. Cut a shallow cross on the bottom. Scrape carrot and cut into
4 diagonal slices. Thread the ginkgo nuts, 3 at a time, on toothpicks.
Sprinkle the *konnyaku* with salt and beat it all over gently with a
rolling pin for a minute or two to release the excess water. Rinse and
cut into 4 triangles. Cook in boiling water 3 or 4 minutes, drain and
skewer with small bamboo skewers. Cut the fish sausages and fish
cakes into halves on the diagonal. If liked, skewer the fish cakes with
small bamboo skewers to make them easier to lift out of the casserole
and to eat. Set aside on a platter.

Halve potatoes crosswise, peel ¼-inch strips round edges and drop
into cold water. Rinse the fried bean curd balls in hot water, then
squeeze out. Cut the broiled bean curd in half, then cut each half in
two diagonally; skewer lengthwise on bamboo skewers. Set the
potatoes, fried bean curd balls, broiled bean curd and treasure bags
aside separately.

In a large saucepan or casserole put the radish, carrot and *konnyaku*
in a single layer, add the soup stock, salt and *sake*. Bring to a boil,
cover, reduce heat to very low and cook at a bare simmer (the liquid
should only just move) for 1½ hours.

Add the potatoes, fish sausages, fish cakes, fried bean curd balls, treasure bags, ginkgo nuts, the sugar and light soy sauce and simmer 1 hour longer. At this point the liquid will be reduced by about a third. Taste for seasoning, and if liked add a little more salt, sugar, *mirin, sake* or light soy sauce.

Serve in deep soup bowls, giving each person some of each ingredient, and pour in some of the liquid. Mix the mustard with hot water and put into a very small bowl or dish. Using chopsticks, put a little of the hot mustard on each ingredient before eating. SERVES 4.

Taichiri

RED SNAPPER AND VEGETABLE CASSEROLE

1½ pounds red snapper, scaled and cleaned, with head and tail left on
1-pound *hakusai* (Chinese cabbage)
Boiling water
Salt
10 ounces spinach (about 5 cups, tightly packed)
6 scallions, trimmed, using white and green parts
8 small *shiitake* (dried Japanese mushrooms)
Sugar
2 ounces *harusame* (bean gelatin noodles)
2 cups *shungiku* (see glossary)
1 *momen tōfu* (bean curd) weighing about ½ pound
4-inch square *kombu* (kelp)
4-inch slice *daikon* (white radish)
1 or 2 dried hot red peppers
4 tablespoons *ponzu* (citrus vinegar)
6 tablespoons soy sauce
6 tablespoons *dashi* (soup stock)
1 or 2 dashes msg

Cut off the fish head and slice it in half. Fillet the fish, leaving the skin on, and cut the fillets into 1-inch diagonal slices. Chop the bones into 5 or 6 crosswise pieces. (Or have the fish store do this.) Drop the fish, fish head, bones and any bits into a saucepan of boiling water; remove from the heat and let stand for 2 or 3 seconds. Drain through a colander, rinse in cold water and drain.

Wash the cabbage and separate the leaves. Drop them into boiling water and simmer, covered, for about 2 minutes. Drain and sprinkle with salt. Roll up each leaf so it will be easier to handle with chopsticks. Wash the spinach and drop it into boiling water for 1 minute. Rinse in 3 lots of cold water and squeeze out.

Make an overlapping layer of cabbage leaves on a *sudare* (bamboo mat) and cover with the spinach. Roll up, squeeze to get rid of excess water and to firm the roll. Unroll and cut the cabbage-spinach into 1-inch slices. Arrange on the platter, cut side up. (A kitchen cloth can be used instead of a bamboo mat.)

Cut 4 of the scallions diagonally into 2-inch pieces and add to the platter. Finely chop the remaining 2 scallions and put into a small bowl. Soak the mushrooms for 30 minutes in warm water with a pinch of sugar, squeeze out and remove the stems. Add to the platter. Soak the bean gelatin noodles in warm water to soften, drain and add to the other ingredients. Rinse the *shungiku* leaves, drain and strip the leaves from the stems. Add to the platter. Cut the bean curd into 8 slices and add to the platter.

Clean the seaweed (kelp) with a damp cloth and cut it into a ½-inch fringe. Put it into a *donabe* (fireproof earthenware casserole) on a table heater, or use an electric skillet on the table. Pour in 4 or 5 cups of water and bring to a boil, removing the seaweed just before the water boils. Add the fish, fish head, bones and any bits, then the cabbage rolls, noodles, scallions, mushrooms, *shungiku* and bean curd. Skim as necessary and cook for about 5 minutes on moderate heat. When the dish is ready, turn the heat to low.

Peel the radish, poke a hole with a chopstick in the center, remove the seeds from the peppers and stuff them into the hole. Grate the radish and place in a small bowl. Mix together the citrus vinegar, soy sauce, soup stock and msg and pour into 4 small bowls so that each diner has a bowl of sauce. Put the garnishes, scallion and radish, which are to be added to the sauce when the dish is served, at the center of the table. Food is lifted out of the pot with chopsticks and dipped into the sauce and eaten. Fish bones are not eaten but Japanese like to suck the meat off them and they give added flavor to the stock.

When all solids are finished, the dish may be rounded out by adding leftover cooked rice with 1 or 2 eggs stirred and poured over the rice, then rice and eggs stirred into the soup. Or rice cakes, 1 per person, cut in half, may be added to the soup with a little salt and cooked until heated through, about 5 minutes. SERVES 4.

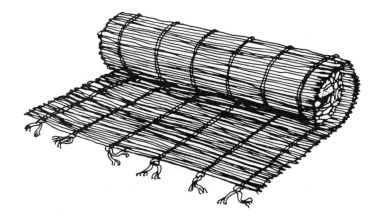

Kaki No Dotenabe

OYSTERS WITH BEAN PASTE

This dish has a much more imaginative name than oysters with bean paste. Dotenabe *is the retaining wall built to protect a river bank and here the oysters are surrounded in their pot by banks of bean paste.*

4 tablespoons red *miso* (bean paste)
8 tablespoons white *miso* (bean paste)
3 tablespoons *mirin*
2 8-ounce containers fresh oysters, or 16 ounces freshly shucked oysters
Salt
2 *yakidōfu* (broiled bean curd)

4 scallions, trimmed, using white and green parts
¼ pound *shūngiku* (see glossary) *or* 2 cups tightly packed fresh spinach
2½ cups soup stock
Shichimi-tōgarashi (seven-flavor spice) *or* ground hot red pepper *or sanshō* (Japanese pepper)

Mix together the red and white *miso* with the *mirin* to make a smooth paste then, using the fingers, make a layer of the paste in the bottom and sides of a *donabe* (earthenware casserole).

Rinse the shucked oysters in salted water and drain. Rinse and drain the bean curd and cut each into 8 squares. Cut the scallions diagonally into ½-inch slices. Wash the *shungiku* and drain. If using spinach wash and trim it and drop for 1 minute into boiling water. Rinse in cold water, drain and squeeze lightly. Arrange all the ingredients in the casserole, ending with *shungiku* or spinach. Put the casserole on a table heater over low heat. Pour in the soup stock little by little. Turn the heat up to moderate and cook, uncovered, for 2 or 3 minutes.

Have a small bowl at each place setting. Eat with chopsticks and ladle out the soup into the bowls to drink. Season the dish with any of the ground peppers. SERVES 4.

VARIATIONS: A beaten egg may be added to each bowl to be mixed with the soup. *Momen tōfu* (bean curd) may be used instead of *yakidōfu* (broiled bean curd). Eight *shiitake* (dried Japanese mushrooms), soaked for 30 minutes in warm water with a pinch of sugar, squeezed out, with stems removed and sliced, may also be added. So may a *konnyaku* (devil's-tongue root cake), sliced.

Kaki No Mizutaki
OYSTERS WITH CHINESE CABBAGE

2 dozen shucked oysters
1 pound *hakusai* (Chinese cabbage)
12 medium-sized fresh mushrooms
4-inch square *kombu* (kelp)
Soy sauce

½ cup grated *daikon* (white radish)
1 lemon cut into 4 wedges
2 small scallions, trimmed, using white and green parts
Shichimi-tōgarashi (seven-flavor spice)

Rinse the oysters in cold salted water and drain. Pull the leaves from the cabbage and wash and drain them. Stack the leaves and cut into 1-inch crosswise slices. If they are very large, cut them in half lengthwise, then slice. Trim the mushroom stems. Arrange the oysters, cabbage and mushrooms on a large platter.

Clean the seaweed (kelp) with a damp cloth and cut into a ½-inch fringe. Put into the bottom of a large fireproof *donabe* (earthenware casserole) and put on a table heater, or use an electric skillet. Pour 4 cups water into the casserole, about half filling it. Start it off on low heat so as not to crack the earthenware. Raise the heat to moderate and bring to a boil, removing the seaweed just before the water boils.

Have the soy sauce in a small jug. Lightly squeeze the moisture out of the radish and put it into a small bowl. Put the lemon wedges into a small bowl or on a plate. Finely chop the scallions and put into a bowl. Put a bowl with chopsticks at each place setting. Group the garnishes together with the seven-flavor spice round the casserole in the center of the table.

Add the cabbage and mushrooms to the casserole and simmer until the cabbage is tender, 10 to 15 minutes. Add the oysters, a few at a time, and cook just long enough to plump them, about 1 minute. To eat take the garnishes as liked and put into the small bowl at the place setting. Use as a dipping sauce for the contents of the casserole, taking more garnishes as needed. SERVES 4.

Ishikari-nabe

SALMON AND VEGETABLE CASSEROLE

12 ounces salmon fillet, with skin
Salt
8 ounces cabbage
Boiling water
1 medium-sized carrot, scraped
    and cut into ¼-inch slices
1 medium-sized potato, peeled
    and cut into ¼-inch slices
1 *konnyaku* (devil's-tongue root
    cake)

4 tablespoons butter
2 medium-sized onions, halved
    and cut into ¼-inch slices
3 to 4 cups *dashi* (soup stock)
6 tablespoons *miso* (bean paste)
    or more to taste
Sanshō powder (Japanese
    pepper)

Halve the salmon lengthwise, cut into 1-inch diagonal slices, sprinkle lightly with salt and set aside.

Separate the cabbage leaves and drop them into a saucepan full of rapidly boiling water. Cook for 2 minutes, drain, cool, then cut or tear the leaves into pieces roughly 2 by 4 inches and roll each up (to make them easy to pick up with chopsticks).

Put the carrot on to cook in a small saucepan of boiling water and simmer, covered, for 5 minutes. Add the potato and cook for 10 minutes longer. Wash the devil's-tongue root cake, then cut it into pieces with a teaspoon, add to the saucepan and cook for 1 minute longer. Drain and arrange the vegetables on a platter.

Add the butter to an earthenware or other flameproof casserole and melt over medium heat on a table heater. Or use an electric skillet on the table. Add the onions and sauté until tender but not browned. Pour the soup stock in. Mix the bean paste with a little stock until smooth and stir into the casserole over low heat without letting the mixture boil. Taste and add 2 more tablespoons if liked. Add the salmon, devil's-tongue cake, cabbage, carrot and potato and cook at just under a simmer until the salmon loses its translucent look, about 3 minutes.

Serve the casserole as a main course with rice and a vegetable dish. Have *sanshō* powder (Japanese pepper) on the table to be used as liked. Guests or family help themselves into bowls. Eat fish and vegetables with chopsticks and drink the soup when the solids are eaten. SERVES 4.

Kashiwa-age Nabe
CHICKEN DEEP-FRIED THEN BOILED

1¾ pounds chicken, cut into
    serving pieces
Flour
Vegetable oil
⅔ cup *mirin*
½ cup soy sauce
¼ cup flaked *katsuobushi* (dried
    bonito)
1 pound *hakusai* (Chinese
    cabbage)

1 *momen tōfu* (bean curd)
12 medium-sized fresh
    mushrooms, optional
4 scallions, trimmed, using white
    and green parts
2 cups *shungiku* (see glossary) *or*
    1 cup tightly packed spinach,
    about 2 ounces
Shichimi-tōgarashi
    (seven-flavor spice)

Rinse chicken pieces; drain. Chop, bone and all, with a cleaver into about 1-inch pieces. Coat lightly with flour and let stand for about 2 minutes. Heat about 3 inches oil in a *tempura* pan or a saucepan to 325°F. on a frying thermometer. There should be enough oil to cover the chicken pieces; add and cook, turning once, for about 12 minutes. Drain on the rack of the *tempura* pan or on paper towels.

In a saucepan combine 2⅔ cups water, the *mirin,* soy sauce and bonito flakes and bring to a boil over moderate heat. Reduce the heat to low and simmer for 4 or 5 minutes, uncovered. Strain through cheesecloth and discard the bonito flakes. Set the stock aside.

Pull the leaves off the cabbage, rinse and drain. Stack and slice the leaves in half lengthwise, then cut across into 1-inch pieces. If using bean curd, cut into 8 pieces. If using mushrooms, wash and drain them, trim the stem, and slice in half diagonally. Slice the scallions diagonally.

Pour the stock into a *donabe* (fireproof earthenware casserole) on a table heater, or into an electric skillet, and bring to a boil. Add the cooked chicken pieces, arranging them around the sides of the pan. Add the Chinese cabbage, the bean curd and mushrooms if using, the scallions, and *shungiku* or spinach and simmer until the cabbage is done, 10 to 15 minutes.

Ladle some of the chicken and vegetables from the casserole into bowls with a little of the stock. Season with *shichimi-tōgarashi* and eat with chopsticks. Drink the soup from the bowls when all the solids are eaten. SERVES 4.

Tori No Mizutaki

CHICKEN AND VEGETABLE CASSEROLE

2½- to 3-pound chicken, cut into
  serving pieces
Boiling water
5 large leaves *hakusai* (Chinese
  cabbage)
8 *shiitake* (dried Japanese
  mushrooms) or large fresh
  mushrooms
Sugar
½ 5-ounce package *harusame*
  (bean gelatin) noodles
1 *momen tōfu* (bean curd) or
  kinugoshi tōfu, (silky bean
  curd)

4 ounces *shungiku* (see glossary)
  or spinach *or* watercress
5 scallions, trimmed, using white
  and green part
1 scallion, trimmed, using white
  and green part
⅔ cup *daikon momijioroshi,*
  (white radish grated with dried
  hot red pepper)
1-inch cube fresh ginger root
⅓ cup rice vinegar
⅓ cup soy sauce
1 tablespoon *ponzu* (citrus
  vinegar)

Using a cleaver or poultry shears cut up the chicken, bones and all;
halve the legs and thighs, cut the wings into 3 pieces, the back into
about 8 pieces and the breasts into 3 pieces. Put the chicken pieces in a
colander and pour boiling water over them. Put 6 cups cold water into
a saucepan, add the chicken pieces, bring to a boil over high heat and
simmer, covered, for 10 minutes. Skim from time to time. Lower the
heat and cook for 30 to 40 minutes or until the chicken is tender. Set
aside.

Wash and drain the cabbage leaves, stack and cut into 1-inch
crosswise slices.

Soak the mushrooms for 30 minutes in warm water with a pinch of
sugar. Drain, remove the hard stems, squeeze out, and cut a shallow
cross in the tops. If using fresh mushrooms, rinse, dry, trim the stems
and cut a shallow cross in the tops.

Soak the noodles in warm water for 10 minutes. Drain. Cut the
bean curd into 6 cubes. Strip the *shungiku* leaves from the stems. If
using spinach or watercress, trim the stems. Slice 4 of the scallions
into 2-inch diagonal pieces.

Put the chicken pieces and about half of the stock into a *donabe*
(fireproof earthenware casserole) on a table heater over low heat.
Gradually increase heat to moderate. Or use an electric skillet on

moderate heat. Add the cabbage, then the mushrooms, noodles, bean curd, *shungiku* or spinach and finally the scallions, and simmer until all the ingredients are done, adding the rest of the stock as needed.

For the garnish, finely chop the remaining scallion and arrange in a small bowl. To grate the radish with the red pepper, peel a slice of radish, poke a hole with a chopstick in the center, stuff in a seeded, dried hot red pepper, and grate the radish. Place in a small bowl. Grate the ginger and place on a small saucer.

For the sauce, combine the rice vinegar, soy sauce and citrus vinegar and stir to mix. Pour into 4 small bowls.

To eat, put the garnishes into the sauce. Using chopsticks lift out pieces of chicken or vegetable and dip in the sauce. Any leftover stock can be ladled into the serving bowls and drunk from the bowls. SERVES 4.

Yudōfu

SIMMERED BEAN CURD

3 *momen tōfu* (bean curds) each weighing about ½ pound, or use *kinugoshi tōfu* (silky bean curd)

2 6-inch squares *kombu* (kelp)

⅓ cup plus ¼ cup flaked *katsuobushi* (dried bonito)

6 tablespoons soy sauce

¼ cup *mirin*

1-inch cube fresh ginger root

2 small scallions, trimmed, using white and green parts

2 sheets *nori* (dried laver seaweed)

Cut each piece of bean curd into quarters and put into a bowl of cold water until ready to use. Clean the seaweed (kelp) with a damp cloth and cut into a ½-inch fringe. Put 1 square into the bottom of a *donabe* (fireproof earthenware casserole) and place on a turned-off electric table heater until ready to cook the dish. Or use an electric skillet.

To make the sauce, put the other square of seaweed (kelp) into a saucepan with ¼ cup water and bring to a boil over moderate heat. Remove the seaweed before the water boils and add the ⅓ cup bonito flakes. Simmer for 2 minutes, then add the soy sauce and *mirin*. Remove from the heat and strain into a small, deep bowl. Set aside. Discard the seaweed and bonito flakes.

To assemble the garnishes, peel the ginger and grate it finely. Place in a small bowl. Slice the scallions finely and put into another small bowl. Toast the dried laver seaweed on both sides for a few seconds over a gas flame or electric burner, fold the 2 sheets into small squares and cut with scissors into julienne strips. Put into a small bowl. Put the ¼ cup bonito flakes in a small bowl. Place the garnishes in the center of the table.

Put enough water into the casserole to cover the bean curd when it is added. Bring to a boil, removing kelp just before the water boils. Add the bean curd and reduce the heat. Put the bowl with the sauce in the center of the casserole to heat through. The bean curd should be cooked only long enough to heat it through. If preferred the sauce can be heated separately on the stove.

To eat have small bowls at each place setting. Lift out the bean curd into the bowls with chopsticks and pour on some of the sauce. Garnish to taste. SERVES 4.

Gyūniku No Oilyaki

SAUTÉED BEEF AND VEGETABLES

1 pound well-marbled boneless
  beefsteak
12 large fresh mushrooms
1 *momen tōfu* (bean curd),
  weighing about ½ pound
4 medium-sized green bell
  peppers
4 scallions, trimmed, using white
  and green parts

½ grated *daikon* (white radish)
1-inch cube ginger root
½ lemon or lime, *or ponzu*
  (citrus vinegar) to taste
Soy sauce
1 tablespoon vegetable oil
1 tablespoon butter

Cut the steak into very thin slices, about 1 by 3 inches, and arrange on a platter. Wipe the mushrooms with a damp cloth and cut into ½-inch slices. Add to the platter. Cut the bean curd into 8 cubes and add to the platter. Cut the stem end from the peppers and remove the seeds; quarter lengthwise, then halve crosswise. Add to the platter. Cut the scallions into 2-inch diagonal slices and add to the platter. Squeeze out the radish and put into a small bowl. Grate the ginger and put into a small bowl. Cut the lemon or lime into 4 lengthwise wedges and place on a small plate. Put all the garnishes in the center of the table. Pour 1 tablespoon soy sauce, adding more as needed, into each of 4 small bowls.

Have ready a shallow iron pan or skillet on a table heater (or an electric skillet). Heat the casserole or skillet to about 400°F. on a frying thermometer. Add the oil and the butter.

Starting with the beef, each diner selects a piece or two and cooks it in the hot butter mixture, turning once, then adds the green pepper, mushrooms and scallions, adding the bean curd last and taking care not to overcook the beef. To eat, add a little lemon, lime or citrus vinegar to the soy sauce, then add the radish and ginger, and use as a dipping sauce for the beef and vegetables. Many other ingredients may be used such as thinly sliced onions, carrots and potatoes. SERVES 4.

Shabu Shabu
SIMMERED BEEF AND VEGETABLES

Shabu shabu *suggests the sound of water being stirred up. In this dish it refers to meat and vegetables, held in chopsticks, being swished back and forth in simmering stock.*

1 pound very thinly sliced fillet of beef, or sirloin steak
1 *momen tōfu* (bean curd), weighing about ½ pound
6-ounce drained-weight package *shirataki* (devil's-tongue-root noodles)
8 medium-sized fresh mushrooms
3 stalks *mitsuba* (trefoil) *or* 2 cups tightly packed spinach, about ¼ pound
6 leaves *hakusai* (Chinese cabbage)
2 scallions, trimmed, using white and green parts

4-inch slice *daikon* (white radish)
4 tablespoons soy sauce
4 tablespoons *ponzu* (citrus vinegar)
4 tablespoons *dashi* (soup stock)
4 tablespoons white sesame seeds
3 tablespoons rice vinegar
3 tablespoons *usukuchi shōyu* (light soy sauce)
3 tablespoons *dashi* (soup stock)
2 teaspoons *mirin*
Piece *kombu* (kelp), about 4 by 6 inches

Slice the steak into bite-sized pieces, about 1 by 2 inches. Halve the bean curd lengthwise, then cut into 1-inch slices. Drop the noodles into boiling water for 1 minute, drain thoroughly, form into a pile and cut in half. Rinse and dry the mushrooms and trim the stems. If trefoil is available, cut into 2-inch slices. Or wash and drain spinach. Wash and drain cabbage leaves and cut into 1-inch slices. Arrange all these ingredients on a platter.

To make the dipping sauces, finely chop the scallions. Grate the radish and squeeze out lightly. Put the radish and scallions in separate little piles in 4 small bowls. Mix the soy sauce with the citrus vinegar and the soup stock and pour over the radish and scallions. Set a bowl at each serving place.

In a skillet toast the sesame seeds until they begin to jump. Put into a *suribachi* (mortar) and grind fine. Scrape out into a bowl, add the rice vinegar, light soy sauce, 3 tablespoons soup stock and *mirin,* stirring to mix well. Pour into 4 small bowls and set at each place. Clean the seaweed (kelp) with a damp cloth, cut it into a ½-inch fringe and put it on the bottom of a *sukiyaki* (round iron) pot, or a cast-iron skillet, or a *donabe* (fireproof earthenware casserole), on a table heater, or use an electric skillet. Pour in enough water to fill the pot ¾ full, about 4 cups. Bring to a boil over moderate heat, removing the seaweed just before the water comes to a boil.

Each diner selects a piece of food from the platter, using chopsticks, and swishes it back and forth in the simmering liquid until it is cooked. It will make a sound like *shabu shabu.* Care should be taken not to overcook the beef, as too much heat will toughen it. The food is then dipped in one or another of the dipping sauces according to taste. Skim the surface of the pot from time to time.

When all the food has been eaten, cooked rice, cooked noodles or rice cakes may be added to the stock and ladled into the bowls to be eaten. Or add a little soy sauce and msg to the pot, stir and ladle the soup into the bowls. Drink the soup from the bowls. SERVES 4.

This is a favorite winter dish. In Japan *nama-shiitake* (fresh Japanese mushrooms) would be used.

Sukiyaki
SAUTÉED BEEF AND VEGETABLES

1 pound well-marbled, tender boneless steak from fillet or club or sirloin

10 scallions, trimmed, using white and green parts

2 *yakidōfu* (broiled bean curd), each weighing about 10 ounces

2 6-ounce drained-weight packages *shirataki* (devil's-tongue-root noodles)

4 ounces *shungiku* (see glossary) *or* spinach leaves, about ½ pound

1 sheet *fu* (wheat gluten cake), 3-by-9-inch size, optional

½ cup soy sauce

½ cup *mirin*

½ cup *dashi* (soup stock)

Msg

3 tablespoons sugar

Beef fat or vegetable oil

4 eggs, optional

Cut the steak into very thin slices about 2 by 1½ inches or have the butcher do it. Cut the scallions into 2-inch diagonal slices. Halve the bean curd pieces lengthwise, then cut into 4 crosswise slices. Drop the *shirataki* into boiling water for 1 minute, drain and cut in half. Strip *shungiku* leaves from stems. Soak the wheat gluten cake in water for a few seconds to soften, then slice in ½-inch strips. Arrange all the ingredients on a platter.

In a small saucepan combine the soy sauce, *mirin,* soup stock, msg to taste and sugar. Bring to a boil, remove from the heat and pour into a small jug.

Put a *sukiyaki* pan or a heavy iron skillet on a table heater in the middle of the dining table; rub the pan with a small piece of beef fat to grease the cooking surface or film with vegetable oil. Leave the piece of fat in the pan. An electric skillet may also be used, in which case start it off at 400°F., then reduce to between 250° and 300°F. when the meat and vegetables are cooked. Do not add all the ingredients at once. Use a little of everything and add more from time to time as needed. Add the beef strips and cook for a minute or two without turning. Add the scallions, then pour half the sauce over the contents of the pan. Add the noodles, bean curd, wheat gluten cake and the *shungiku* or spinach, stirring with chopsticks. Cook only for 3 or 4 minutes, stirring occasionally.

Break the eggs into 4 small bowls and stir with chopsticks to blend thoroughly. When eating the *sukiyaki,* lift out pieces of beef, vegetable or noodles and dip in the egg. Add the remaining ingredients and cook as before.

This is a traditional dish, but it is also a very flexible one and many nontraditional ingredients may be added. Thinly sliced onions, carrots or bamboo shoots may be used, and the egg may be omitted.

When the dish is finished, boiled rice, rice cake or boiled noodles may be added to the pan and heated through with any of the sauce that is left. SERVES 4.

Meats and Poultry

It was only with the Meiji period, little more than a century ago, that the Japanese kitchen really welcomed meat and poultry. It was after a long, virtually meatless era, although before the introduction of Zen Buddhism these foods had been regularly eaten. All the dishes in this section are therefore relatively new and bear the influence of the kitchens of the Western world.

All meats and poultry are cut into bite-sized pieces so they can be eaten with chopsticks. Cutting up cooked meat at the table seems bizarre to the Japanese so the cutting is done in the kitchen. Japanese cooking methods and culinary style changed the imported Western dishes beyond recognition. The result is a number of original and very attractive dishes to choose from in this untraditional field.

Agebuta
DEEP-FRIED PORK

1 pound boneless pork loin   Soy sauce
Vegetable oil
White pepper *or sansho*
  (Japanese pepper)

Cut the pork in half so that it will fit into a medium-sized saucepan. Heat 3 inches oil in a saucepan to between 345°F. and 350°F. on a frying thermometer, or until bubbles form on wooden chopsticks stirred in the oil. Add the pork to the saucepan. The oil must cover the pork completely. Cook over low to moderate heat for 20 to 25 minutes, or until the pork is tender. Lift out the pork and sprinkle with either white pepper or *sanshō* pepper and a little soy sauce, rubbing the mixture thoroughly into the meat. Cut into 1- to 1½-inch slices and serve either as an appetizer or as a main dish. SERVES 4 AS A MAIN COURSE, 8 AS AN APPETIZER.

Buta No Gomayaki
PORK WITH TOASTED SESAME SEEDS

¾ pound lean boneless pork loin
2 teaspoons plus 2 tablespoons soy sauce
½ teaspoon fresh ginger juice
2 tablespoons vegetable oil
2 tablespoons black sesame seeds
2 tablespoons *sake*

½ tablespoons sugar
1 teaspoon *katakuriko or* cornstarch
Cucumber salad (see *Jabara Kyuri* in *Tori No Teriyaki* recipe, page 158)

Thinly slice the pork, then cut diagonally into 1-by-2-inch pieces. Put into a bowl and mix with the 2 teaspoons of soy sauce and the ginger juice. Let stand for a few minutes.

In a skillet heat the oil and sauté the pork pieces until lightly browned on both sides. Do not overcrowd the pan; the pork should be in a single layer so that it cooks thoroughly. Set aside.

In a small skillet lightly toast the sesame seeds until they begin to jump. Transfer to a *suribachi* (mortar) and grind finely.

In a small saucepan combine the 2 tablespoons of soy sauce with the *sake,* sugar and *katakuriko* mixed with a teaspoon of water. Add the sesame seeds and cook, stirring, over low heat until the mixture is smooth. Spread the sesame paste on the pork slices, arrange on plates and garnish with the cucumber salad. SERVES 4.

Butaniku No Teriyaki

GLAZED PORK

½ tablespoon fresh ginger juice
½ tablespoon *sake*
3½ tablespoons soy sauce
1 pound boneless pork loin cut
   into 4 slices

Vegetable oil
2 tablespoons *mirin*
2 teaspoons sugar

Sprinkle the ginger juice, *sake* and 1½ tablespoons of the soy sauce over the pork slices, turning to coat both sides. Let stand at room temperature for 30 minutes.

Heat a heavy skillet large enough to hold the pork slices comfortably. Pour in just enough oil to coat the pan. Add the pork and sauté over high heat for 3 or 4 minutes, or until browned, on both sides. Reduce the heat to low and cook for 5 minutes longer. Lift the pork slices out of the pan and onto a plate.

Add the *mirin,* the remaining 2 tablespoons of soy sauce, sugar and 1 tablespoon of water to the pan, mix well and bring to a boil. Return the pork slices to the pan and cook over high heat, turning the pieces frequently until the liquid has evaporated and the pork is glazed, about 2 minutes. Remove from the skillet and cut into ½-inch diagonal slices. Arrange on individual plates or platters. If liked, serve with pickled cucumber slices, tomato wedges and pickled ginger. SERVES 4.

VARIATION: For *Gyūniku No Teriyaki* (Glazed Beef) marinate ½ pound sirloin or club steak, trimmed of fat, in mixture of 1 tablespoon each *mirin* and soy sauce for 10 minutes, turning 2 or 3 times. Drain and reserve the marinade. Sauté in a skillet for 1 minute on each side, lift out of the skillet, wipe pan, add the reserved marinade and glaze the steak on both sides, cooking for a minute or two longer for rare steak. Cut steak into ½-inch slices, arrange on an oblong platter or plate, and garnish with pickled ginger or small lettuce leaves. SERVES 1 OR 2.

Butaniku No Shōgazukeyaki
GINGER-MARINATED PORK WITH VEGETABLES

¾ pound boneless pork loin
1 teaspoon fresh ginger juice
1 tablespoon *sake*
4 tablespoons soy sauce
3 ounces green beans
½ teaspoon dry mustard,
   preferably Japanese
Boiling water
8 small radishes

1 dried hot red pepper
2 teaspoons rice vinegar
1 teaspoon sugar
½ teaspoon salt
Flour
Vegetable oil
2 teaspoons fresh ginger juice
2 tablespoons *mirin*

Thinly slice the pork, then cut the slices into bite-sized pieces. Put into a bowl. Sprinkle with the ginger juice, *sake,* and 2 tablespoons of the soy sauce. Mix and leave to marinate for 20 minutes.

Trim the washed beans and drop into boiling water. Cook for 3 minutes, drain and cut into 1-inch pieces. Mix the mustard with a little boiling water to a paste and stir into 1 tablespoon of soy sauce. Pour over the beans and mix.

Trim and thinly slice the radishes and put into a bowl. Seed and chop the pepper and mix with the radish slices, rice vinegar, sugar and salt.

Lift the pork pieces out of the marinade and reserve it. Coat the pork lightly with the flour. In a heavy 10-inch skillet heat 2 table-spoons of oil, add the pork pieces and sauté until browned on both sides. Do in batches, adding more oil if necessary. The pork pieces should not overlap. When all the pork pieces are browned, wipe the pan with paper towels. Add the ginger juice, 1 tablespoon soy sauce, *mirin* and the reserved marinade. Bring to a boil and add the pork. Cook, stirring, over fairly high heat until the pork is glazed. Arrange the pork on a platter.

Drain the beans and radishes and add to the platter. This looks very attractive with the brown pork, pink and white radish and green beans. Serve as a main course with rice. SERVES 4.

Butahikiniku No Kamaboko
GROUND PORK SAUSAGE

2 *shiitake* (dried Japanese
  mushrooms)
Sugar
1 slice firm white bread
¾ pound ground lean pork loin
1 egg
Soy sauce
1 teaspoon sugar
¼ teaspoon salt

1 tablespoon *sake*
Flour
Vegetable oil
2 tablespoons *mirin*
¼ pound green beans
1 teaspoon dry mustard,
  preferably Japanese
Boiling water

Soak the mushrooms in warm water with a pinch of sugar for 30 minutes. Squeeze out, remove the hard stems and chop finely. Soak the bread in cold water for a few minutes, squeeze out. In a large bowl combine the mushrooms, bread, pork, egg, 2 teaspoons of soy sauce, sugar, salt and *sake* and mix thoroughly. Place a *sudare* (bamboo mat) on a board and cover with a kitchen cloth or double piece of cheesecloth wrung out in cold water. Form the pork mixture into a roll and place at one end of the mat. Roll it up, pressing firmly into a sausage shape. Remove the mat. Twist the ends of the cloth firmly and tie with kitchen string. Put into a steamer over boiling water and steam for 30 minutes. Remove from the steamer and cool. Very carefully remove the cloth casing and discard. Coat with flour.

Heat 1 tablespoon of oil in a skillet and sauté the sausage until golden brown all over. Add the *mirin,* spooning it over the sausage while cooking for a minute or two longer to give the sausage a nice shiny glaze.

Trim the washed beans, drop into boiling water and cook for 6 minutes. Drain and slice lengthwise on an angle. Wipe out the sausage skillet with paper towels, add another tablespoon of oil and sauté the beans, stirring, for 2 or 3 minutes.

Mix the mustard to a paste with boiling water.

Slice the sausage and arrange the slices on plates. Garnish with the beans and the mustard. Pour a little soy sauce over the mustard and dip the sausage in the mustard mixture.

Green bell peppers, seeded and cut into julienne strips and cooked in the same way as the beans, may be used instead of the beans. This is good for a buffet. SERVES 4.

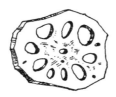

Yudebutaniku No Nikomi
BOILED PORK

1½ pounds boneless pork loin
1½-inch cube fresh ginger root
2 tablespoons *sake*
4 tablespoons soy sauce

1 tablespoon plus 1 teaspoon
  sugar
2-inch piece scallion, using
  white part only

Cut the pork in half crosswise and put it into a saucepan into which it fits comfortably. Add enough water barely to cover, bring to a boil, lower the heat and simmer, uncovered, for about 1 hour. Drain, discard the stock, and rinse out the pan. Cool the pork slightly and cut into 1-inch cubes. Return to the pan.

Peel the ginger and slice it thinly. Add it to the pork in the cooking pan with the *sake,* 2 tablespoons of the soy sauce and 1 tablespoon of sugar and water barely to cover. Simmer, covered, over moderate heat, for 10 minutes. Add the remaining soy sauce and 1 teaspoon of sugar and cook, uncovered, until the liquid has all evaporated.

Serve the pork in small deep bowls or plates. Finely chop the scallion and sprinkle over the pork. SERVES 4.

Sakeni-nabe
PORK SIMMERED WITH RICE WINE

¾ to 1 pound boneless pork loin
1 teaspoon fresh ginger juice
Salt
4 fresh mushrooms *or* 4 *shiitake*
  (Japanese dried mushrooms)
2 *konnyaku* (devil's-tongue-root
  cake)
1-inch cube fresh ginger root
5 scallions, trimmed, using white
  and green parts

8-inch slice *daikon* (white
  radish)
¾ cup *sake*
2 tablespoons *usukuchi shōyu*
4 cups *shungiku* (see glossary) *or*
  spinach leaves
Soy sauce

Thinly slice the pork and put into a bowl. Sprinkle with the ginger and 1 teaspoon salt, mix and set aside.

Trim the stems of the fresh mushrooms and cut the mushrooms in half. If using dried mushrooms, soak them for 30 minutes in warm water with a pinch of sugar, squeeze out, remove the hard stems and halve the mushrooms. Drop the *konnyaku* into boiling water, simmer for 2 or 3 minutes, drain, cut in halves, then into ¼-inch slices. Put into a colander to continue draining.

Peel the ginger, and cut in half; thinly slice one half, grate the other. Cut the scallions into 1-inch pieces. Peel and grate the radish, and squeeze out lightly, reserving the juice.

To a *sukiyaki* pan or iron skillet over moderate heat add the *sake*, radish juice and sliced ginger. When heated through add the *konnyaku*, light soy sauce, ½ teaspoon salt, mushrooms and pork. Cook over moderate heat, turning the pork pieces from time to time until they are done, about 10 minutes. Add the scallion and cook for a minute or 2 longer, then add the *shungiku* or the spinach and cook 2 or 3 minutes longer. If there is not enough liquid, add a little more *sake* and ginger juice.

Divide the radish among 4 small dishes, put the grated ginger on top of each portion of radish and pour a little soy sauce, about 1 teaspoon, over each. Use as a dipping sauce.

Put the *sukiyaki* pan in the center of the table, or if using an iron skillet, transfer the contents of the pan to a warmed platter. Eat with the sauce. SERVES 4.

Yudebuta
BOILED PORK WITH MUSTARD SAUCE

1 pound boneless pork loin in one picce
½ medium-sized onion
1-inch slice fresh ginger root
¼ cup rice vinegar

2 teaspoons dry mustard, preferably Japanese
Boiling water
4 tablespoons soy sauce
⅛ teaspoon msg

Choose a saucepan just large enough to hold the pork comfortably. Cut the peeled onion into thin lengthwise slices. Wash and thinly slice the ginger root. Add the onion, ginger and rice vinegar to the saucepan with 1½ cups water. Bring to a boil over moderate heat, add the pork and cover with an *otoshibuta* (inner wooden lid), or a smaller saucepan lid, or use a plate. Cook over moderate heat for about 50 minutes, or until pork is tender. Remove from the heat and let the pork cool in the liquid. When cooled, lift out and thinly slice the pork. Arrange the slices on a platter.

To make *Karashi-Jōyu* (Mustard Sauce), mix the mustard to a paste with boiling water and mix with the soy sauce and the msg. Pour into 4 tiny individual bowls. Place the platter in the center of the table and a bowl of sauce at each place setting. Using chopsticks, dip the pork slices into the sauce to eat. The pork may be served on individual plates if preferred. SERVES 4.

Hikiniku-Dango

MEATBALLS

2-inch slice *daikon* (white radish), about 3 ounces
Salt
2 tablespoons rice vinegar
2 tablespoons dry red wine
Sugar
½ dried hot red pepper
2 *shiitake* (dried Japanese mushrooms)
¾ pound ground beef

1 teaspoon finely chopped fresh ginger root
1 egg, stirred
4 tablespoons bread crumbs
2 tablespoons plus 1 teaspoon soy sauce
1 tablespoon *sake*
Cornstarch
Vegetable oil
2 tablespoons *mirin*

First make the garnish, *Kikuka-Daikon* (Chrysanthemum Looking Radish Flowers). Peel the slice of radish. Place on a board with a chopstick on each side and slice thinly. (See *kikukagiri* illustration in Introduction.) The chopsticks will prevent the knife cutting through the radish, leaving about ¼ inch holding the slices together. Turn the radish around and cut across again, forming tiny squares. Sprinkle with salt and place 1 or 2 plates on top of the radish and let stand for 30 minutes to get rid of some of the moisture. Drain the radish and rinse under cold running water. Squeeze very carefully in a cloth so as not to break. Cut into quarters.

Mix together the rice vinegar, red wine, 1 tablespoon sugar and ¼ teaspoon salt. Pour over the radish. Leave for 15 minutes. Take the radish quarters out of the marinade carefully. Separate the "petals" to form a flower, pushing a finger down into the center. Shake the seeds out of the hot pepper and chop it finely. Put the chopped pepper in the center of the radish flowers. Set aside. To make the meatballs, soak the mushrooms in warm water with a pinch of sugar for 30 minutes. Drain, squeeze out and remove the hard stems. Chop the mushrooms finely. In a bowl combine the mushrooms, beef, ginger, egg, bread crumbs, ½ teaspoon salt, 1 teaspoon of the soy sauce and the *sake* and mix well. Shape the mixture into 16 small balls, ¾ to 1 inch across. Roll in cornstarch.

Heat 2 to 3 inches of vegetable oil in a *tempura* pan or a saucepan to 350°F. on a frying thermometer and add the meatballs. Cook, turning once, for 2 to 3 minutes. Drain on the rack of the *tempura* pan or on paper towels.

In a skillet combine 2 tablespoons sugar, the 2 tablespoons of soy sauce and the *mirin,* bring to a boil, add the meatballs and cook over moderate heat, turning the meatballs so that they are coated all over with the sauce. Cook until all the liquid has evaporated. Remove from the heat and shake the pan two or three times to stop the meatballs sticking. Thread the meatballs 2 at a time on *takegushi,* small bamboo skewers. Lay 2 skewers diagonally across each of 4 platters.

Place the radish flowers on the platters with the meatballs. Eat the radish with chopsticks and the meatballs off the skewers. The red wine gives the radish a pretty pink color. SERVES 4.

Gyūniku No Misozuke-Yaki
GRILLED BEEF WITH BEAN PASTE

¾ pound rump steak cut into 4
  slices
1 cup red or white *miso* (bean
  paste)

4 tablespoons sugar
2 tablespoons *sake*
Lettuce
Pickled ginger

Score the edge of the slices once on each side, then make 2 small cuts in the surface. Put the bean paste in a bowl with the sugar and *sake* and mix to a soft paste. Choose a dish large enough to hold all the steaks in one layer and spread half the bean paste mixture on the bottom. Cover with a layer of double cheesecloth cut to fit the dish. Arrange the steaks on top and cover with a second layer of cheese-cloth spread with the rest of the bean paste mixture. Cover tightly with aluminum foil and refrigerate for 1 or 2 days. To cook, lift out the steaks, scrape the bean paste off the cheesecloth and reserve for another use.

Heat a grill, reduce the heat to moderately low and grill the steaks 2 minutes on each side, or until lightly browned, or to the desired degree of doneness. Cut into bite-sized diagonal slices, arrange on an oblong platter and serve garnished with the lettuce and ginger placed at the front of the dish. The meat will be tenderized and flavored by the bean paste.

The steaks may also be broiled under moderate heat for about 2 minutes a side. SERVES 4.

Gyūniku No Negimaki
SCALLION-STUFFED BEEF ROLLS

¾ pound beef: London broil, top
  round, or similar cut
2 tablespoons soy sauce
1 tablespoon *mirin*
1 teaspoon finely grated fresh
  ginger root

3 scallions, trimmed, using white
  and green parts
Flour
Vegetable oil
½ lemon, cut into 4 wedges

Cut the beef into pieces about 5-by-3-by-⅛-inch thick. This is easier to do if the beef has been partially frozen. Place the beef slices in a dish. Combine the soy sauce, *mirin* and ginger and pour over the beef, mixing well. Marinate for 30 minutes.

Cut the scallions into pieces as long as the beef is wide. Divide the scallions so that there will be some white and some green to stuff each roll.

Lift the beef slices out of the marinade and lay the scallions on the beef and roll up. Dab a little flour on the end of each beef strip to hold the rolls together. Coat the rolls with flour, shaking to remove the excess.

Heat 2 to 3 inches oil in a *tempura* pan or a saucepan to about 340°F. on a frying thermometer, or until bubbles form on wooden chopsticks stirred in the oil. Fry the rolls, a few at a time, for about 2 minutes, turning once or twice. Drain on the rack of the *tempura* pan or on paper towels. Garnish with the lemon wedges and squeeze the lemon over the beef rolls. Serve hot and as freshly cooked as possible. SERVES 4.

VARIATION: Instead of being deep fried, the beef rolls may be sautéed, in which case do not coat them with flour. Heat 2 tablespoons oil in a skillet and sauté the rolls over fairly brisk heat, turning to brown all over, about 3 to 4 minutes. The flavor is surprisingly different.

VARIATION: For *Butaniku No Negimaki* (Scallion-stuffed Pork Rolls) cut 1 pound boneless pork loin into ⅛-inch slices and marinate for 30 minutes in mixture of 1 teaspoon ginger juice, 1 tablespoon *sake* and 2 tablespoons soy sauce. Turn several times. Make into rolls the same way as the beef, using 4 large scallions. Sauté the same way as the beef variation. When the rolls are cooked mix 2 tablespoons each *sake,* soy sauce and sugar with 1 tablespoon *mirin,* add to the skillet and shake over fairly brisk heat to glaze the rolls all over. Cut in half diagonally, if liked. This looks very pretty as the scallion can be seen.

Iridori

FRIED CHICKEN AND VEGETABLES

½ pound boned chicken thighs, skin left on
¼ pound *gobō* (burdock root)
¼ pound carrots
½ *konnyaku* (devil's-tongue-root cake)
Salt
Boiling water
4 *shiitake* (dried Japanese mushrooms)

Sugar
12 snow-pea pods, trimmed
¼ pound *renkon* (lotus root)
Rice vinegar
2½ tablespoons oil
2 teaspoons *mirin*
3½ tablespoons soy sauce
1½ cups *dashi* (soup stock)

Cut the chicken into diagonal bite-sized pieces. Scrape the burdock root with the back of a knife under cold running water, then slice *rangiri* (see illustration in Introduction) and drop into a bowl of cold water. Scrape the carrots and cut *rangiri*. Rub the *konnyaku* on both sides with salt, rinse and tear with the fingers into 8 pieces. Drop into a saucepan of boiling water, bring back to a boil and drain.

Soak the mushrooms for 30 minutes in warm water with a pinch of sugar, squeeze out, cut off the hard stems and cut the mushrooms into quarters. Drop the snow-pea pods into boiling salted water, bring back to a boil and cook for 2 minutes. Drain. Slice the lotus root *rangiri* and put it to soak in cold water to cover with 1 tablespoon of vinegar.

To cook, assemble all the ingredients, drained where necessary, on a plate. Add 1 tablespoon of oil to a wok or a heavy skillet and stir fry the chicken on high heat for 2 minutes, or until it changes color, using chopsticks to stir. Remove the chicken pieces to a bowl and sprinkle with 1 teaspoon sugar, the *mirin,* and 1 tablespoon of the soy sauce. Mix well and set aside.

Add 1½ tablespoons oil to the wok and cook the burdock root over high heat for 1 minute, stir frying, then add the carrot and cook 1 minute more, then the lotus root and again cook for 1 minute longer. Add the *konnyaku* and mushrooms, lower the heat to moderate and cook for 2 minutes, still moving the ingredients around with chopsticks. Add the soup stock, bring to a boil, cover and cook for 7 minutes, then add 1 teaspoon sugar and the remaining 2½ tablespoons of soy sauce and cook for 10 minutes longer. Add the chicken and the marinade and cook uncovered, stirring with chopsticks, over fairly brisk heat for about 3 minutes, or until almost all the liquid has evaporated. Add the snow-pea pods and cook for ½ minute longer, still stirring. Serve in bowls. SERVES 4.

This is popular for lunch boxes, also for New Year, and indeed at any time.

Toriniku No Tatsuta-age
DEEP-FRIED MARINATED CHICKEN

¾ pound skinned and boned chicken breast
½-inch cube fresh ginger root
½ cup soy sauce
3 tablespoons *sake*

Katakuriko or cornstarch
Vegetable oil
2 scallions, trimmed, using white and green parts

Cut the chicken into bite-sized pieces and place in a bowl. Grate the ginger finely and mix with the chicken. Pour on the soy sauce and *sake* and mix. Marinate for 30 minutes. Lift out the chicken pieces and roll in the *katakuriko,* shaking to remove the excess.

Heat 2 to 3 inches of oil in a *tempura* pan or a saucepan to about 340°F. on a frying thermometer, or until bubbles form on wooden chopsticks stirred in the oil. The heat should be a little lower than moderate.

Fry the chicken pieces, a few at a time, until golden brown. Drain on the rack of the *tempura* pan or on paper towels. Arrange on a platter.

Cut the scallions into 1-inch crosswise pieces, then cut into fine lengthwise strips. Crisp for a few minutes in cold water, then squeeze dry in a kitchen cloth. Add to the platter with the chicken. SERVES 4.

Mushidori To Ika No Gomazu

CHICKEN, SQUID AND VEGETABLE PLATTER

4 small half chicken breasts,
  boned with skin on
2 teaspoons *sake*
Salt
1 squid, cleaned and without
  tentacles
Rice vinegar
4 8-inch fronds *wakame*
  (lobe-leaf seaweed)
2 scallions, trimmed, using white
  and green parts

1 medium-sized cucumber
2-inch slice medium-sized carrot
4 tablespoons white sesame
  seeds
1 clove garlic
1 tablespoon soy sauce
1 tablespoon *mirin*
1 tablespoon mayonnaise
Tōgarashi-ko (ground hot red
  pepper)

Prick all over the skin of the chicken breasts with a fork. Put into a shallow dish, sprinkle with *sake* and salt and put into a steamer over boiling water. Steam over moderate heat for 15 minutes. Remove from the steamer, cut into 1-inch diagonal slices, return to dish and allow to cool in the liquid. Cut the squid open and score all over in a diamond pattern. Cut into 1-inch squares and drop into boiling water for 2 or 3 seconds, rinse in cold water and drain. Sprinkle with a little rice vinegar and salt.

Soak the seaweed in cold water for 10 to 15 minutes. Drain, drop into boiling water for a few seconds, rinse in cold water and drain. Cut away the hard ribs, squeeze out and cut into 1-inch slices.

Cut the scallions into 2-inch slices, then cut these very thinly lengthwise and crisp for a few minutes in cold water. Drain and squeeze dry in a cloth.

Peel the cucumber in alternate strips, slice thinly lengthwise, then cut into thin crosswise strips. Rinse in cold water and drain.

Scrape the carrot, slice thinly lengthwise, cut in half crosswise, then into thin lengthwise strips. Rinse in cold water and drain.

Toast the sesame seeds in a skillet until they begin to pop. Transfer to a *suribachi* (mortar) and grind. Crush the clove of garlic with the blade of a knife and grind with the sesame seeds. Add 1 teaspoon salt, the soy sauce, 5 tablespoons rice vinegar, the *mirin,* the mayonnaise and the liquid in which the chicken has been cooling. Add a dash or two of the hot pepper and mix until smooth. Pour into a bowl.

On a large platter arrange the chicken slices, the squid, seaweed, carrot, cucumber and scallions. Place in the center of the table with the sauce. Diners serve themselves from the platter with chopsticks into small bowls, taking a little of everything as the meal proceeds, and add some of the sauce, served with a spoon. This is a very attractive dish in hot weather for either lunch or dinner. SERVES 4.

Torikimo No Tamago-toji
CHICKEN LIVERS AND PEPPERS WITH EGG

10 ounces chicken livers	1 tablespoon sugar
8 medium-sized hot green peppers	4 tablespoons soy sauce
2 tablespoons *mirin*	
2 tablespoons vegetable oil	1 egg
¾ cup *dashi* (soup stock)	

Wash the chicken livers in 2 or 3 changes of cold water, drain, halve them, then slice in half again, diagonally. Seed the peppers and cut into ½-inch slices.

In a saucepan heat the oil and sauté the chicken livers over high heat, turning constantly until lightly browned. Reduce the heat to moderate and sauté for 1½ minutes longer. Add the soup stock, sugar, soy sauce and *mirin* and cook for 2 or 3 minutes. Skim, add the peppers and bring to a boil. Cover with an *otoshibuta* (inner wooden lid), or a smaller saucepan lid, or use a plate; reduce the heat to low and cook for 2 or 3 minutes. Remove the *otoshibuta,* and skim. Break the egg into a cup and stir with chopsticks until well blended but not foamy. Pour the egg over the chicken liver mixture in a thin stream to cover the whole surface of the pan. Cover and cook until the egg is just set, about 1 minute. Serve in 4 small bowls with the liquid from the pan poured over the livers. SERVES 4.

NOTE: Nibble a tiny piece of a hot pepper and if it is very hot, soak the peppers in cold salted water for 15 minutes, then rinse and drain. This will take out the excess heat.

Torikimo No Shōgajōyu
CHICKEN LIVERS WITH GINGER AND SOY SAUCE

10 ounces chicken livers
Salt
1-inch cube fresh ginger root

½ cup grated *daikon* (white radish)
Soy sauce

Wash and drain the livers and drop into boiling salted water. Simmer 4 or 5 minutes, drain and cool. Slice diagonally and divide among 4 small plates.

Peel and grate the ginger and add to the plates in little heaps. Squeeze out the radish to remove excess liquid and put small mounds of radish beside the ginger. Pour a little soy sauce over both ginger and radish. SERVES 4.

For a spicier garnish, the radish may be grated *momijioroshi*, that is, stuffed with a seeded, dried hot red pepper.

Toriniku Dango No Terini
GLAZED CHICKEN BALLS

½ pound finely ground raw chicken
2 tablespoons flour
Soy sauce
½ egg, stirred

Boiling water
1 tablespoon sugar
1½ tablespoons *mirin*
1 teaspoon poppy seeds

Put the chicken into a *suribachi* (mortar) and pound the chicken until smooth and light. Add the flour, 1 teaspoon soy sauce and egg and mix thoroughly. Form into 1-inch balls and drop into a saucepan with 1¼ cups boiling water. Bring back to a boil, reduce the heat and cook for 2 or 3 minutes. Add the sugar, *mirin* and 3 tablespoons soy sauce to the pan. Shake to mix, cover and continue cooking for 5 or 6 minutes. Remove the lid, raise the heat and cook until the liquid has evaporated and the chicken balls are glazed. Thread the balls, three at a time, on bamboo skewers, sprinkle with the poppy seeds and serve. SERVES 4.

Torisashi
CHICKEN SASHIMI

8 *tori-sasamī* (bamboo-leaf
  chicken breasts—see
  glossary)
Salt
1 medium-sized cucumber
1 medium-sized tomato
5 tablespoons white *miso* (bean
  paste)

1 tablespoon sugar
⅓ cup *dashi* (soup stock)
1 egg yolk
½ teaspoon dry mustard,
  preferably Japanese
Boiling water
2½ tablespoons rice vinegar

Sprinkle the chicken lightly with salt and let stand a few minutes. Drop the chicken into boiling water for 2 or 3 seconds, then transfer quickly to a bowl of ice water and cool for a minute or two. Lift out of the water and refrigerate.

If the cucumber is waxed, peel it, otherwise leave it unpeeled. Cut it into 3 or 4 lengthwise slices, then cut the slices into crosswise strips. Peel the tomato and cut it into 8 wedges. Refrigerate the vegetables.

To make the sauce combine the bean paste, sugar and soup stock in a small saucepan and mix well with the egg yolk. Cook over moderate heat, stirring, until heated through but do not let the mixture boil. Cool. Mix the mustard with ½ tablespoon of boiling water and the rice vinegar and stir into the sauce. Divide among 4 small dishes and use as a dipping sauce.

Cut the chicken pieces into ¼-inch diagonal slices and arrange at one end of an oblong serving dish or on 4 small individual dishes. Put the cucumber in the middle and the tomato wedges at the other end. Using chopsticks, dip the chicken and vegetables into the sauce.
SERVES 4.

VARIATION: Another popular sauce is *Wasabi-Jōyu* (Green Horse-radish Sauce) made by mixing 2 teaspoons *wasabi* (green horseradish powder) to a paste with a little water, then mixing it with 4 table-spoons soy sauce and 6 tablespoons *dashi* (soup stock). For *Shōga-Jōyu* (Ginger Sauce) mix 2 tablespoons grated fresh ginger root with 4 tablespoons soy sauce and 6 tablespoons *dashi* (soup stock).

Wakadori No Nanbanyaki

SPICED, GRILLED YOUNG CHICKEN

1 pound boned chicken thighs
 with skin left on
3 tablespoons soy sauce
1 tablespoon *mirin*
1 tablespoon *sake*
2 scallions, trimmed, using white
 and green parts

2 dried hot red peppers
1 egg yolk
12 small fresh hot green peppers
Vegetable oil
Salt

Prick the skin of the chicken thighs all over with a fork and put into a bowl. Add the soy sauce, *mirin* and *sake* and marinate for 10 minutes, turning 2 or 3 times. Thread the thighs on a skewer. Reserve the marinade.

Chop the scallions. Seed and chop the dried peppers. Grind the scallions and peppers in a *suribachi* (mortar) until smooth. Add the reserved marinade and mix, then beat in the egg yolk. Set aside.

Using a *hibachi* or an electric or other grill, grill the chicken on both sides until about half done, about 4 minutes on each side. Using a pastry brush paint the chicken with the scallion sauce, return to the grill and cook for 1 minute on each side. Continue until the sauce is used up and the chicken is done.

Cut the stems from the fresh green peppers. If they are very hot (check by nibbling a tiny slice), remove the seeds as well. Rinse, dry and paint with oil. Grill, turning once, for about 1 minute. Sprinkle lightly with salt.

Slice the chicken diagonally and arrange on platters; garnish with the peppers. SERVES 4.

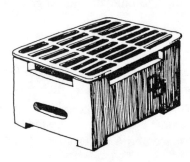

Tori No Sakamushi

CHICKEN STEAMED WITH RICE WINE

2 boned whole chicken breasts,
    skin left on
4 tablespoons *sake*
2 teaspoons soy sauce
¼ teaspoon salt
½ scallion, trimmed, using white
    or green part

1-inch cube fresh ginger root
1 medium-sized cucumber
2 teaspoons dry mustard,
    preferably Japanese

Pierce the chicken skin all over with a fork. Place the chicken breasts in a bowl. Mix the *sake,* soy sauce and salt and pour over the chicken. Marinate for 20 minutes.

Chop the scallion, then crush with the blade of a knife. Peel the ginger and crush. Put the scallion and ginger on top of the chicken breasts. Place the bowl in a steamer over boiling water and steam for 10 to 15 minutes. Cool to room temperature and cut all diagonally into ½-inch slices. Arrange the chicken slices in bowls with the cooking liquid poured over them.

Peel the cucumber, cut it in half lengthwise and scrape out the seeds. Cut into 2-inch slices crosswise, then slice each piece finely lengthwise. Put into cold water to crisp for 5 minutes, drain thoroughly and divide among the bowls with the chicken.

Mix the mustard with boiling water to a paste and place a small mound beside the slices of chicken breast. This is a summer dish. SERVES 4.

If small unwaxed cucumbers are available, use 4 and leave them unpeeled.

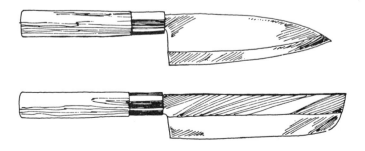

Toriniku No Jibuni

CHICKEN AND VEGETABLE STEW

½ pound boned chicken thighs,
　skin left on
3 tablespoons soy sauce
1 tablespoon *sake*
1-inch cube fresh ginger root
4 small *shiitake* (dried Japanese
　mushrooms)
Sugar
2 large scallions, trimmed, using
　white and green parts

½ medium carrot, using top part
Dashi (soup stock)
½ teaspoon salt
½ teaspoon sugar
Flour
2 tablespoons *mirin*
12 cooked ginkgo nuts, canned or
　bottled
Lime peel

Cut the chicken diagonally into bite-sized pieces. In a bowl combine 1 tablespoon of the soy sauce and the *sake*. Peel and grate the ginger and squeeze the juice into the bowl. Add the chicken pieces and marinate at room temperature until ready to use.

Soak the mushrooms for 30 minutes in warm water with a pinch of sugar. Squeeze out and remove the hard stems.

Cut the scallions into 1-inch pieces crosswise and grill on top of the stove or broil until lightly browned, about 1 minute.

Make 5 evenly spaced small, shallow, wedge-shaped cuts the length of the carrot by placing a sharp knife at an oblique angle when cutting. Cut into 8 slices crosswise. The slices will look like conventionalized plum or cherry blossoms. If it is easier, slice the carrot and cut the slices into flower shapes with a tiny cooky cutter.

In a medium-sized saucepan combine the scallions, carrot, mushrooms and enough soup stock to cover. Add the salt and sugar and cook, covered, over moderate heat until the liquid has evaporated and the carrot is tender.

Lift the chicken out of the marinade. Coat the chicken pieces with flour, shaking to remove the excess. Pour the *mirin* into a medium-sized saucepan and bring to a boil. Immediately add 1½ cups soup stock and the remaining 2 tablespoons soy sauce and bring back to a boil. Add the chicken pieces, one at a time, keeping them separate. There should be only one layer. Simmer for about 3 minutes, or until the chicken is tender.

Arrange the chicken pieces in 4 bowls, add the vegetables and ginkgo nuts in a decorative pattern round the chicken, remembering to turn the mushrooms up so that the dark side shows. Pour the stock from the chicken over the bowls and decorate with a tiny strip of lime peel. The lime peel may be cut into a very thin strip and tied in a knot, or cut into a V-shape to represent a pine needle. This is a very pretty dish with the brown of mushrooms, orange of carrot, pale yellow of ginkgo nuts, green of scallion and gold of chicken. SERVES 4.

Toriniku No Goma-Goromo-age
DEEP-FRIED SESAME-COATED CHICKEN

¾ pound boned and skinned
chicken breasts
1 teaspoon fresh ginger juice
2 tablespoons soy sauce
1 tablespoon *mirin*
4 fresh hot green peppers

1 egg
1 tablespoon *sake*
2 or 3 dashes msg
1 tablespoon black sesame seeds
½ cup flour
Vegetable oil

Slice the chicken diagonally into bite-sized pieces. In a bowl mix together the ginger juice, soy sauce and *mirin*. Add the chicken, mix and leave to marinate for 20 minutes.

Cut off the stem ends and scrape out the seeds of the peppers. Cut them in half, crosswise, if they are large. Pat dry.

Break the egg into a bowl and stir with chopsticks until it is well blended but not foamy. Stir in the *sake,* 2 tablespoons of water, msg and sesame seeds. Sift the flour into the egg, mixing lightly.

Heat 2 to 3 inches oil in a *tempura* pan or saucepan to 350°F. on a frying thermometer, or until bubbles form on wooden chopsticks stirred in the oil. Add the peppers and fry for 1 minute. Lift out and drain on the rack of the *tempura* pan or on paper towels. Drain the chicken pieces, dip into the batter and add to the pan in batches, taking care not to crowd the pan. Cook, turning, for about 2 minutes. Drain with the peppers.

Line an oblong platter with a paper napkin, arrange the chicken pieces on the platter and garnish with the peppers. SERVES 4.

Tori No Teriyaki
GLAZED CHICKEN

1 large or 2 small cucumbers	¾ pound boned chicken breast
Salt	with skin left on
2 tablespoons rice vinegar	2 tablespoons vegetable oil
Soy sauce	¼ cup *mirin*
Sugar	2 dashes msg

Cut a thin slice from each end of the cucumber and rub the cut surfaces with the peel side of the slices for a minute or so. Sprinkle a chopping board with salt and roll the cucumber back and forth for 2 or 3 minutes. This process removes the bitterness. Peel the cucumber in alternate strips, then place between two chopsticks and slice finely. The chopsticks will prevent the knife cutting right through the cucumber. Sprinkle the cucumber lightly with salt, let stand for 10 minutes, then rinse carefully so as not to break. Drain.

Mix together the vinegar, 1 tablespoon soy sauce and ½ teaspoon sugar and pour it over the cucumber. Marinate for 20 minutes.

Halve the chicken breast lengthwise and score the pieces very lightly at ½-inch intervals. Heat the oil in a skillet and sauté the chicken until it is lightly browned on both sides, about 3 minutes. Lift out the chicken. Wipe the pan with paper towels and return the chicken to the pan, off the heat. In a small saucepan combine ¼ cup soy sauce, *mirin,* 2 tablespoons sugar and msg and heat, stirring, until the sugar has dissolved. Pour the mixture over the chicken and cook over moderate heat for a minute or two, turning several times. Arrange the chicken on individual plates.

Lift the cucumber out of the marinade, cut into 4 slices and add to the plates with the chicken. Boned chicken leg may also be used for this recipe. SERVES 4.

Cucumber salad made in this way is called *Jabara Kyūri.*

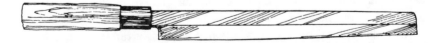

Nikumiso

CHICKEN AND VEGETABLES PICKLED IN BEAN PASTE

1 medium-sized onion
1 medium-sized green bell
  pepper
4 *shiitake* (dried Japanese
  mushrooms)
Pinch sugar
1 medium-sized carrot
1-inch cube fresh ginger root

2 tablespoons green peas
Vegetable oil
½ pound ground chicken, using
  any part
⅔ cup firmly packed *miso* (bean
  paste)
⅛ teaspoon ground hot red
  pepper

Finely chop the peeled onion. Seed and finely chop the green pepper. Soak the mushrooms for 30 minutes in warm water with the sugar. Drain, squeeze out, remove the stems, and chop finely. Scrape and finely chop the carrot. Peel and finely chop the ginger root. Drop the peas into boiling water and simmer for 4 minutes. Drain.

Pour just enough oil into a medium-sized saucepan to film the bottom. Add the chicken and cook over moderate heat, stirring with 4 or 5 chopsticks held in a bunch in one hand for 2 or 3 minutes. Then add the onion, green pepper, mushrooms, carrot and ginger, one by one, cooking for 2 or 3 minutes after each addition. Stir in the bean paste and cook for 4 or 5 minutes, or until the mixture is smoothly blended. Add the peas and cook for 2 or 3 minutes. Season with the hot pepper. Cool and store in a covered container. The mixture will keep for up to 3 weeks, refrigerated. It is eaten as a garnish on rice or in small bowls accompanied by rice and is popular for lunch boxes. It may also be eaten by putting some rice on a lettuce leaf, adding a little *nikumiso,* folding up the lettuce and eating by hand. This use represents a Korean influence in the Japanese kitchen. SERVES 8.

Tori-Dango No Nimono

CHICKEN BALLS

½ pound ground chicken
⅓ cup dry bread crumbs
1 egg, stirred
1 tablespoon white *miso* (bean paste)
1 tablespoon plus 1¼ cups *dashi* (soup stock)
1 teaspoon plus 1½ tablespoons soy sauce

Salt
Dash msg
1 large potato
Boiling water
3 cups loosely packed *shungiku* (see glossary) *or* spinach leaves
3 tablespoons *mirin*

Put the chicken into a *suribachi* (mortar) and pound with the pestle until it is smooth and light. Add the crumbs, egg and bean paste and pound together until the mixture is very smooth. Add the tablespoon of soup stock, little by little, mixing well. If the mixture is too loose, add more bread crumbs. Form into 12 balls. Bring 3½ cups water to a boil in a saucepan with the teaspoon of soy sauce, a pinch of salt and the msg. Drop in the chicken balls, reduce the heat to low and poach, uncovered, for 2 or 3 minutes. Drain in a sieve or colander and set aside. Discard the stock.

Peel the potato and let it stand in cold water for a few minutes, then slice it into 8 lengthwise wedges. Drop the slices into boiling salted water and cook until barely tender, about 5 minutes.

Thoroughly wash the *shungiku* or spinach, drop into boiling salted water and cook, uncovered, 1 minute for the *shungiku* or 2 minutes for the spinach. Rinse in cold water, squeeze out, form into a roll and cut into 1-inch pieces.

Pour the remaining 1¼ cups soup stock into a medium-sized saucepan, add the remaining 1½ tablespoons soy sauce and the *mirin,* and bring to a boil. Add the chicken balls and potato slices and cook, uncovered, over low heat for about 10 minutes to blend the flavors. Just before removing from the heat add *shungiku* or the spinach to heat through. Divide among 4 medium-sized bowls. (The sauce will not be abundant.) SERVES 4.

Vegetables, Salads and Bean Curd Dishes

VEGETABLES AND SALADS

The Japanese were not always vegetarians. They became vegetarians primarily during the Zen Buddhist era, but for the last 100 years or so, they have reverted to a diet which includes fish, fowl and meat. All the same, the Japanese have an unsurpassed appreciation of vegetables and include more of them in their daily diet than do most people.

The distinction between vegetables and salads is not very clearly defined; many dishes that would be served hot in western kitchens as vegetable dishes, are served at room temperature as salads in Japan. No matter what a vegetable dish is called, it will be part of a meal with a main course of fish, poultry or meat, soup, rice and so on.

Vegetable and salad dishes can be complicated or very simple, but all have the same aim: a fresh, natural taste. The cooking method is geared only to enchance, never to mask, nature's flavors, though many flavors may be harmoniously present in a single dish.

Vegetable and salad dishes, like almost all dishes in the Japanese kitchen are eaten with chopsticks.

Kabocha No Ankake
WINTER SQUASH WITH THICK SAUCE

1½ pounds winter squash (acorn, hubbard, butternut or calabaza—West Indian pumpkin)
1 tablespoon sugar
1 teaspoon soy sauce
1 teaspoon salt

2 or 3 dashes msg
¼ pound ground chicken
1 teaspoon ginger juice squeezed from grated fresh ginger root
½ tablespoon *katakuriko or* potato starch

Cut the squash, unpeeled, into 1-inch pieces. Using a small sharp knife, carefully trim a thin strip of peel from around the edge of each piece to prevent it breaking up while cooking.

Put the squash in a saucepan with the sugar, soy sauce, salt, msg and enough water to cover and bring to a boil over high heat. Reduce the heat and simmer gently, uncovered, until the squash is tender and the liquid reduced to half, about 15 minutes. Lift out the squash onto a platter and keep warm.

To the liquid remaining in the saucepan add the ground chicken and ginger juice and cook, stirring, for 2 or 3 minutes. Mix the potato starch with ½ tablespoon water and add to the saucepan, stirring, until the sauce is thickened. Taste for seasoning, adding a little more salt or sugar if necessary. Arrange the squash pieces on 4 small oblong platters or plates and pour the sauce over it. SERVES 4.

VARIATION: For *Kabocha No Itameni* (Fried and Boiled Winter Squash) cut and prepare the squash as above. Put into a saucepan or skillet large enough to hold all the pieces in a single layer, heat 4 tablespoons of vegetable oil and sauté the squash over moderate heat on both sides. Add water to cover, ½ cup flaked *katsuobushi* (dried bonito), 4 tablespoons sugar, or to taste, and 2 tablespoons *mirin*. Bring to a boil and cover with an *otoshibuta* (inner wooden lid) or use a smaller saucepan lid to fit closely on top of the squash, or use a plate. Reduce the heat and simmer for 10 minutes. Add 4 tablespoons soy sauce and cook, uncovered, over low heat until the squash is tender, basting once or twice with the cooking liquid. Serve with sauce in small bowls. SERVES 4.

VARIATION: For *Kabocha No Soboroni* (Winter Squash with Chicken or Meat Sauce) cut and prepare the squash as above. Heat 2 tablespoons vegetable oil in a skillet, add ½ pound ground chicken, pork or beef and 2 teaspoons finely chopped fresh ginger root and cook, stirring, over high heat for about 3 minutes. Add the squash and continue to cook, stirring, for 2 minutes longer. Add water to cover, bring to a boil, cover, reduce the heat and cook until the squash is tender, about 10 minutes. Skim if necessary. Add 1 tablespoon sugar, 2 tablespoons *mirin* and cook 5 minutes longer over moderate heat. Stir in 3 tablespoons soy sauce and cook, uncovered, over low heat until the liquid is reduced to about a third. Serve with sauce in small bowls. SERVES 4.

Nasu No Misoni
EGGPLANT WITH BEAN PASTE

8 small eggplants, about 3 inches long by 1½ inches wide, or cut up large eggplant to same size	1 tablespoon sugar
	5 tablespoons vegetable oil
	1 teaspoon finely chopped fresh ginger root
3 tablespoons *miso* (bean paste)	2 tablespoons *sake*
3 tablespoons *dashi* (soup stock) *or* water	1 teaspoon white sesame seeds

Cut the washed eggplants, unpeeled, into ½-inch slices and soak in cold water for 20 minutes. Drain and pat dry.

In a small bowl mix together the bean paste, soup stock and sugar until smooth. Set aside.

In a large skillet heat the oil, add the eggplant slices and ginger and sauté, turning the eggplant slices from time to time until they are lightly browned, 10 to 15 minutes. Add the bean paste mixture and the *sake* and continue cooking over medium heat until the liquid has evaporated. Arrange the eggplant slices on 4 small platters or dishes.

In a small skillet toast the sesame seeds until they begin to jump. Sprinkle them over the eggplant. Either white or red *miso* (bean paste) may be used for this dish. SERVES 4.

Nasu No Shigiyaki
BROILED EGGPLANT

½ medium eggplant, about 12
    ounces
Vegetable oil
4 tablespoons *miso* (bean paste)

3 tablespoons sugar
4 tablespoons *dashi* (soup stock)
White sesame seeds

Halve the washed eggplant crosswise, then cut it into 1-inch lengthwise slices. If very small eggplants are available, use four. Trim them and halve lengthwise. Thread the eggplant slices on 4 metal skewers and brush with oil on all the cut surfaces. Broil 3 or 4 inches from the source of heat until the eggplant is cooked and browned all over, about 5 minutes.

The eggplant may be fried, in which case heat 4 tablespoons of oil in a skillet and fry until cooked and browned, about 5 minutes.

Arrange the eggplant on 4 small oblong platters.

In a small saucepan combine the *miso,* sugar and soup stock and cook, stirring constantly, over low heat until the mixture is smooth and hot. Do not let it boil. Pour the sauce over the eggplant and garnish with white sesame seeds, about ½ teaspoon, toasted in a skillet until they begin to jump. SERVES 4.

Yakinasu
BROILED EGGPLANT

6 small eggplants (4 by 1½
    inches) or 1 medium
Msg

4 teaspoons flaked *katsuobushi*
    (dried bonito)
2 teaspoons soy sauce

Grill the eggplants on top of the stove or broil under medium heat, turning frequently, until the peel is blackened and blisters and the eggplants are tender, about 12 minutes for the small ones, longer for a medium-sized one. As soon as the eggplant is cool enough to handle, cut off the stems, peel off the skin, and tear or pull the eggplant into lengthwise strips. Sprinkle the strips with a little msg. Arrange on 4 small dishes. Sprinkle with the bonito flakes and the soy sauce and eat at room temperature. SERVES 4.

Mushi Hakusai
STUFFED CHINESE CABBAGE

8 large or 12 small leaves *hakusai* (Chinese cabbage)
Boiling water
Vegetable oil
Salt
1 small onion, finely chopped
¼ pound ground beef
¼ pound ground pork
1 teaspoon grated ginger

3 tablespoons bread crumbs
1 egg
Soy sauce
Katakuriko or potato starch starch
⅔ cup *dashi* (soup stock)
4 tablespoons *mirin*
Grated lime peel

Cut away and discard the stalk end of the cabbage leaves. Wash and drain. Put a few drops of oil into a saucepan of boiling salted water, add the cabbage, bring back to a boil and cook for 1 minute. Lift out the cabbage and drain in a colander.

In a small skillet (about 7 inches) heat 2 teaspoons of oil and sauté the onion until it is tender and lightly browned. Let it cool. In a bowl mix together the onion, beef, pork, ginger, bread crumbs and the egg, stir with 1 teaspoon soy sauce and ½ teaspoon salt. Divide the mixture into 4 patties.

Squeeze any excess moisture out of the cabbage leaves. Place a cabbage leaf in a small bowl (4 to 4½ inches wide, 2 inches deep), and sprinkle lightly with starch. Add another leaf or two according to whether there are 8 large or 12 small leaves, then add a pattie, sprinkle with starch. Repeat until all the ingredients are used up, ending with a cabbage leaf. Fold the leaves into a neat package. Place the stuffed cabbage, in the bowl, in a steamer. Steam, over high heat, for 20 to 25 minutes.

In a small saucepan combine the soup stock, *mirin,* and 3 tablespoons soy sauce. Mix ½ tablespoon starch with ½ tablespoon cold water and stir into the sauce. Cook this sauce over moderate heat, stirring, until it is lightly thickened.

Turn the stuffed cabbage out of the bowl onto a platter or dish, bottom side up. Cut a cross in the top and pour the sauce over the cabbage. Sprinkle with the lime peel. To serve, cut into quarters with chopsticks and place in small individual bowls with the sauce. SERVES 4.

Hakusai No Ohitashi
CABBAGE WITH BONITO FLAKES

8 large *hakusai* (Chinese
   cabbage) leaves
Boiling water
Salt
1 tablespoon rice vinegar

1 tablespoon soy sauce
4 tablespoons *dashi* (soup stock)
2 tablespoons *katsuobushi* (dried
   bonito flakes)

Place the cabbage leaves in boiling salted water in a saucepan large enough to hold them comfortably and simmer until tender, about 5 minutes. Drain and arrange the leaves on a *sudare* (bamboo mat), or use a kitchen cloth. Allow to cool to room temperature. Roll up the mat and squeeze gently to get rid of the excess moisture. Unroll and cut the cabbage into 4 slices. Set aside.

In a small bowl combine the rice vinegar, soy sauce, soup stock and a little salt. Mix well and pour over the cabbage slices. Put the cabbage slices into 4 small shallow dishes and garnish with the bonito flakes. SERVES 4.

This is a winter vegetable dish and, with similar vegetable dishes, is very popular in Japan because of its simple, natural flavor.

Okura No Sanbaizu
OKRA WITH VINEGAR DRESSING

20 small okra
Boiling water
2 tablespoons rice vinegar
4 tablespoons *dashi* (soup stock)

½ teaspoon salt
2 teaspoons soy sauce
2 teaspoons sugar

Rinse the okra and drop into boiling salted water and boil, uncovered, for 3 to 4 minutes. Drain, rinse quickly in cold water, cut off stem end and cut the okra into ½-inch slices. Transfer to a bowl.

Mix the vinegar, soup stock, salt, soy sauce and sugar together and pour over the okra, tossing lightly to mix. Serve in small bowls. SERVES 4.

Sato-imo To Toriniku No Umani
TARO WITH CHICKEN AND VEGETABLES

1½ pounds (8 small) *sato-imo* (taro—a starchy root)
1½ cups *dashi* (soup stock)
3 tablespoons *sake*
1 tablespoon sugar
½ teaspoon salt
1 tablespoon plus 1 teaspoon soy sauce
1 tablespoon plus 1 teaspoon *mirin*

1 teaspoon ginger juice squeezed from grated fresh ginger root
5 ounces skinned and boned chicken, cut into diagonal bite-sized pieces
⅓ large carrot (about 2 ounces), scraped
6 large green beans, trimmed and cut into thin lengthwise slices
2 teaspoons grated lime peel

Peel the washed taro, rub with salt and rinse in cold water. If small taro are not available, cut larger ones into 8 even-sized pieces. In a saucepan large enough to hold the taro in a single layer, combine the soup stock, 2 tablespoons of the *sake,* and the sugar and salt. Add the taro, cover with a double piece of cheesecloth wrung out in water. Bring to a boil, reduce heat to low and simmer, uncovered, until the liquid is reduced to about one third and the taro is tender, 20 to 35 minutes. Remove the cheesecloth, add 1 teaspoon of the soy sauce and the tablespoon of *mirin.* Simmer for a few minutes, remove from the heat and set aside.

In a saucepan combine the ginger juice, the remaining tablespoon of *sake* and the tablespoon of soy sauce. Bring to a boil and add the chicken. Cook, stirring, over very low heat until the liquid is absorbed and the chicken tender, 3 or 4 minutes. Set aside.

Flute the carrot, cutting 5 small wedges at even intervals down its length. Cut it into 12 slices, or slice and cut into flower shapes with a small cooky cutter. Cook in salted water to cover by about 1 inch with a pinch of sugar until tender and the water evaporated, about 15 minutes.

Drop the beans into boiling salted water and cook for 8 minutes. Drain, sprinkle with a little salt and the teaspoon of *mirin.* Set aside.

Arrange the taro on a serving platter, top with the chicken and any sauce from both the chicken and the taro. Garnish with the carrots and beans and sprinkle the lime peel on the taro. Eat at room temperature. If preferred arrange on 4 small dishes. SERVES 4.

Saya-Ingen No Shōyuni
GREEN BEANS WITH SOY SAUCE

12 ounces green beans, trimmed	2 tablespoons *mirin*
1 cup *dashi* (soup stock)	Dash msg
2 tablespoons soy sauce	

Break the washed beans into 2-inch pieces and put into a saucepan with the soup stock, soy, *mirin* and msg. Simmer, uncovered, over moderate heat until the liquid has all evaporated and the beans are tender, about 15 to 20 minutes. Serve in 4 small bowls. SERVES 4.

Saya-ingen No Miso-ae
GREEN BEANS WITH BEAN PASTE

Saya refers to the outside of the green beans, not the beans inside. Translated, the word means the scabbard of the sword—hence the scabbard of the bean.

¾ pound green beans	3 tablespoons sugar
Boiling water	3 tablespoons *mirin*
4 tablespoons either red or white	
miso (bean paste)	

Drop the washed beans into a large saucepan of boiling salted water, bring back to a boil and cook, uncovered, for 6 minutes. Drain and trim the ends of the beans. Slice diagonally into 2 or 3 pieces according to the size of the bean.

In a small saucepan combine the bean paste, either red or white according to taste as either is traditionally used, with the sugar and *mirin* and cook, stirring, over very low heat until the mixture is smooth but without letting it come to a boil. Cool.

Mix the beans with the sauce and serve in 4 small dishes. SERVES 4.

Saya-Ingen No Goma-ae
GREEN BEANS WITH WHITE SESAME SEEDS

1 tablespoon salt
Boiling water
½ pound green beans, washed
and trimmed
3 tablespoons white sesame
seeds

1½ tablespoons sugar
2 tablespoons soy sauce
Flaked *katsuobushi* (dried
bonito)

Add the salt to a saucepan with 5 cups boiling water, drop in the beans and bring back to a boil over high heat. Boil for 2 to 3 minutes according to the degree of crispness desired. Rinse the beans under cold running water and drain. Cut each bean into 2 or 3 diagonal slices, according to size.

In a skillet toast the sesame seeds until they begin to jump. Transfer them to a *suribachi* (mortar) and crush them coarsely. Scrape them into a bowl. Add the sugar and soy sauce and stir to mix. Add the beans and toss lightly. Serve at room temperature in 4 small bowls. Garnish with some bonito flakes, if liked. Do not chill. SERVES 4.

VARIATION: For *Saya-Ingen No Kurumi-ae* (Green Beans with Walnuts) use 8 whole walnuts or 4 tablespoons broken walnut meats, coarsely crushed, instead of the white sesame seeds.

VARIATION: For *Saya-Ingen No Peanuts-ae* (Green Beans with Peanuts) use 3 tablespoons coarsely crushed peanuts instead of the white sesame seeds.

VARIATION: For *Saya-Ingen No Kuro Goma-ae* (Green Beans with Black Sesame Seeds) cook the beans as above and put in a bowl with 1 tablespoon soy sauce. In a skillet toast 3 tablespoons black sesame seeds until they begin to jump. Transfer them to a *suribachi* (mortar) and crush them coarsely. Scrape them into a bowl and add 2 tablespoons soy sauce, 2 teaspoons *mirin* and ⅛ teaspoon msg. Stir to mix and pour over the beans, tossing lightly. Serve at room temperature in small bowls. SERVES 4.

Furofuki Daikon
STEAMED WHITE RADISH

This is a winter dish and is eaten hot. The radish holds the heat so that when it is cut with chopsticks steam rises from it, which is why it is called "a blow-on-it-to-cool-it dish."

¾ pound *daikon* (white radish)
1 teaspoon salt
2-by-5-inch piece *kombu* (kelp)
4 tablespoons black sesame seeds
3¼ tablespoons red *miso* (bean paste)

4 tablespoons *dashi* (soup stock)
4 tablespoons sugar or to taste
1 tablespoon *mirin*
Lime peel cut into 4 V-shapes
Poppy seeds (optional)

Peel the radish and cut it into 4 slices. Peel a very thin strip from the top and bottom edges of each slice to prevent the radish breaking up in cooking. Cut a shallow cross in one side of each slice and arrange, cut side down, in a saucepan. Cover with cold water and add the salt. Clean the seaweed (kelp) with a damp cloth, cut it into a ½-inch fringe and add to the saucepan. Cover with an *otoshibuta* (an inner wooden lid) or use a smaller saucepan lid that will fit closely on top of the radish, or use a plate. Just before the water comes to a boil, remove the seaweed. Replace the *otoshibuta* with a lid and cook on low heat until the radish is tender, about 45 minutes.

In a skillet lightly toast the sesame seeds until they begin to jump. Transfer to a *suribachi* (mortar) and grind them to a fine paste. Scrape out into a bowl with chopsticks and set aside.

In a small saucepan combine the red bean paste with the soup stock, sugar and *mirin* and heat gently, stirring until smooth and well blended. Add the sesame seed paste and stir to mix, off the heat. Keep the sauce warm until the radish is tender.

Arrange the radish slices in 4 warmed dishes and pour any cooking liquid over them. Spread the bean paste sauce on top of each slice so that a little of it runs down the sides. Put a lime-peel pine needle on top. Sprinkle with poppy seeds if liked. The effect is extremely pretty as the radish is very white, the paste red-brown and the lime a vivid green. SERVES 4.

Kiriboshi-Daikon No Nitsuke

DRIED RADISH AND FRIED BEAN CURD

This is an old traditional dish, which is no longer seen very often. Nowadays, fresh daikon *(white radish) is available all year round and no one has to wait until autumn or winter for it, so that the dishes that rely on the dried version are being neglected. A pity, as this recipe is unusual and the dish is very good.*

1½ ounces *kiriboshi daikon* (dried radish strips)	2 dried hot red peppers, seeded and chopped
4 pieces *aburaage* (fried bean curd)	2 cups *dashi* (soup stock)
3 tablespoons vegetable oil	1½ tablespoons sugar
	1½ tablespoons soy sauce

Soak the dried radish strips in cold water for 30 to 40 minutes. Drain and squeeze out the water gently. Rinse the dried bean curd in hot water to remove the oil, and slice, crosswise, into ¼-inch slices.

In a medium-sized saucepan heat the oil, add the peppers, then the radish strips. Cook, stirring, for about 1 minute. Add the fried bean curd and stir to mix. Add the soup stock, stir and bring to a boil. Add the sugar and cover with an *otoshibuta* (inner lid) or use a smaller saucepan lid. Simmer over low heat for 30 minutes, then add the soy sauce, cover with the *otoshibuta* again and simmer over low heat until the liquid has almost evaporated, about 20 minutes. Stir to mix 3 or 4 times during the final cooking. Serve in small bowls. SERVES 6 TO 8.

Kabu No Oroshimushi
GRATED STEAMED TURNIPS

¼ pound peeled raw shrimp, coarsely chopped

¼ pound skinned and boned chicken breast, coarsely chopped

2 teaspoons *usukuchi shōyu* (light soy sauce)

2 teaspoons *sake*

2 eggs, stirred

1½ cups finely grated white turnips, about 4 small, drained through a sieve

4 small *shiitake* (dried Japanese mushrooms), soaked 30 minutes in warm water with a pinch of sugar

½ tablespoon raw green peas

Salt

1 teaspoon sugar

4 teaspoons *mirin*

1½ cups *dashi* (soup stock)

1½ tablespoons soy sauce

2 teaspoons *katakuriko or* arrowroot *or* cornstarch

2 teaspoons grated fresh ginger root

Sprinkle the shrimp and chicken with the light soy sauce and *sake* and let stand 5 minutes. In a bowl combine the eggs, turnips, mushrooms (squeezed out, stems removed and quartered), the chicken and shrimp and any liquid, the peas, ½ teaspoon salt, sugar, and 2 teaspoons of the *mirin*. Mix well. Pour the mixture into 4 deep bowls large enough so that they are only ¾ full, leaving room for the sauce. Place in a steamer over boiling water and steam over high heat for about 12 minutes.

In a small saucepan combine the soup stock, ¼ teaspoon salt, 1½ tablespoons soy sauce, the remaining 2 teaspoons of *mirin* and the *katakuriko* mixed with 2 teaspoons of water and bring to a boil. Simmer, stirring, until the sauce is lightly thickened. Pour the sauce over the turnips and garnish each bowl with a little mound of grated ginger. SERVES 4.

Kokabu No Torimisokake
TURNIPS WITH BEAN PASTE AND CHICKEN SAUCE

12 small white turnips, washed
   and peeled
1½ cups *dashi* (soup stock)
1 teaspoon salt
1 teaspoon soy sauce
6 ounces skinned and boned
   chicken breast
1 teaspoon finely chopped fresh
   ginger root

2 tablespoons *mirin*
4 tablespoons *miso* (bean paste)
2 teaspoons *katakuriko or*
   cornstarch *or* arrowroot
1 scallion, trimmed, using white
   and green parts

Cut a shallow cross on the bottom of each turnip. In a saucepan large enough to hold the turnips in a single layer combine the soup stock, salt, soy sauce and turnips. Cover, bring to a boil, lower the heat and simmer until the turnips are tender, about 20 to 25 minutes. Drain, set the turnips aside and reserve the stock.

Put the chicken twice through the fine blade of a meat grinder. Put the chicken into another saucepan with the ginger root and 1 tablespoon of the *mirin* and cook, stirring constantly, over moderate heat until the chicken is cooked, 3 to 4 minutes. Add the bean paste and the remaining tablespoon of *mirin,* stir to mix and add ¾ cup turnip stock, making up the quantity with soup stock, if necessary. Mix the *katakuriko* or other starch with 2 teaspoons of cold water and stir into the sauce. Cook over moderate heat, stirring, until lightly thickened. Put the turnips into 4 small bowls and cover with the sauce.

Finely chop the scallion, crisp for a few minutes in cold water and squeeze dry in a towel. Sprinkle it over the turnips. This is an autumn or winter vegetable dish. SERVES 4.

Kabu No Tsumemushi
STEAMED STUFFED TURNIPS

4 small white turnips, peeled
2 *kikurage* (jelly mushrooms)
12 cooked ginkgo nuts
3 ounces fillet of sole *or* red
    snapper *or* striped bass, thinly
    sliced on the diagonal

Salt
¾ cup *dashi* (soup stock)
½ teaspoon *usukuchi shōyu*
    (light soy sauce)
2 teaspoons arrowroot *or*
    cornstarch

Cut a small slice from the top of the washed and peeled turnips and using a sharp spoon (a grapefruit spoon is ideal) hollow them out leaving a shell about ½ inch thick. Slightly hollow out the slice from the tops to make a lid.

Soak the mushrooms until tender, about 10 minutes. Drain and slice thinly.

In a bowl combine the mushrooms, ginkgo nuts and fish; season with salt and stuff into the turnips. Cover with the turnip lids. Put into a steamer over boiling water and steam over high heat for 20 minutes.

In a small saucepan combine the soup stock, light soy sauce and ⅛ teaspoon salt. Mix the arrowroot with 2 teaspoons water and add to the saucepan. Bring to a boil, stirring constantly, and simmer until the sauce is lightly thickened. Arrange the turnips on a warmed platter or put into 4 shallow bowls with covers. Remove the turnip lids and balance them at the side of the vegetables. Pour the sauce over the turnips. SERVES 4.

Endō No Aoni
PEAS IN SOUP STOCK

3⅔ cups water
2¼ teaspoons salt
1½ cups fresh green peas
1½ cups *dashi* (soup stock)

1 teaspoon *usukuchi shōyu* (light
    soy sauce)
1½ teaspoons *mirin*

In a saucepan combine the water with 2 teaspoons of the salt, bring to a boil, add the peas and cook, uncovered, over moderate heat until tender, about 10 minutes. Drain and set aside.

In another saucepan combine the soup stock, the remaining ¼ teaspoon salt, the light soy sauce and *mirin* and bring to a boil. Add the peas, bring back to a boil, then remove from the heat. Stand the saucepan in very cold water, with ice cubes, changing the water from time to time to keep it very cold. Let stand for 2 or 3 hours. Pour the soup and peas into bowls. SERVES 4.

This method of cooling gives the peas a beautiful fresh color, hence the name of the recipe as *ao* means blue green and *ni* means boiled. The peas also absorb the flavor of the soup stock.

Endō No Nataneni
GREEN PEAS WITH CHICKEN AND EGGS

This dish, which means literally "peas looking like the seeds of rape greens," gets its name from the green of the peas and the yellow of the eggs. The combination succeeds in looking like rape greens when the yellow flowers are running to seed.

1⅓ cups fresh green peas	1 teaspoon sugar
Boiling water	1 tablespoon *usukuchi shōyu*
2½ teaspoons salt	(light soy sauce)
5 ounces skinned and boned	1 tablespoon *mirin*
chicken, coarsely chopped	3 eggs, stirred until well blended
1½ cups *dashi* (soup stock)	

Drop the peas into a saucepan of boiling water with 2 teaspoons of the salt and cook, uncovered, over moderate heat for 8 minutes. Drain and let stand in cold water until ready to use.

Add the chicken to a small saucepan with the soup stock and cook for 4 or 5 minutes over moderate heat. Add the sugar, the remaining ½ teaspoon, salt, light soy sauce and *mirin,* skimming the surface if necessary. Drain the peas and add to the chicken mixture. Bring to a boil, then pour the eggs in a thin stream over the whole surface of the pan. Cover, turn off the heat and let stand for a minute or two until the egg is set. Serve hot in bowls. SERVES 4.

Wakatakeni

BOILED BAMBOO SHOOTS

This is a spring dish, at which time in Japan fresh young bamboo shoots are available. Whole canned bamboo shoots can be used instead.

3 cups *dashi* (soup stock)
3 tablespoons *usukuchi shōyu* (light soy sauce)
2 tablespoons sugar
⅛ teaspoons msg
½ pound skinned and boned chicken, sliced diagonally into bite-sized pieces

1½ pounds bamboo shoots, cut into ¼-inch slices
6 8-inch fronds *wakame* (lobe-leaf seaweed)
2 tablespoons *mirin*

In a saucepan combine the soup stock, light soy sauce, sugar and msg. Add the chicken pieces and cook over low heat for 2 minutes. Remove the chicken and set aside. Add the bamboo shoots and cook over low heat for 20 to 30 minutes, or until the shoots are tender.

Soak the seaweed in cold water for 10 to 15 minutes, drain, cut away any tough ribs and chop into 1-inch slices. Add to the saucepan. Add the reserved chicken and *mirin* and simmer, covered, for 5 minutes over low heat. Serve in small deep bowls. SERVES 4.

In Japan the dish would be garnished with a leaf of *sansho,* Japanese pepper.

Kinpira

BURDOCK ROOT AND CARROT WITH SESAME SEEDS

¾ pound *gobō* (burdock root)
1 medium-sized carrot
1 or 2 dried hot red peppers, to taste

1¼ tablespoons vegetable oil
1 tablespoon sugar
2½ tablespoons soy sauce
2 teaspoons white sesame seeds

Scrape the burdock root with the back of a knife under cold running water, cut it into 2-inch pieces, then slice each piece thinly lengthwise. Drop into cold water until ready to use. Scrape the carrot and cut the same way as the burdock root.

Seed the peppers and if they are very dry, soak for a minute or two in cold water to soften. Then cut into diagonal strips.

In a large saucepan heat the oil. Add the peppers and sauté for a few seconds. Drain and add the burdock root and sauté over moderate heat, stirring from time to time, for about 10 minutes. Then add the carrot and sauté for 5 minutes longer. Add 2 tablespoons water, cover and cook for 2 or 3 minutes, or until the carrot is tender. Add the sugar and soy sauce and stir to mix. Bring to a boil and cook over moderate heat, stirring with chopsticks, until the liquid has evaporated, about 5 minutes.

In a small skillet toast the sesame seeds until they begin to jump. Serve the burdock root and carrot mixture in bowls and sprinkle with the sesame seeds. This has a very natural taste and although it is a New Year dish it is also very popular for lunch boxes, and indeed at any time. SERVES 4 TO 6.

Na-No-Hana No Goma-ae
RAPE BLOSSOMS WITH SESAME SEEDS

10 ounces rape blossoms, washed, drained and with tough stems removed
Boiling water

3 tablespoons white sesame seeds
2½ tablespoons soy sauce
1 tablespoon sugar

Drop the rape blossoms into a large saucepan of boiling water and cook, uncovered, over high heat for 4 minutes. Drain and put into a large bowl of cold water. When cool, drain, squeeze out any excess moisture and chop into ½-inch pieces.

In a skillet toast the sesame seeds until they begin to jump, then transfer them to a *suribachi* (mortar) and grind to a paste. Add the soy sauce and sugar and mix, scraping down the sides of the mortar with chopsticks to remove any sesame paste. Just before serving toss the cooked rape blossoms with the dressing and divide among 4 small bowls. SERVES 4.

Tamanegi No Goma Ankake
ONIONS IN SESAME SEED SAUCE

4 medium onions, about
   2-inches across, peeled and
   halved crosswise
Boiling water
1⅓ cups *dashi* (soup stock)
1 tablespoon *mirin*
1½ tablespoons plus 2 teaspoons
   soy sauce

1 tablespoon vegetable oil
6 ounces ground chicken
msg
1 tablespoon potato starch *or*
   cornstarch
2 tablespoons white sesame
   seeds

Arrange the onions in a saucepan large enough to hold them in a single layer and pour in enough boiling water to cover. Bring back to a boil over moderate heat and cook for 3 minutes. Add the soup stock, *mirin* and 1½ tablespoons soy sauce. Cover and simmer until tender, about 10 minutes. Lift out the onions and place in 1 large or 4 small serving bowls. Measure the liquid and make up the quantity to 1½ cups with more soup stock if necessary. Set aside.

In another saucepan heat the vegetable oil, add the chicken and fry, stirring with chopsticks, for a minute or two. Add the reserved stock, the 2 teaspoons soy sauce, 1 or 2 dashes of msg and the potato starch mixed with 1 tablespoon of cold water. Cook, stirring, until the sauce is lightly thickened.

In a skillet toast the sesame seeds until they begin to jump. Crush coarsely and add to the sauce. Stir and pour the sauce over the onions. SERVES 4.

Tamanegi No Sunomono
ONION SALAD

2 medium onions, peeled and
   halved lengthwise
4 tablespoons rice vinegar

4 tablespoons soy sauce
4 tablespoons flaked *katsuobushi*
   (dried bonito)

Slice the onions very thinly lengthwise and put to soak in ice water for 15 to 30 minutes according to how strongly flavored they are. Drain. Transfer the onions to a bowl and mix with the vinegar, soy sauce and 3 tablespoons of the bonito flakes. Place in small serving bowls and sprinkle with the remaining tablespoon of bonito. SERVES 4 TO 6.

Warabi-Zansetsu
STICKY YAM AND FERNBRAKE SALAD

This salad has a very poetic name which describes it as looking like lingering snow from winter on the mountains and fields of spring, and the description is really very apt.

8 to 10 ounces *shiozuke warabi* (ready-packaged salted fernbrake)
1 pound *yamaimo* (sticky yam)
1 tablespoon rice vinegar
1 sheet *nori* (dried laver seaweed)
1 tablespoon *ponzu* (citrus vinegar) *or* 1 tablespoon lime or lemon juice
1 tablespoon soy sauce

Soak the fernbrake in cold water for about 1 hour, changing the water several times. Cut off and discard any hard stems. Cut into 1-inch pieces and squeeze in a kitchen cloth to remove excess water.

Peel the yam fairly thickly under cold running water and drop into a bowl with 4 cups water and the rice vinegar as it discolors very quickly. Let it stand for 30 minutes. Drain, pat dry and transfer to a *suribachi* (mortar) and grate it. It will turn into a white foamy liquid. Or chop and reduce in a blender.

Toast the *nori* on both sides for a few seconds on top of the stove then cut into small pieces with scissors.

Mix the fernbrake with the grated yam and divide among 4 small bowls. Top with the *nori*. Mix the citrus vinegar or the lime or lemon juice with the soy sauce and pour over the salad. SERVES 4.

Yamaimo No Sunomono
STICKY YAM SALAD

½ pound *yamaimo* (sticky yam)
2 tablespoons plus 1 teaspoon
  sake
6 tablespoons rice vinegar
2 teaspoons sugar

⅛ teaspoon salt
2 or 3 dashes msg
1-inch piece lime peel, finely
  sliced

Peel the yam, slice very thinly, then stack the slices and cut into julienne strips. Put in a bowl with 2 tablespoons of the *sake* and 4 tablespoons of the rice vinegar, toss thoroughly and set aside.

In a bowl combine the remaining 2 tablespoons of rice vinegar, the sugar, the remaining teaspoon of *sake,* the salt and msg and mix well.

Drain the yam, discard the liquid and put the yam into 4 small bowls. Pour the vinegar mixture over the yam strips and garnish with the lime peel. SERVES 4.

Yamaimo no Tororokobu-kake
STICKY YAM SALAD WITH SEAWEED

1 *yamaimo* (sticky yam)
  weighing about 14 ounces
3 tablespoons rice vinegar
4 tablespoons *tororo kombu*
  (shredded kelp)

1 to 2 teaspoons *wasabi* (green
  horseradish powder)
2 tablespoons soy sauce

Peel the yam and put to soak for 10 minutes in cold water with 1 tablespoon rice vinegar to prevent it from discoloring. Drain, pat dry with paper towels and cut into 1½-inch slices. Stack the slices and cut crosswise into ½-inch slices. Divide among 4 small bowls and top with the *tororo kombu.*

Mix the horseradish with a little water and place a small mound on the yam.

Mix the remaining 2 tablespoons of rice vinegar with the soy sauce and pour over the yam. SERVES 4.

Moyashi No Karēsu-ae
CURRIED BEAN SPROUT SALAD

14 ounces bean sprouts
Boiling water
⅓ cup rice vinegar
⅓ cup *mirin*
1 teaspoon salt

1½ teaspoons curry powder
2 teaspoons *usukuchi shōyu*
  (light soy sauce)
2 teaspoons sugar

Wash and drain the bean sprouts. Drop into boiling salted water and cook, uncovered, for 2 minutes. Drain in a colander and transfer to a bowl. Mix together all the remaining ingredients and pour over the bean sprouts, tossing lightly to mix. Let stand for 30 minutes. Serve in 4 small bowls. SERVES 4.

Kaki No Sunomono
OYSTER SALAD

20 medium-sized shucked fresh
  oysters
⅓ cup grated *daikon* (white
  radish)
3 tablespoons rice vinegar
8 cups *shungiku* (see glossary) *or*
  raw spinach leaves

Salt
1½ teaspoons sugar
1 tablespoon soy sauce
½ teaspoon msg

Put the oysters in a bowl with the grated radish and mix gently with the fingers for a minute or two. Add cold water to cover, lift out the oysters and rinse. Discard the radish. Return the oysters to the bowl and pour 1 tablespoon of the rice vinegar over them.

Drop the *shungiku* into boiling salted water and simmer for 2 or 3 minutes. Drain, rinse under cold water, drain again and form into a roll on the end of a *sudare* (bamboo mat) or a kitchen cloth. Roll up and squeeze lightly to get rid of the excess water. Unroll and cut into 1-inch slices.

In a bowl mix together the remaining 2 tablespoons of rice vinegar, the sugar, soy sauce and msg. Arrange the oysters and *shungiku* in 4 small bowls and pour the sauce over them. SERVES 4.

Kyūrimomi
CUCUMBER SALAD

2 medium cucumbers
Salt
2 tablespoons rice vinegar
2 teaspoons soy sauce

1 teaspoon sugar
⅛ teaspoon msg
1 teaspoon white sesame seeds

Cut the ends off the cucumbers and rub both ends of the cucumbers with cut-off slices for a minute or two. Sprinkle a chopping board with salt and roll the cucumbers in the salt for a few minutes. This is called *itazuri* and removes any bitter taste. If the cucumbers have been waxed, peel them; otherwise leave them unpeeled. Slice them thinly, sprinkle with a teaspoon of salt, mix and let them stand for 10 minutes, then squeeze out lightly. This is the *momi* of the title.

Put the cucumber in a sieve and pour cold water over the slices, drain thoroughly and again squeeze out. Transfer to a bowl.

Mix the vinegar, soy sauce, sugar and msg and pour over the cucumbers, mixing lightly. Toast the sesame seeds in a skillet until they begin to jump. Crush coarsely. Serve the salad in 4 small bowls and sprinkle with the sesame seeds. This is a very old traditional recipe. SERVES 4.

Wakame To Kyuri No Sumiso-ae
SEAWEED AND CUCUMBER SALAD

3 8-inch fronds *wakame*
   (lobe-leaf seaweed)
3 tablespoons rice vinegar
1 medium cucumber
Salt
4 tablespoons white *miso* (bean
   paste)

1 tablespoon *mirin*
1 teaspoon sugar
1 teaspoon Japanese mustard
   mixed with hot water

Soak the seaweed in cold water until soft, about 10 to 15 minutes. Cut away any hard ribs, squeeze out and chop into 1-inch pieces. Rinse these pieces in hot water, then in cold water, drain and squeeze out. Put into a bowl and sprinkle with 1 tablespoon of the vinegar. Set aside.

Cut the ends off the cucumber and rub the ends with the cut-off slices. Sprinkle a chopping board with salt and roll the cucumber in the salt for 2 or 3 minutes. This removes the bitter taste. Rinse the cucumber and if it is waxed, peel it. If unwaxed, do not peel. Slice the cucumber very thinly. Soak in cold, salted water for a few minutes, drain and squeeze out. Set aside.

In a small saucepan combine the *miso, mirin* and sugar and heat through, stirring, without letting the mixture boil. Cool. Add the mustard and the remaining 2 tablespoons of rice vinegar and mix well. Add the seaweed and cucumber to the bean paste mixture and toss lightly to mix. Serve in small bowls as a salad. SERVES 4.

Kyūri To Moyashi No Goma-ae
CUCUMBER AND SOY BEAN SPROUTS WITH SESAME SEEDS

½ pound bean sprouts, rinsed
and cleaned
Boiling water
1 medium cucumber
Salt
1 tablespoon rice vinegar

1 tablespoon sesame oil
2 tablespoons soy sauce
1 tablespoon white sesame seeds
Shichimi-tōgarashi
(seven-flavor spice)

Drop the bean sprouts into a saucepan of boiling water and cook for 2 minutes. Drain and cool. Peel the cucumber and cut in half lengthwise. Scrape out the seeds and slice thinly crosswise. Put the cucumber slices in a bowl and sprinkle lightly with salt. Mix well, squeezing the cucumber gently to get rid of the water. If cucumber is not waxed, do not peel.

In a bowl combine the vinegar, sesame oil and soy sauce and mix well. Season to taste with salt, add the bean sprouts and the cucumber and mix lightly. In a skillet toast the sesame seeds until they begin to jump. Sprinkle over the bean sprout and cucumber mixture. Serve in small bowls and sprinkle with *shichimi-tōgarashi* powder. This is a summer dish. SERVES 4.

Kyūri To Wakame No Sunomono
CUCUMBER SALAD WITH LOBE-LEAF SEAWEED

1 medium cucumber, weighing
   about ½ pound
Salt
6 8-inch fronds *wakame*
   (lobe-leaf seaweed)

1½ tablespoons rice vinegar
2 teaspoons sugar
1 teaspoon soy sauce
2 dashes msg

Cut the ends off the cucumber and using the cut-off slices rub both ends of the cucumber for a minute or so. Sprinkle a chopping board generously with salt and roll the cucumber in the salt for 2 or 3 minutes. This takes away any bitterness. If the cucumber is waxed, peel it, otherwise leave it unpeeled. Cut the cucumber in half lengthwise and place on a chopping board with the flat sides down. Place a pair of cooking chopsticks, the kind that are tied together at the top, on each side of the cucumber and slice it finely on the diagonal. The chopsticks will prevent the knife cutting completely through the cucumber, which will remain in one piece. Repeat with the other half. Sprinkle with 1 teaspoon salt and pour 2 tablespoons of water over the cucumber halves. Let stand a minute or two, then drain and squeeze gently. Cut in half crosswise, then slice each piece into 3 diagonal slices, which makes 1 serving. Arrange on 4 small platters or plates.

Put the seaweed to soak in cold water for 10 to 15 minutes. Rinse, squeeze out the water and chop coarsely. Arrange on the platters at the side of the cucumber.

In a small bowl combine vinegar, sugar, soy sauce, msg and ¼ teaspoon salt and stir to mix. Pour over the cucumber and seaweed. SERVES 4.

Green Asparagus No Kimijōyukake
GREEN ASPARAGUS SALAD

10 ounces green asparagus, about
   20 thin stalks
Boiling water
Salt

1 tablespoon black sesame seeds
1 egg yolk
2 tablespoons soy sauce

Cut the hard ends from the washed and drained asparagus. Drop it into a large saucepan of boiling salted water, bring back to a boil and simmer for 5 minutes. Lift out the asparagus into a *zaru* (bamboo colander), or a sieve and plunge into cold water for 1 minute. Drain.

Toast the black sesame seeds in a skillet until they begin to jump. Set aside.

Put the egg yolk into a small bowl and stir in the soy sauce, mixing thoroughly but not beating. Cut the asparagus stalks in half. Lay the end halves on 4 small oblong platters and arrange the tips diagonally across them. Pour the egg-yolk mixture over them and top with the sesame seeds. Serve at room temperature. Do not chill. SERVES 4.

Toriniku No Oroshi-ae

CHICKEN AND VEGETABLE SALAD

½ pound *tori-sasami* (bamboo leaf chicken breasts) (see glossary)
Salt
1 teaspoon *sake*
4 medium-sized fresh mushrooms
1 medium-sized stalk celery
1 large or 2 small sprigs flat Italian parsley

Boiling water
½ pound *daikon* (white radish)
2½ tablespoons rice vinegar
½ teaspoon *usukuchi shōyu* (light soy sauce)
¼ teaspoon salt
Dash msg

Sprinkle the chicken breasts lightly with salt and *sake* and grill or broil until cooked, 3 to 4 minutes. Shred into lengthwise strips.

Trim the rinsed mushroom stems, sprinkle the mushrooms with salt, and grill or broil until cooked, about 5 minutes. Slice thinly.

Remove any strings from the washed celery and cut into 1-inch pieces, then cut into julienne strips.

Drop the parsley into boiling salted water and simmer for 2 minutes. Rinse in cold water and cut into 1-inch pieces.

Grate the radish finely and squeeze out the excess moisture.

Mix the rice vinegar with the light soy sauce, salt and msg. Combine all the ingredients in a bowl, pour on the dressing and mix lightly. Serve in individual bowls. SERVES 4 TO 6.

Hōrensō No Ohitashi
SPINACH SALAD

5 cups tightly packed spinach
Boiling water
1 teaspoon sugar
1 teaspoon plus 2 tablespoons soy
  sauce

Dash msg
¼ cup *dashi* (soup stock)
2 tablespoons flaked *katsuobushi*
  (dried bonito)

Wash and drain the spinach. Drop into a large saucepan of boiling water with the sugar, bring back to a boil over high heat and cook, uncovered, for 2 minutes. Drain in a colander, then rinse under cold running water. Drain and squeeze out. Place in a bowl and sprinkle with the teaspoon of soy sauce and the msg. Let stand for a minute or two, then arrange along the bottom edge of a *sudare* (bamboo mat), or use a kitchen cloth about 10 inches wide. Roll up and gently press out any remaining liquid while forming the spinach into a sausage-shaped roll. Unroll and cut into 1- to 1½-inch slices.

Place in 4 small bowls. Mix together the soup stock and remaining 2 tablespoons of soy sauce and pour over the spinach. Garnish with the bonito, crumbled with the fingers. Serves 4.

VARIATION: For *Hōrensō No Shiro-ae* (Spinach with Bean Curd) cook 6½ cups tightly packed spinach (1 10-ounce package) exactly as above and put into a bowl. Cut 1 *momen tōfu* (bean curd) weighing about ½ pound in half, reserving one half for another use. Cook the bean curd in boiling water for 1 minute, drain through cheesecloth, and squeeze to break up. Set aside.

In a skillet toast 3 tablespoons white sesame seeds until they begin to jump. Transfer to a *suribachi* (mortar) and grind to a paste. Scrape down the sides of the mortar with chopsticks, add the bean curd, 1 tablespoon sugar and ½ teaspoon salt and mix well. Add to the spinach and mix with chopsticks. Place in 4 small bowls and serve at room temperature as a vegetable. SERVES 4.

BEAN CURD DISHES

Though the soy bean is the youngest of the bean family, going back only to about 3500 B.C. while other beans in the Middle East go back to 7000 B.C. and in Mexico to 5000 B.C., it makes up in versatility what it lacks in age. In its various forms it is essential to the Japanese kitchen as soy sauce, bean paste and many types of bean curd (listed in the glossary). For the most part the bean curd dishes belong to Japan's vegetarian period. They are subtle in flavor and very high in protein.

Hijiki To Aburaage No Nimono
FRIED BEAN CURD WITH KELP FLAKES

4 tablespoons *hijiki* (kelp flakes), about ½ ounce

2 pieces *aburaage* (fried bean curd)

2½ tablespoons vegetable oil

⅔ cup *dashi* (soup stock)

2½ teaspoons sugar

2 tablespoons soy sauce

Wash the *hijiki* (kelp flakes) in cold water, then soak for 1 hour. Drain, drop into a saucepan of boiling water and boil for 1 minute. Drain, and set aside.

Wash the fried bean curd in hot water to remove the excess oil. Slice lengthwise in half, stack and cut into ⅓-inch slices. Set aside.

In a medium-sized saucepan heat the oil, add the kelp flakes and sauté, stirring with chopsticks for 1 minute, then add the fried bean curd and soup stock and simmer, uncovered, for 4 or 5 minutes. Add the sugar and soy sauce and continue cooking, uncovered, until all the liquid has evaporated, about 10 minutes. Serve in small, deep bowls. SERVES 4.

This is a very refreshing and attractive dish.

Yūzendōfu

SOLE WITH BEAN CURD

Literally translated, Yōzen Dōfu means "printed-silk-used-for-kimonos bean curd." The sole and bean curd make a subtle off-white background which is flecked with the green of beans, the orange of carrot, and the dark brown of mushrooms. The resulting pattern is as pretty as a silk print.

7 ounces fillet of sole
1 *momen tōfu* (bean curd),
   weighing about ½ pound
Boiling water
Sugar
Salt
1 teaspoon soy sauce
2 tablespoons *katakuriko or*
   potato starch
4 *shiitake* (dried Japanese
   mushrooms)

4 green beans
2-inch slice medium carrot
Dashi (soup stock)
1 tablespoon *mirin*
¼ teaspoon salt
2 teaspoons soy sauce
1½ teaspoons arrowroot *or*
   potato starch
1-inch cube fresh ginger root,
   grated

Chop the sole coarsely, transfer to a *suribachi* (mortar) and grind with a pestle until smooth. Drop the bean curd into a saucepan of boiling water and immediately remove from the heat. Let stand for 2 or 3 minutes in the hot water, then drain in a kitchen towel and squeeze out all the moisture, crushing the bean curd. Add to the fish with 1 tablespoon sugar, or to taste, 1 teaspoon salt and the soy sauce; mix well with a wooden spoon. Push the mixture through a sieve and add the *katakuriko* or potato starch. Set aside.

Soak the mushrooms for 30 minutes in warm water with a pinch of sugar. Squeeze out, remove the stems and slice thinly.

Drop the green beans into boiling salted water and boil, uncovered, for 2 or 3 minutes. Drain, trim the ends and cut into very thin diagonal slices.

Scrape the carrot and slice it thinly lengthwise, then cut into thin strips crosswise. In a small saucepan combine ½ cup soup stock, 2 teaspoons sugar, salt to taste and a few drops of soy sauce. Add the carrot and the mushrooms and bring to a boil. Cook, uncovered, until the carrot is tender and the liquid almost evaporated, about 5 minutes. Add the green beans and cook until the mixture is quite dry, 2 or 3 minutes longer. Fold into the bean curd-fish mixture, mixing lightly but thoroughly.

Pack the mixture into a *nagashikan,* about 3 by 5 inches: this is a stainless steel loaf pan with a removable tray that makes unmolding this sort of dish very easy. Otherwise use a lightly oiled loaf pan. Place in a steamer and steam over moderate heat for 20 minutes or until firm.

To make the sauce combine 1 cup soup stock, *mirin,* salt, soy sauce and arrowroot mixed with 1½ teaspoons water in a saucepan. Stir to mix, bring to a boil, stirring, and remove from the heat.

To serve cut the steamed sole and bean curd into slices and place in 4 bowls. Pour the sauce over them and top each with a little ginger. Eat with chopsticks and drink any leftover sauce. SERVES 4.

In Japan fresh mushrooms would be used. In this recipe it is better to use *shiitake* (dried Japanese mushrooms) than U.S. fresh local mushrooms because of the color effect the darker Japanese mushrooms give.

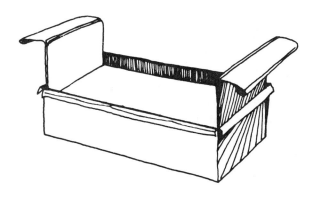

Katsuomabushi Age-dōfu

DEEP-FRIED BEAN CURD WITH BONITO FLAKES

2 *momen tōfu* (bean curd), each
    weighing about ½ pound
1 cup flaked *katsuobushi* (dried
    bonito)
Flour
1 egg

Vegetable oil
2 teaspoons *mirin*
⅓ cup soy sauce
1 or 2 dashes msg
½ cup *dashi* (soup stock)
1-inch cube fresh ginger root

Rinse the bean curd and dry in a cloth. Wrap in the cloth and set a plate with a cup or bowl on top of the bean curd for about 20 minutes to press out excess liquid. Cut the bean curd into quarters.

Heat a heavy skillet and when it is hot, turn off the heat. Add the dried bonito flakes and shake the pan 2 or 3 times. Put the bonito flakes into a bowl.

Dip the bean curd pieces in flour and shake to remove the excess. Break the egg into a bowl and stir with chopsticks until it is well blended but not foamy. Dip the bean curd in the egg, then roll it in the bonito flakes.

Heat about 3 inches of oil in a *tempura* pan or a saucepan to 350°F. on a frying thermometer, or until bubbles form on wooden chopsticks stirred in the oil. The oil should completely cover the bean curd. Add the bean curd and fry for about 2 minutes. Lift out, drain on paper towels and put onto 4 plates.

Mix together the *mirin,* soy sauce, msg and soup stock and pour into 4 small, deep bowls.

Peel the ginger, cut it into julienne strips and put it in a small mound beside the bean curd. To eat, cut the bean curd into bite-sized pieces with chopsticks, mix the ginger into the sauce and dip the bean curd in the sauce. It is perfectly polite to lift up the whole piece of bean curd in the chopsticks, dip it in the sauce, take a bite, and dip it in the sauce again, and so on until it is finished. But this requires very great skill with chopsticks. This is a splendid cold weather dish.
SERVES 4.

Kōyadōfu To Shiitake No Takiawase
DRIED BEAN CURD WITH VEGETABLES

4 *kōyadōfu* (dried bean curd)
2½ cups *dashi* (soup stock)
3 tablespoons sugar
1 teaspoon salt
1½ tablespoons *sake*
2 teaspoons *usukuchi shōyu*
  (light soy sauce)

8 *shiitake* (dried Japanese
  mushrooms)
1 tablespoon *mirin*
2 tablespoons soy sauce
8 medium-sized green beans

Put the bean curd into a baking dish, cover with hot water and weight with a wooden spatula or spoon to keep the curd covered with water. Soak for about 3 minutes, or until soft, turning once or twice. Lightly squeeze out in cold water, changing the water 5 or 6 times until it runs clear. Squeeze out. In a saucepan large enough to hold the bean curd in a single layer, combine the soup stock, 2 tablespoons of the sugar, the salt, *sake* and light soy sauce. Add the bean curd, cover with an *otoshibuta* (inner wooden lid) or a shallow saucepan lid, or use a plate, and cook over low heat for 1 hour. Remove from the heat and let stand for 2 hours.

Soak the mushrooms in warm water with a pinch of sugar for 30 minutes. Squeeze out and cut off the hard stems. Put into a saucepan with enough of the water in which they have soaked to cover, cover with an *otoshibuta* (inner wooden lid) and cook over moderate heat for 2 or 3 minutes. Add the remaining tablespoon of sugar and the *mirin* and cook another 3 minutes, then add the soy sauce. Lift out the mushrooms onto a *zaru* (bamboo plate), or a plate, turn so that the brown side is up and fan quickly to make the mushrooms glisten.

Trim the beans and boil in salted water for 3 to 5 minutes or until tender. Drain and cut in half diagonally.

When the bean curd has stood for 2 hours, squeeze out the liquid and cut each into quarters. Reserve the liquid. Arrange on 4 plates with the mushrooms and beans and pour 2 tablespoons of the reserved cooking liquid over each serving. SERVES 4.

This is popular for lunch boxes, for New Year, or at any time.

Kūya-mushi
BEAN CURD, CHICKEN AND VEGETABLE CUSTARD

Buddhist monks of the Kūya sect are believed to have created this recipe during the Heian period, from 794 to 1192. The monks could not have been very strict since the dish contains chicken and Buddhists are vegetarians. Perhaps the chicken was a later addition.

1 *momen tōfu* (bean curd), weighing about ½ pound
4 *shiitake* (dried Japanese mushrooms)
Sugar
¼ pound skinned and boned chicken breast
Usukuchi shōyu (light soy sauce)
4 okra *or* 4 sprigs *mitsuba* (trefoil), if available

2 large eggs
Dashi (soup stock)
Salt
1 teaspoon *mirin*
Pinch msg
½ teaspoon *katakuriko or* potato starch
Lime peel

Drop the bean curd into boiling salted water, bring back to a boil and cook just long enough to heat the bean curd through, a minute or so. Lift the bean curd out of the water and pat dry with a cloth. Cut in quarters.

Soak the mushrooms in lukewarm water with a pinch of sugar for 30 minutes. Squeeze out and remove the hard stems.

Cut the chicken breast into ½-inch diagonal slices and sprinkle with 1 teaspoon of the light soy sauce.

Cook the okra in boiling salted water for 3 minutes. Drain, trim and cut in halves. If using trefoil, cut the sprigs into 1-inch pieces.

Break the eggs into a bowl and stir with chopsticks until well blended but not foamy. Measure the eggs and mix with 4 times the amount of soup stock. Add ½ teaspoon salt, 1 teaspoon light soy sauce, the *mirin* and msg.

In 4 bowls arrange the bean curd, mushrooms, chicken, okra or trefoil, and pour the egg mixture over them. If there are any bubbles on the surface, break them with chopsticks; otherwise the finished custard will have a pitted, instead of a smooth, surface. Place the bowls in a steamer over boiling water, reduce the heat to moderate and steam for 20 minutes, or until the custard is set.

To make the sauce combine ¾ cup soup stock, ¼ teaspoon salt, and ¼ teaspoon light soy in a small saucepan. Mix the *katakuriko* with a teaspoon of water and stir into the stock. Bring to a boil and cook until lightly thickened.

Cut a piece of lime peel into 4 V shapes for a garnish.

Pour the sauce over the custard, garnish with the peel and eat with chopsticks and a spoon. SERVES 4.

Yakidōfu To Toriniku No Nimono
SIMMERED BEAN CURD AND CHICKEN

½ pound skinned and boned chicken thighs
2 *yakidōfu* (broiled bean curd), each weighing about 10 ounces
1½ cups *dashi* (soup stock)
½ teaspoon salt
1 tablespoon *mirin*

1 tablespoon *usukuchi shōyu* (light soy sauce)
2 scallions, trimmed, using white and green parts
Vegetable oil
1 teaspoon grated fresh ginger root

Cut the chicken into bite-sized pieces. Rinse the bean curd and cut each piece into 6 cubes. Put into a bowl of cold water until ready to use.

Pour the soup stock into a medium-sized saucepan and bring to a boil over moderate heat. Add the salt, *mirin*, light soy sauce, chicken and the drained bean curd. Cover with an *otoshibuta* (inner wooden lid) and simmer over low heat for 20 minutes. Skim any froth that rises to the surface.

Cut the scallions into 1-inch pieces and thread on 2 metal skewers. Brush lightly with oil and grill or broil about 2 to 3 minutes. Remove from the skewers.

Divide the chicken and bean curd mixture among 4 individual bowls with the stock in which they were cooked; garnish with the ginger and scallions. Eat with chopsticks and drink the soup from the bowls. SERVES 4.

Takara Bukuro
TREASURE BAGS

4 pieces *aburaage* (fried bean curd)

½ 10-ounce package *shirataki* (devil's-tongue-root noodles)

1 *shiitake* (dried Japanese mushroom)

3 tablespoons *sake*

1 tablespoon soy sauce

1 tablespoon plus 2 teaspoons sugar

¼ pound ground chicken thighs or breast

1 teaspoon finely chopped fresh ginger root

8 canned ginkgo nuts

8 strips *kanpyō* (dried gourd shavings), about 6 inches long

1⅓ cups *dashi* (soup stock)

1½ tablespoons *mirin*

3 tablespoons soy sauce

2 teaspoons cornstarch

Rinse the bean curd in hot water to remove any oil, pat dry and cut into halves crosswise. The bean curd can then be opened into 8 little bags.

Drain the noodles, cut into pieces about 1½ inches long and drop into boiling water. Bring back to a boil over high heat and cook for 2 minutes. Drain.

Soak the mushroom for 30 minutes in warm water with a pinch of sugar, squeeze out, remove the hard stems and chop finely.

In a saucepan combine 1 tablespoon of the *sake,* the soy sauce and 2 teaspoons of sugar and bring to a boil. Lower the heat and add the chicken. Stir to mix and add the ginger, ginkgo nuts, mushroom and noodles and cook, stirring, over low heat for 2 or 3 minutes. Allow to cool slightly and stuff into the bean curd bags.

Rub the dried gourd shaving strips with a little salt, wash and put to soak for a few minutes to soften. Gather up the tops of the bean curd bags, run the gourd strips twice around and tie with a single knot. Prick the bags in 3 places with a toothpick.

In a medium-sized shallow saucepan combine the soup stock, the remaining 2 tablespoons of *sake,* 1 tablespoon of sugar, the *mirin* and soy sauce. Stir to mix. Bring to a boil, place the bean curd bags upright in the pan in a single layer, cover with an *otoshibuta* (inner wooden lid), reduce the heat to moderate and cook for 15 minutes.

Lift the bags out carefully and put into 4 small shallow bowls.

Mix the cornstarch with 2 teaspoons of water and stir into the sauce in the pan. Cook, stirring, until the sauce has thickened lightly, then pour it over the bean curd bags. To eat, untie the bags with chopsticks and eat the string. Then eat the contents of the bag and finally the bag itself. This is a winter dish. SERVES 4.

Tōfu No Shirō-ae
MIXED VEGETABLES WITH BEAN CURD

1 medium carrot
½ *konnyaku*
   (devil's-tongue-root cake)
Boiling water
3 or 4 *kikurage* (jelly
   mushrooms)
⅓ cup *dashi* (soup stock)
2 teaspoon sugar

3 tablespoons *usukuchi shōyu*
   (light soy sauce)
1 *momen tōfu* (bean curd), about
   ½ pound
¼ teaspoon salt
½ teaspoon soy sauce
1 teaspoon *sake*

Scrape the carrot and slice it thinly. Stack the slices and cut into julienne strips. Thinly slice the *konnyaku*, stack and cut into thin strips. Drop into boiling water and cook 10 seconds. Drain. Soak the jelly mushrooms in cold water for 1 hour or in warm water for 20 minutes. Drain and drop into boiling water for 10 seconds. Drain and slice thinly. In a saucepan combine the soup stock, 1 teaspoon of the sugar and the light soy sauce and bring to a boil. Add the carrot, *konnyaku* and mushrooms and cook, covered, 5 to 6 minutes over moderate heat, drain and set aside.

Rinse the bean curd, cut it into quarters, add it to a saucepan of boiling water and simmer for 3 minutes. Drain through cheesecloth and squeeze to break it up. Push it through a sieve. Put it into a *suribachi* (mortar) and add the remaining teaspoon of sugar, the salt, soy sauce and *sake*. Grind until smooth and well mixed with a pestle, then add to the carrot mixture, and mix lightly with chopsticks. Serve in small bowls. SERVES 4.

Hiya-Yakko

GARNISHED COLD BEAN CURD

2 *momen tōfu* (bean curd), each
   weighing about ½ pound
2-by-4-inch piece *kombu* (kelp)
1 scallion, trimmed, using white
   and green parts, *or* 1 sprig
   shiso (beefsteak plant),
   chopped, *or* 1½ teaspoons
   grated lime peel, *or* 2
   tablespoons grated ginger, *or*
   1 teaspoon *wasabi* (green
   horseradish powder), *or* use
   them all

Soy sauce

Rinse the bean curd and cut each piece into quarters. Put the seaweed (kelp) into a saucepan and add water to a depth that will cover the bean curd. Bring to a boil over moderate heat, removing the seaweed just before the water boils. Reduce heat to low, add the bean curd and poach for 4 minutes, being careful not to let the water boil. Drain and chill the bean curd quickly by putting it into a bowl of cold water for about 5 minutes. Drain and put into a bowl, preferably glass, with water to cover and about 6 ice cubes. Surround the bowl with the garnishes in small dishes.

Pour a little soy sauce into each of 4 bowls. To eat, add the garnishes to the soy sauce and, using chopsticks, dip the pieces of bean curd into the sauce. If preferred the bean curd can be served in 4 small individual bowls with cold water to cover. This is a summer dish. SERVES 4.

Kinugoshi tōfu (silky bean curd) may also be used.

Kikukadōfu

CHRYSANTHEMUM-FLOWER BEAN CURD

2 *momen tōfu*, each weighing about ½ pound
Salt
2 canned quail eggs, cooked and shelled
1 cup *dashi* (soup stock)
½ teaspoon *usukuchi shōyu* (light soy sauce)
2 teaspoons *mirin*
2 teaspoons arrowroot *or* cornstarch
Few leaves *shungiku* (see glossary) *or* raw spinach, optional
2 teaspoons grated fresh ginger root

Wrap the bean curd in a kitchen cloth and weight with a light board or a plate for 20 minutes to remove excess moisture and firm up the bean curd. Add the bean curd to a saucepan of boiling salted water, reduce the heat and simmer for 3 minutes. Lift the bean curd carefully out of the saucepan with a spatula and place on a board. Cut each bean curd in half and transfer to 4 shallow bowls large enough to hold the bean curd comfortably, but not much larger.

Slice the pieces of bean curd ¾ way through at about ⅔-inch intervals, then slice the opposite way, giving the look of a chrysanthemum flower. Cut the quail eggs in half and place cut side up in the center of each bean curd "chrysanthemum" flower.

In a small saucepan heat together the soup stock, light soy sauce, ¼ teaspoon salt, and *mirin*. Mix the arrowroot or cornstarch with 2 teaspoons cold water and stir into the soup stock mixture. Cook over low heat until the sauce is lightly thickened. Pour over the bean curd.

Garnish with the *shungiku* or spinach leaves and ginger, placed in little mounds beside each "flower." Eat with chopsticks, holding the bowl quite near the face to lessen the distance as the bean curd is very soft. SERVES 4.

Nabeyaki Denraku
BEAN CURD WITH WHITE AND RED BEAN PASTE

2 *momen tōfu* (bean curd), each weighing about ½ pound
2 tablespoons vegetable oil
3 tablespoons white *miso* (bean paste)
1½ tablespoons *mirin*
4½ tablespoons sugar
3 tablespoons red *miso* (bean paste)
½ tablespoon *sake*

Wrap the bean curd pieces in a cloth and weight with a light board or plates for 20 minutes to press out excess liquid. Cut the bean curd into 4 crosswise slices, giving 8 pieces in all. In a 9-inch skillet heat the oil and sauté the pieces of bean curd until they are lightly browned all over, about 2 minutes. Arrange in 4 bowls.

Put the white bean paste into a small saucepan with the *mirin* and 2 tablespoons of the sugar. Put the red bean paste into another small saucepan with the remaining 2½ tablespoons of sugar and the *sake*. Cook the bean-paste mixtures over low heat, stirring constantly, until smooth. Do not let them boil.

Spread half the slices of bean curd with white bean paste, the other half with red bean paste so that each serving has a red and a white slice.

In Japan the slices topped with white bean paste would be garnished with the small, very pretty serrated leaf of the Japanese pepper, *sansho,* and the slices topped with red bean paste would be sprinkled with poppy seeds. SERVES 4.

Niku-Dōfu
PORK WITH BEAN CURD

2 *kinugoshi tōfu* (silky bean curd), each weighing about ½ pound
Boiling water
¼ pound boneless pork loin
3 scallions, trimmed, using white and green parts
½-inch cube fresh ginger root
2 tablespoons vegetable oil
⅓ cup *dashi* (soup stock)
2 teaspoons *miso* (bean paste)
3 tablespoons soy sauce
1½ tablespoons *sake*
1 tablespoon sugar

Cut the pieces of bean curd in half and put into a shallow pan with just enough boiling water to cover. Let stand ½ minute, drain and set aside.

Coarsely chop the pork. Thinly slice the scallions diagonally. Peel and finely chop the ginger root.

In a medium-sized saucepan heat the vegetable oil and add the ginger. Stir, then add the pork and scallions and sauté, stirring, over moderate heat until the pork has lost all its pink color, 3 to 4 minutes.

In a bowl mix together the soup stock, bean paste, soy sauce, *sake* and sugar and add to the saucepan. Reduce the heat to low and add the bean curd pieces (taking care not to break them) and cook, covered, for 15 to 20 minutes longer. Divide among 4 bowls and serve as a main course. SERVES 4.

Ni-Yakko
BEAN CURD WITH DRIED BONITO FLAKES

1 scallion, trimmed, using white and green parts

4 2-inch squares *kombu* (kelp)

2 pieces *momen tōfu* (bean curd), each weighing about ½ pound

8 tablespoons flaked *katsuobushi* (dried bonito)

2 teaspoons grated fresh ginger root

Soy sauce

Finely chop the scallion, put to soak in cold water for a few minutes to crisp; drain and squeeze out in a piece of cheesecloth. Set aside.

Clean the seaweed with a damp cloth and put into the bottom of a medium-sized saucepan. Pour in water to a depth that will cover the bean curd and bring to a boil over moderate heat, removing the seaweed just before the water boils. Put the squares of seaweed into 4 small, shallow bowls.

Cut the pieces of bean curd in half and add to the saucepan. Simmer for 4 minutes over low heat, then lift out and place on top of the seaweed in the bowls. Sprinkle the scallions on top of the bean curd, then cover with the dried bonito flakes and the ginger. Pour soy sauce into 4 small saucers to use as a dipping sauce. Have a small jug of extra soy sauce on the table to be poured onto the bean curd to taste. Eat with chopsticks. This is a winter dish and should be served hot. SERVES 4.

Eggs

The Japanese show the same originality in cooking eggs as they do in every other aspect of the cuisine, from the light and delicious egg custard to the rolled omelette.

The omelettes can be made in any omelette pan, but they are much easier to make and look much neater if made in the oblong Japanese omelette pan called a *tamago-yaki nabe*. They are surprisingly easy to make and serve, especially if rolled up with chopsticks. They make, in either a western or a Japanese context, a splendid appetizer or accompaniment to drinks.

Ebiiri-Tamago-Yaki
SHRIMP OMELETTE

8 medium-sized raw shrimp,
  peeled and deveined
⅓ cup *dashi* (soup stock)
¾ teaspoon salt
2 eggs, stirred to mix well

½ tablespoon sugar
1 tablespoon *sake*
1 teaspoon arrowroot
Vegetable oil

Chop the shrimp to a paste with the back of a heavy knife. Put into a small saucepan with the soup stock and ½ teaspoon salt, bring to a boil and cook over moderate heat for 1 minute. Cool, drain, and set the shrimp aside.

Combine the eggs with the sugar, *sake,* ¼ teaspoon salt, the arrowroot mixed with a teaspoon of water and the reserved shrimp.

Heat a *tamago-yaki nabe* or an omelette pan and add just enough oil to film the surface. Pour in the egg mixture and tilt the pan so that it covers the whole surface. When the omelette is lightly browned on one side, turn it and brown on the other side. Slide the omelette out of the pan onto a *sudare* (bamboo mat) or a kitchen cloth and roll it up. When the omelette is cool, remove the bamboo mat and cut the omelette into ½-inch slices. Serve on an oblong platter as an appetizer. SERVES 4.

Hōrensō Tamago Maki

EGG ROLL STUFFED WITH SPINACH

10 ounces spinach (5 cups tightly packed), stems removed	2 or 3 dashes msg
1 teaspoon sugar	2 eggs
½ tablespoon soy sauce	¼ teaspoon salt
	Vegetable oil

Wash the spinach, drain, drop into a large saucepan of boiling water with the sugar and boil for 2 minutes. Rinse 3 times in cold water, squeeze out the moisture, sprinkle with the soy sauce and msg, form into a roll, divide into 2 pieces and set aside.

Break the eggs into a bowl, add the salt and stir with chopsticks until thoroughly blended but not foamy. Heat an 8-inch skillet and add just enough oil to film the surface. Pour in half of the egg and tilt the pan quickly so that the egg covers the whole surface. When the egg is set and lightly browned on the bottom, lift out carefully onto a *sudare* (bamboo mat) or a cloth. Lay one of the spinach rolls along the edge of the omelette and, using the bamboo mat, roll up the spinach in the omelette. Squeeze lightly to firm. Repeat with the remaining egg and spinach. Cut the omelette rolls into 1-inch slices. Serve at room temperature. SERVES 4.

Dashi-Maki Tamago
ROLLED OMELETTE WITH SOUP STOCK

6 eggs
Dashi (soup stock)
Salt
½ teaspoon *usukuchi shōyu*
  (light soy sauce)
2 teaspoon *mirin*

2 dashes msg
Vegetable oil
½ cup grated *daikon* (white
  radish), lightly squeezed
4 teaspoons soy sauce

Break the eggs into a bowl and stir with chopsticks until well blended but not foamy. Measure the eggs. Add ¼ the amount of cold soup stock to the eggs, then add salt to taste, light soy sauce, *mirin* and msg and stir to mix.

Heat a *tamago-yaki nabe* or omelette pan and pour in just enough oil to film the surface. Pour in ⅓ of the egg mixture, tilt the pan so that the egg covers the whole surface and cook over moderate heat until the egg is set. Using chopsticks, or a spatula, roll up the omelette to the end of the pan. Add more oil and another ⅓ of the egg mixture, tilting the pan as before so that the egg runs down to the cooked omelette. When the second omelette is set, roll it towards the handle of the pan, incorporating the first omelette. Repeat with the remaining egg, rolling the 3 omelettes towards the end of the pan.

Carefully lift the omelette roll out of the pan and place it on a *sudare* (bamboo mat) or a kitchen cloth and roll up very gently. Weight with a plate until it is cold, then cut into 12 slices. Serve 3 slices per person on small platters. Garnish with a mound of white radish with the soy sauce poured over it. SERVES 4.

VARIATION: For *Tamago Yaki* (Rolled Omelette) break 6 eggs into a bowl and stir with chopsticks until well blended but not foamy. Add 6 tablespoons freshly cooked peas, 2 tablespoons *sake,* 2 teaspoons sugar and ½ teaspoon salt to the eggs and stir to mix. Make into an omelette following the instructions above. The omelette can accompany a main dish at a meal or be served as an appetizer. It is a special favorite for picnics. It can be made, if preferred, without the peas.

Chawan-Mushi
STEAMED EGG CUSTARD

4 *shiitake* (dried Japanese
  mushrooms)
Sugar
¼ pound boned and skinned
  chicken breast
½ teaspoon *sake*
1¼ teaspoons *usukuchi shōyu*
  (light soy sauce)
4 large leaves spinach *or mitsuba*
  (trefoil) if available

Boiling water
4 medium-sized raw shrimp
8 canned ginkgo nuts
4 slices *kamaboko* (fish
  sausage), ¼ inch thick
3 eggs, about ⅔ cup
2⅔ cups *dashi* (soup stock)
Salt
4 small pieces lime peel

Soak the mushrooms in warm water with a pinch of sugar for 30 minutes, drain, remove tough stems and squeeze out.

Cut the chicken breast into diagonal slices about 1½ by ½ inch. Put into a small bowl and mix with the *sake* and ½ teaspoon of the light soy sauce.

Drop the spinach leaves into boiling water for 1 minute, drain, rinse in cold water and squeeze lightly.

Peel and devein the shrimp, leaving the tails on.

Place the chicken, ginkgo nuts, mushrooms, shrimp, spinach and fish sausage, divided equally, in four 8-ounce custard cups or bowls.

Stir the eggs thoroughly with chopsticks but do not beat as they must not be foamy. Stir in the soup stock, a little salt, and the remaining ¾ teaspoon light soy sauce. Strain and divide among the custard cups. If there are any bubbles on the surface, break them with chopsticks as they will otherwise pit the surface of the finished custard. Garnish with the lime peel, cover with lids or with aluminum foil and arrange in a steamer over boiling water. Partially cover the steamer and cook the custards over moderate heat for 15 to 20 minutes, or until set. The custard, unlike other dishes where only chopsticks are used, is eaten with a spoon and chopsticks. SERVES 4.

Takenoko No Tamago-Toji
EGGS WITH BAMBOO SHOOTS

4 medium-sized mushrooms
10-ounce can whole bamboo
  shoots
¼ pound boned and skinned
  chicken breast
1 medium-sized onion

2 cups *dashi* (soup stock)
6 tablespoons soy sauce
½ cup *mirin*
⅛ teaspoon msg
10 snow peas
4 eggs, stirred to blend

Slice the washed mushrooms thinly. Halve the bamboo shoots lengthwise, then slice thinly. Slice the chicken thinly on the diagonal. Halve the peeled onion lengthwise, then slice finely. Place the mushrooms, bamboo shoots, chicken and onion in a saucepan with the soup stock, soy sauce, *mirin* and msg. Bring to a boil, lower the heat and simmer, uncovered, for about 4 minutes. Slice the snow peas thinly on the diagonal and add to the saucepan. Pour the eggs in a thin stream over the entire surface of the pan. Cover the pan, turn the heat to low and cook for about a minute, or until the eggs are set. Serve in bowls. SERVES 4.

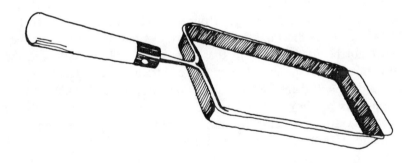

Fukusa Yaki

OMELETTE WITH SHRIMP AND MUSHROOMS

The fukusa *are very old dishes whose name signifies dishes whose taste everyone enjoys. The name also signifies tender or happy.*

1 *momen tōfu* (bean curd),
   weighing about ½ pound
4 *shiitake* (dried mushrooms)
Sugar
4 eggs, stirred
½ teaspoon salt
2 teaspoons *mirin*
1 teaspoon *usukuchi shōyu* (light
   soy sauce)

Pinch msg
5 ounces tiny peeled shrimp
1 tablespoon green peas
1 tablespoon vegetable oil
⅓ cup grated *daikon* (white
   radish)

Roll the bean curd in a *sudare* (bamboo mat) or a kitchen cloth and weight with 2 plates for about 5 minutes to remove excess liquid. Pat dry.

Soak the mushrooms for 30 minutes in warm water with a pinch of sugar, squeeze out, remove the stems and slice the mushrooms into julienne strips.

Put the bean curd in a bowl and mash it with a whisk or a fork. Add the eggs, salt, *mirin*, light soy sauce, 1 teaspoon sugar and msg, and mix well. Add the mushrooms, shrimp and peas, folding in lightly.

Heat an 8-by-6-inch *tamago-yaki nabe* (rectangular skillet) or a medium-sized skillet with the oil. Pour in the bean curd mixture, smoothing the surface, and cook over low heat, covered, for about 7 minutes. Turn and cook 5 minutes longer. Turn the omelette out on to a board and cut into slices about 1½ by 2 inches. Arrange the omelette pieces in 4 dishes. Squeeze out the radish and put a little of it on top of each slice of omelette. Serve at room temperature. SERVES 4.

Pickles

Pickles are immensely popular in Japan, where they play a far more important role than they do in the Western world. The mouth-puckering *umeboshi* (small pickled plums), ginger shoots, and *warabi* (pickled fernbrake or bracken, also known as fiddleheads) are all best bought ready prepared, in stores selling Japanese food. There are other pickles that can be prepared easily at home here. Pickles made from *hakusai* (Chinese cabbage) and *beni-shōga* (ginger root, which is usually colored red with vegetable coloring) and vegetables pickled in *miso* (bean paste) present no problems of technique, equipment, or ingredients.

Pickles are used with many dishes as a garnish to enhance both appearance and taste. They particularly enliven plain boiled rice; their sharp flavor contrasts the blandness of the rice.

Hakusai No Shiozuke
PICKLED CHINESE CABBAGE

Generally in Japan this is made on a sunny day in late autumn or early winter. A sunny day is required for the drying of the cabbage, which is at its peak during the later months of the year.

1 *hakusai* (Chinese cabbage), weighing about 2 pounds
3 tablespoons or more salt
½ large or whole small lime, sliced

3 dried hot red peppers
3-inch square *kombu* (kelp)
msg
Soy sauce

Cut through the stem end of the cabbage, then tear in half with the hands. Then tear into lengthwise quarters. Wash the cabbage pieces in cold water, and drain thoroughly. Put the cabbage in a large colander to dry in the sun for half a day.

Sprinkle a little salt in the bottom of a glass bowl. Salt the cabbage quarters, sprinkling inside the leaves. Reserve a little salt. Pack the cabbage into the bowl and layer with the lime slices. Split the peppers, leaving the seeds on. Clean the seaweed (kelp) with a damp cloth and bury the peppers and seaweed in the middle of the cabbage. Sprinkle with the remaining salt, then put an *otoshibuta* (wooden lid) or a plate on top of the cabbage and put a weight (about 5 pounds) on top. Stand in a cool place or in the refrigerator for 2 days. At the end of this time the cabbage will have given off quite a lot of liquid. Do not pour it off, but reduce the weight to about 3 pounds. Leave for 2 or 3 days longer. It is then ready to eat. Take out as needed and store for use in a covered container in the refrigerator.

To eat, lift the cabbage out of the brine, squeeze lightly to get rid of excess water, and cut into bite-sized pieces. Serve with rice as an accompaniment to a main dish. If liked, sprinkle with msg and a little soy sauce.

In Japan a lidded wooden pickle barrel would be used, but a bowl does very well, and fresh limes are an excellent substitute for the citrus *yuzu* that is used in Japan. Lemons may also be used as a substitute.

Kyuri No Inrōzuke
PICKLED CUCUMBERS

ınrō is a small box that was used to hold pills in the days of old Tokyo, then called Edo, before the city became the imperial and administrative capital of modern Japan. The halved cucumbers in the recipe are put together and look like small boxes which is why they are called inrōzuke.

4 medium cucumbers, about 1¼ pounds	2 tablespoons *shiso* seeds (beefsteak plant), optional
Salt	2 or 3 dashes msg
4 large leaves cabbage	*Kombu* (kelp)
1-inch cube fresh ginger root	

If the cucumbers are waxed, peel them, otherwise leave unpeeled. Halve them lengthwise and scrape out the seeds with a spoon. Sprinkle with 2 teaspoons of salt. Place on a plate, cut side down, cover with another plate and weight. The weight should be about double that of the cucumbers. Leave for 1 hour.

Wash and dry the cabbage and cut it finely as for cole slaw. Peel the ginger and cut it into julienne strips. Mix the cabbage and ginger with 2 teaspoons of salt, rinse in cold water and drain. Mix in the *shiso* seeds and a dash of msg if available.

Pat the cucumber dry. Stuff the seed cavity of half the cucumbers with the cabbage mixture, pressing down firmly, then top with the other half to make an *inrō*, little box.

Cut 2 pieces seaweed (kelp), each large enough for the cucumbers to fit on. Clean with a damp cloth. Lay one of the pieces of seaweed in a large shallow dish and put the cucumbers on top. Sprinkle with a little salt and the msg, then cover with the second piece of seaweed. Put a plate on top of the cucumbers and weight with a 4-pound weight. Press for 4 or 5 hours in a cool place. Remove the seaweed and cut the cucumbers into ½-inch slices. Serve on small plates. SERVES 6 TO 8.

Hakusai To Ninjin No Kaorizuke

CHINESE CABBAGE AND CARROT PICKLES

1¾ pounds *hakusai* (Chinese cabbage)
3-inch slice from top of a large carrot
Boiling water

1 medium clove garlic
1 dried hot red pepper
1½ tablespoons salt
4-inch square *kombu* (kelp)

Pull the leaves from the cabbage, rinse, drain and cut into 1-inch crosswise slices. Scrape the carrot, slice thinly, then cut into julienne strips. Drop the cabbage and carrot into boiling water and cook, stirring with chopsticks, for 1 minute. Drain and cool. Squeeze, by the handful, to remove excess water. Transfer to a bowl.

Crush the garlic lightly with the blade of a knife, then chop it finely. Remove the seeds from the pepper and chop it finely. Mix the garlic and pepper with the cabbage, carrot and salt.

Clean the seaweed (kelp) with a damp cloth, cut into a ½-inch fringe and bury in the cabbage mixture. Cover the cabbage with an *otoshibuta* (inner wooden lid) or a plate and put a 5-pound weight (about) on top. Stand in a cool place overnight or refrigerate. Drain; discard the seaweed. Serve the pickles in a small dish to be eaten with rice served in separate bowls. SERVES 4 TO 6.

The pickles will be ready to eat in 24 hours but will keep, refrigerated in a covered container, for a week or more.

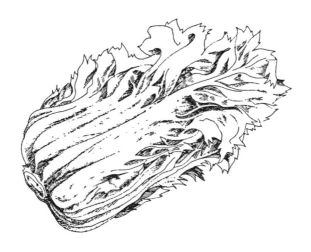

Sokuseki Misozuke
INSTANT PICKLED VEGETABLES WITH BEAN PASTE

¾ cup firmly packed *miso* (bean
   paste)
2 tablespoons soy sauce
2 tablespoons *mirin*
2 small cucumbers or 1 medium

1 small eggplant, about 3 inches
4 small white radishes
4 small okra, *or* 1 green bell
   pepper, *or* 4 stalks asparagus

Mix the bean paste with the soy sauce and *mirin* and put into a bowl large enough to hold all the vegetables comfortably.

Wash and dry the whole vegetables and mix with the bean paste. Leave for a day in a cool place.

To use, lift the vegetables out of the bean paste mixture, scraping the paste off with chopsticks. Slice the vegetables and arrange on 4 small dishes. Eat with rice. Reserve the bean paste to use again.

To re-use the bean paste, pour off any liquid from the vegetables, put the paste into a saucepan, stir over low heat and add a little more bean paste until the paste is again of the original consistency. It can be used several times to make these pickles. This dish allows for plenty of variations and personal choice. SERVES 4 OR MORE.

Shōga No Suzuke
PICKLED GINGER

¼ pound fresh ginger root (a
   piece about 3 by 2 inches)
Boiling water
Salt
½ cup rice vinegar

1½ tablespoons sugar
½ teaspoon *usukuchi shōyu*
   (light soy sauce)
Red vegetable coloring

Wash and peel the ginger root and cut with the grain into very thin slices. Put into a bowl, cover with cold water and let stand for 30 minutes. Drain the ginger, then drop it into a saucepan of boiling water. Bring the water back to a boil over high heat, then drain and cool. Sprinkle with a little salt and place in a bowl.

In a saucepan combine the rice vinegar, sugar, ½ teaspoon salt and light soy sauce; stir to mix. Bring to a boil and simmer just until the sugar has dissolved. Cool and add just enough red food coloring to color the liquid a light pink. Pour the liquid over the ginger and mix well. Let the ginger stand for at least an hour before using it as a garnish with *sushi* (vinegared rice dishes) or other dishes. It will keep indefinitely in a covered jar in the refrigerator. YIELD: 1 cup.

Hakusai No Suzuke

PICKLED CHINESE CABBAGE WITH RICE VINEGAR

¾ to 1 pound *hakusai* (Chinese cabbage)
Boiling water
1 teaspoon salt

2 or 3 dried hot red peppers
2 tablespoons vegetable oil
3 tablespoons soy sauce
5 to 6 teaspoons rice vinegar

Carefully pull the leaves from the cabbage, rinse, drain and stack the leaves. Cut crosswise into 1-inch slices, then cut into approximately 1-inch squares, halving the narrow part of the leaf and cutting the wide part into thirds.

Drop the cabbage pieces into a large saucepan of boiling water. Bring back to a boil over high heat and cook, uncovered, for 2 minutes. Drain in a colander and sprinkle with the salt. Transfer to a bowl.

Remove the seeds from the peppers, rinse and chop finely.

In a small saucepan heat the vegetable oil with the soy sauce and peppers. When the mixture comes to a boil, remove from the heat and stir in the vinegar. Pour the hot liquid over the cabbage and mix well with chopsticks. Cool, put into a covered container, and refrigerate for 2 or 3 days. Eat as an accompaniment to rice. SERVES 4.

Desserts, Snacks and Beverages

Desserts play a minor role in the Japanese kitchen. There are a few, most of which by Western standards could be considered snacks rather than actual desserts. These snacks are varied, unusual and sweet; they are served with tea when guests call or between meals at any time of the day.

Nowadays in Japan all the usual Western drinks are served, and wine is becoming increasingly popular. However, *sake* (rice wine) remains the national drink. *Sake* sets consisting of tiny china bowls and a small matching flask holding about ½ pint are traditionally used. The drink is served lukewarm, either before or during meals.

Tea is the other great drink of Japan, from *matcha*, the powdered green tea of the formal tea ceremony, to the green tea of everyday use. This unfermented tea is always taken plain and is both stimulating and refreshing. There are a number of grades: *Gyokuro*, the first new leaves on the tea bush, is the best, with *sencha* the second best. *Bancha* or *hōjicha* is used for everyday tea. *Mugicha*, made from roasted barley and served chilled, is a popular and wonderfully refreshing summer "tea."

Koshi-an
RED BEAN PASTE

1½ cups red *azuki* (adzuki) beans

Wash and pick over the beans and put into a large saucepan with 6 cups cold water. Cover and bring to a boil over high heat. Cook until the beans begin to rise to the surface, then reduce the heat to moderate, add ¾ cup cold water and bring back to a boil. Add ¾ cup cold water, and repeat the process, adding ¾ cup cold water twice more. Reduce the heat to low and cook, covered, until the beans are tender, about 30 minutes.

Drain the beans, reserving the cooking liquid. Push the beans through a fairly coarse sieve and discard the skins. Using a Japanese wooden pestle, the *surikogi* that goes with the *suribachi* (mortar), makes this go very quickly. Return the beans to the cooking liquid, and mix. Pour the mixture through a fine sieve and discard any skins that may have gone through the coarse sieve. Pour the mixture through a double thickness of cheesecloth set over a large saucepan. After the liquid has dripped through the cheesecloth, twist the cloth to remove as much liquid as possible, leaving a firm paste. This makes about 3 cups and is the basis for many desserts. The paste will keep, refrigerated, 3 or 4 days or frozen for several weeks.

The bean paste can be bought ready-made in powder form, needing only the addition of water to reconstitute it. The difference in flavor between the homemade and the commercial article, in my opinion, justifies the work.

Zenzai

BEAN PASTE WITH RICE CAKES

¾ cup red *azuki* (adzuki) beans   1 tablespoon arrowroot
1 to 1½ cups sugar to taste   5 *mochi* (rice cakes)

Wash and pick over the beans, put into a saucepan with 5 cups cold water. Bring to a boil, covered, over high heat, then reduce the heat to moderate and simmer for about 40 minutes, or until the beans are tender. Drain, set aside.

Rinse out the saucepan and add the sugar with ¼ cup water, stir to mix and cook, stirring from time to time, over low heat for 5 minutes. Add the beans to the syrup and cook, mashing the beans into the syrup with a wooden spoon or spatula until they form a smooth, heavy paste, about 30 minutes. Add 2 cups water, mixing well over moderate heat. Mix the arrowroot with 1 tablespoon water and stir into the beans. Cook until thickened.

Cut each of the rice cakes into quarters and toast in a grill or under a broiler until lightly browned and tender. Put 3 pieces of rice cake into the bottom of 6 small bowls. Cover with about 1 cup of the bean paste. There will be 2 rice cake squares left over, a little extra for someone. This is a snack and can be eaten at any time. SERVES 6.

Chamanjū

BEAN PASTE DUMPLINGS

1 cup *koshi-an* (bean paste), see   1 cup sifted all-purpose flour
  preceding recipe   1 teaspoon baking soda
⅔ cup sugar   ½ cup brown sugar
¼ teaspoon salt

In a saucepan combine the bean paste, sugar and salt and cook, stirring constantly, over low heat until the paste is quite stiff. Cool and form into ten 1½-inch balls.

Sift the flour with the baking soda and brown sugar into a bowl and mix to a fairly stiff dough with 3 tablespoons of water, adding a little more if necessary. Roll out the dough on a lightly floured board and cut ten 3-inch circles. Put a ball of bean paste into the center of each circle of dough and fold up into a dumpling, covering the paste completely. Place a 1-inch square of aluminum foil over the join and turn the dumplings over so that the foil is on the bottom. Bring the water in a steamer to a boil, lay a kitchen cloth on the steamer tray and arrange the dumplings on top of the cloth. Steam over moderate heat for 13 minutes, or until done. Let the dumplings cool a little before eating by hand. Serve with tea. SERVES 10.

Mizuyōkan

RED BEAN JELLY

¼ ounce *kanten* (agar-agar) ¼ teaspoon salt
1 cup sugar
1 cup *koshi-an* (red bean paste),
  see preceding recipe

Wash the agar-agar in cold water, squeeze out and shred with the fingers. Put into a saucepan with 1¾ cups water and soak for about 1 hour. Cook over moderate heat, stirring from time to time until the agar-agar is dissolved. Add the sugar and cook, stirring, until the sugar is dissolved. Strain the mixture through a fine sieve or cheesecloth, return to the saucepan and stir in the bean paste. Add the salt and cook, stirring, over moderate heat until the mixture comes to a boil. Remove from the heat, cool slightly and pour into a 4-by-6-inch loaf pan rinsed out in cold water. Set in a pan of cold water or refrigerate until set, about 1 hour.

To serve, cut into 1-by 2-inch slices, and put on small plates. Eat with cake forks. Traditionally this dish would be garnished with a pickled cherry leaf though today a plastic leaf might be used. Serve with cold *mugicha*, roasted barley tea. This is a summer dessert. SERVES 8 TO 12.

Ohagi
SWEET RICE EGGS

1 cup sweet rice
¼ cup rice
2 cups *koshi-an* (red bean paste),
   see preceding recipe

1 cup sugar
¼ teaspoon salt

Wash the sweet rice and the rice, drain and put into a saucepan with 1⅓ cups water. Soak for at least 1 hour. Bring to a boil over high heat, reduce the heat to moderate and cook for 5 to 6 minutes, then reduce the heat to low and cook for 10 minutes. Let the rice stand for 10 minutes then mash it to a paste with a pestle. While it is still warm form it with wet hands into 12 egg-shaped balls, patting them smooth.

In a saucepan combine the bean paste, sugar and salt and cook, stirring, until it forms a firm paste. Let the paste cool a little and form it into 12 balls. Fold a piece of cheesecloth into quarters, wet it and wring it out thoroughly. Flatten a ball of bean paste on the cloth and put a rice egg in the center. Very carefully pat the paste all over the rice to cover it, using the cheesecloth to help smooth the paste. Continue until all the rice balls are covered. Serve on small square platters traditionally used for snacks, or on small plates. Eat with chopsticks. SERVES 4 TO 12.

VARIATION: For each rice egg, in a small skillet toast 2 teaspoons black sesame seeds until they begin to jump. Transfer to a *suribachi* (mortar) and grind coarsely. Add 1 teaspoon sugar and a pinch of salt and mix thoroughly. Take a rice ball and flatten it, add a half-size ball of bean paste and, with wet hands, cover the paste with the rice. Then roll it in the sesame seed mixture.

VARIATION: Roll the stuffed rice ball in a mixture of ½ teaspoon soy bean flour, ½ teaspoon sugar and a pinch of salt.

If all three types are served on one platter the snack is called *Sanshoku Ohagi* (Three-Color Rice Eggs).

This is a favorite for the autumn equinox holiday, Shūbun No Hi, on September 24. Formerly a Buddhist festival, it is now a public holiday in Japan. Rice eggs can of course be eaten at any time.

TEA

Gyokuro
BEST TEA

Put 1½ tablespoons *gyokuro* tea leaves into a small teapot. Warm 4 small tea bowls. In a tea kettle bring water to a boil, then let it stand 3 or 4 minutes to cool it to a temperature of about 160°F. It should not be at the boiling point. Pour ½ to ⅔ cup of the water into the teapot and let it stand for about 1 minute. Pour it into the bowls. SERVES 4.

Sencha
SECOND-BEST TEA

Put 2 tablespoons *sencha* tea leaves into a small teapot. Warm 4 medium-sized tea bowls. In a tea kettle bring water to a boil, then let it stand 2 or 3 minutes to cool to a temperature of about 170°F. It should not be at the boiling point. Pour 1¼ to 1¾ cups water into the teapot and let it stand for about 30 seconds. Pour it into the bowls. SERVES 4.

Bancha or Hōjicha
EVERYDAY TEA

Put 3 tablespoons *bancha* tea leaves or *hōjicha* into a teapot. In a tea kettle bring water to a boil and pour 1⅔ to 2⅓ cups water into the teapot. It should be at boiling point. Let it stand for a few seconds, then pour it into large tea bowls. SERVES 4.

Mugicha (roasted barley tea) is made in the same way as *bancha*. It is served cold as a summer drink.

New Year Dishes

Nowhere in the Japanese calendar is there a festival more important than New Year, when special dishes are abundant and varied. Houses are given a special cleaning, visits are made to Shinto shrines to honor ancestors, bells in Buddhist temples ring out the old year and welcome the new, and people pay visits to their friends.

It is a very happy holiday and involves a good deal of preparation since the shops close for three days. In the past, before refrigeration was widely available, families cooked for three days ahead, choosing dishes that could be kept unrefrigerated. Today, many of the traditional New Year foods reflect this former necessity. Special attention is paid to the preparation of holiday foods, and there is an exciting array. None of the dishes is difficult to cook, though some require patience.

New Year foods are presented in a special, ceremonial way. They are arranged in *jūbako*, layer boxes which stack one on top of the other and are kept in a larger box. Each layer is divided by partitions. These traditional boxes are made of lacquer and are very beautiful. Nowadays boxes are often made of plastic, but even these are handsome. Foods, both sweet and salty, are arranged decoratively in the boxes, which are presented buffet style. They are all in small portions so each guest, with a bowl and chopsticks, may fill his plate much as we do at a cocktail buffet. Especially traditional dishes are *kuromame* (black beans), and *gomame* (glazed dried sardines); it would not be New Year in Japan without them. There are also a number of modern dishes that are special to the holiday.

Tea and *sake* are customarily served, and nowadays many Western drinks, such as wine and whisky, are too. The most traditional drink for New Year's Day, however, is *toso,* a cold spiced *sake* made by infusing *mirin* with a mixture of spices. The spices are sold ready-packaged and include *sanshō* (Japanese pepper), cinnamon, orange peel and broad bellflower. The drink, which is said to prolong life and keep evil away, has been popular since the Heian period (9th to 12th centuries).

Gomame
GLAZED DRIED SARDINES

1½ cups *tazukuri* (dried sardines), about 1½ ounces
4 tablespoons soy sauce

3½ tablespoons sugar
1 tablespoon *mirin*

Clean the sardines if necessary and put them into a medium-sized saucepan over low heat and toast, turning from time to time, until they are crisp, about 25 to 30 minutes.

In a medium-sized saucepan combine the soy sauce, sugar and *mirin* and bring to a boil. Add the sardines and cook, stirring, over high heat until almost all the liquid has evaporated and the sardines are glazed, about 2 minutes. Be careful not to let the sardines get too dry. Put on a platter as part of a New Year buffet and serve at room temperature. SERVES 8 TO 10.

Kuromame
BLACK SOY BEANS

This is a congratulatory dish and symbolizes an active, healthy life.
Mame, *the word for bean, also means healthy.*

2 cups black soy beans	2 tablespoons soy sauce
½ teaspoon salt	1¼ cups sugar
½ teaspoon baking soda	

Wash and pick over the beans. Pour 4½ cups water into a large saucepan. Bring to a boil over high heat and add the salt, baking soda, soy sauce, sugar and beans. Remove from the heat and let stand 4 or 5 hours, covered.

Bring to a boil over moderate heat, skim, and add ½ cup cold water. Bring back to a boil and add another ½ cup cold water. Skim again. Reduce the heat to very low and put an *otoshibuta* (inner wooden lid) or a smaller saucepan lid or plate over the beans. Cover with the saucepan lid. Cook for 7 to 8 hours, using one or two asbestos mats if necessary to keep the heat very low. The water will reduce to barely cover the beans. On no account lift the lid during the cooking process. Let the beans stand, off the heat, overnight. The beans are now ready to eat but will keep for a week or more refrigerated. They come out very shiny and the liquid is not thick as it would be if other types of black bean were used.

Serve in small deep bowls and eat with chopsticks at room temperature. For guests the beans may be threaded 5 or more at a time on small bamboo skewers. SERVES 8 TO 10 for the family, but serves a great many more guests as they will be offered a wide variety of different dishes.

Kodai No Nanbanzuke
PICKLED PORGIES

8 porgies, each weighing 3 to 4
  ounces, scaled and cleaned but
  with heads and tails left on
Salt
Katakuriko or cornstarch
Vegetable oil
4 tablespoons sugar
¼ cup soy sauce

¼ cup *dashi* (soup stock)
¼ cup *sake*
¼ cup rice vinegar
1½ tablespoons *mirin*
1 tablespoon dry red wine
½ scallion
2 dried hot red peppers
4 thin slices fresh ginger root

Wash the fish in salted water, pat dry and sprinkle lightly with salt inside and out and set aside for 20 minutes. Pat dry again and coat with *katakuriko*. Heat 2 to 3 inches oil in a *tempura* pan or a saucepan to 350°F. on a frying thermometer, or until bubbles form on wooden chopsticks stirred in the oil. Drop the fish into the oil a few at a time and fry for 8 minutes, turning once.

Combine the sugar, soy sauce, soup stock, *sake,* rice vinegar, *mirin,* and dry red wine in a large shallow dish, such as a glass baking dish. Grill or broil the scallion until lightly browned and add to the marinade. Seed and chop the peppers and add with the ginger to the marinade. Stir to mix and arrange the fish in the marinade. Refrigerate for 1 or 2 days, turning the fish from time to time.

To serve, lift the fish out of the marinade and place in a layer box with the heads to the left, or serve on a platter, always placing the fish so that the head is to the left. SERVES 8. This is a modern New Year dish.

Kōhaku-Namasu
WHITE RADISH AND CARROT SALAD

¾ pound *daikon* (white radish)   6 tablespoons rice vinegar
1 medium-sized carrot   2 tablespoons sugar
Salt   ½ teaspoon msg

Peel the radish and cut into 2-inch julienne strips. Scrape the carrot and cut into the same size julienne strips. Put both vegetables into a bowl with a little salt and mix gently with the fingers for about a minute. Set aside for about 3 minutes, then squeeze out into a sieve, discarding the liquid. Set aside to drain.

In a bowl mix together the rice vinegar, sugar, msg and salt to taste. Add the radish and carrot mixture and toss lightly to mix. Cover and refrigerate until ready to use. The salad will keep for a week, refrigerated. Serve in small bowls. SERVES 8.

Kinton
MASHED SWEET POTATO AND CHESTNUT DESSERT

2 pounds *satsuma-imo* (white   ½ teaspoon salt
   sweet potato, *boniato*)   5 tablespoons *mirin*
2 cups sugar   1-pound can chestnuts in syrup

Peel the washed sweet potatoes, cut into ¼-inch slices, and drop into a bowl of cold water. Drain and drop into a saucepan of boiling water and cook for 5 minutes. Drain, return to the saucepan, add cold water to cover and simmer, partially covered, until tender, about 15 minutes. Add the sugar and salt and cook, stirring and mashing with the back of a wooden spoon, until the mixture forms a heavy paste, about 15 minutes. Push the mixture through a fine sieve and spread in the bottom of a shallow casserole or heavy skillet. Stir in the *mirin* and ½ cup syrup from the chestnuts. Cook, stirring, over moderate heat until thick, about 10 minutes. Add chestnuts as liked. A serving consists of 1 or 2 sweet potato-coated chestnuts, so the number used is a matter of taste. Stir to mix, remove from the heat and put into a covered serving dish. Serve on small dishes. Eat with chopsticks. SERVES 8 TO 10.

Zōni

RICE CAKES WITH CHICKEN AND VEGETABLES

½ chicken breast, boned and
skinned, about 3 ounces
2 cups spinach, tightly packed,
about ¼ pound
4 *shiitake* (dried Japanese
mushrooms)
Sugar
3 cups plus 3 tablespoons *dashi*
(soup stock)

½ tablespoon plus ½ teaspoon soy
sauce
4 *mochi* (rice cakes)
1 teaspoon salt
msg
Lime peel cut into 4 V-shapes

Cut the chicken breast into bite-size diagonal slices. Drop the spinach
into boiling salted water for 1 minute, drain, rinse in cold water, drain
again and squeeze dry. Form into a roll and cut into 4 pieces.

Soak the mushrooms in warm water with a pinch sugar for 30
minutes, squeeze out and cut away the hard stems. Put into a small
saucepan with the tablespoon of soup stock and the ½ teaspoon of soy
sauce and simmer, uncovered, for 2 minutes.

Grill or broil the rice cakes for 5 minutes, or until lightly toasted. Drop
into boiling water for 1 minute to heat through just before serving.

Pour the soup stock into a saucepan and bring to a boil. Reduce the
heat to moderate, add the chicken and simmer for 2 or 3 minutes, then
add the remaining ½ tablespoon soy sauce, the salt and a dash of msg. To
serve, put a rice cake in each of 4 bowls, with a quarter of the chicken, a
mushroom and a slice of spinach. Pour the soup stock into the bowls and
garnish with the lime peel. SERVES 4.

Umani

TEN-INGREDIENT DISH

¾ pound *sato-imo* (taro)
Dashi (soup stock)
Sugar
Salt
Sake
Soy sauce
Mirin
5 ounces *gobō* (burdock root)
Vegetable oil
¼ pound lotus root
Rice vinegar

8 *shiitake* (dried Japanese
   mushrooms)
4 *kōyadōfu* (dried bean curd)
msg
½ pound small whole bamboo
   shoots, about 4
1 medium carrot
16 snow-pea pods
8 medium-sized shrimp

I

Peel the taro, cut into cork shapes, then cut a very thin strip from the edge at one end. Drop into boiling water and cook, uncovered, for 5 minutes. Drain. Return to the saucepan with enough soup stock, 1 to 1½ cups, to cover, 2 tablespoons sugar, ¾ teaspoon salt and 1 teaspoon *sake*. Cut a circle of wax paper to fit the pan and put it on top of the taro. Simmer 10 to 15 minutes or until tender. Then add ½ teaspooon soy sauce and 1 tablespoon *mirin* and cook, uncovered, until all the liquid has evaporated. Transfer to a bowl and set aside.

II

Scrape the burdock root with the back of a knife under running water, cut *rangiri* (see illustration in Introduction) and drop into cold water as it discolors quickly. Put into a saucepan of boiling water and cook for 10 minutes. Drain. In a small saucepan heat 2 teaspoons oil and sauté the burdock for 2 or 3 minutes. Add ¾ cup soup stock and cook, covered, for 5 minutes. Add 3 teaspoons sugar, ½ teaspoon salt, 1 teaspoon *sake* and 1 teaspoon soy sauce, stir to mix and cook over low heat, covered, for 15 minutes. Put into a bowl with remaining cooking liquid and set aside.

III

Peel the lotus root and cut it into ⅕-inch slices. Put into a saucepan with boiling water mixed with rice vinegar in the proportion of 1 cup water to 1 teaspoon vinegar. Cover and cook 3 minutes. Drain, rinse in cold water. In the saucepan combine ⅓ cup soup stock, 1¼ tablespoons sugar and ½ teaspoon salt; bring to a boil, add the lotus root slices and cook 3 to 4 minutes on high heat. Lift out the lotus root and put into a small bowl. When cool pour the cooking liquid over it and set aside.

IV

Soak the mushrooms overnight in lukewarm water with a pinch of sugar. Lift out the mushrooms. Reserve the soaking water. Remove the tough stems from the mushrooms and cut a shallow cross in the top of each one. Strain the soaking water and pour 1 cup into a saucepan. Add 1 teaspoon sugar and the mushrooms and cook, uncovered, over moderate heat until the liquid has evaporated and barely covers the mushrooms. Add 2 tablespoons soup stock, 4 teaspoons sugar, 1 tablespoon soy sauce and ½ teaspoon salt and cook 3 minutes. Add 1 tablespoon *mirin* and cook, uncovered, over moderate heat until all the liquid has evaporated. Put into a bowl and set aside.

V

Soak the bean curd in warm water for 3 minutes. Rinse and squeeze out in 5 or 6 changes of cold water. Cut each slice into quarters. Pour 2 cups soup stock into a saucepan, add 5 tablespoons sugar, ½ teaspoon salt, 2 or 3 dashes msg, ½ tablespoon soy sauce and the bean curd and cook, covered with an *otoshibuta* (inner wooden lid) or a smaller saucepan lid or a plate, over moderate heat for 30 minutes. Pour into a bowl and set aside.

VI

Wash the bamboo shoots and cut into quarters. Pour ¾ cup soup stock into a saucepan, add 2 tablespoons sugar, 1 tablespoon soy sauce, ½ teaspoon salt, and the bamboo shoots and cook, covered with an *otoshibuta* (inner wooden lid), over moderate heat until the liquid is reduced to half. Add 1 tablespoon *mirin* and cook, uncovered, until all liquid has evaporated. Put into a bowl and set aside.

VII

Scrape the carrot and flute it lengthwise at 5 evenly spaced intervals, then cut into ¼-inch slices, or slice and cut into flower shapes with a tiny cooky cutter. Put into a pan with boiling salted water to cover and cook for 2 or 3 minutes. Drain, add ¾ cup soup stock to the saucepan with 1 tablespoon sugar, a pinch of salt and the carrot slices. Cover with an *otoshibuta* (inner wooden lid) and cook, covered, over low heat until tender. Add 1 tablespoon *mirin* and ½ teaspoon soy sauce and cook, uncovered, over moderate heat until all the liquid has evaporated. Put into a bowl and set aside.

VIII

Trim the snow-pea pods, rinse, and boil in salted water for 2 or 3 minutes. Drain, cool, and set aside.

IX

Peel and devein the shrimp, remove the heads and rinse. In a saucepan combine 3 tablespoons *sake,* 1 tablespoon *mirin,* ½ teaspoon salt, and ½ teaspoon soy sauce. Bring to a boil, add the shrimp, cover with an *otoshibuta* (inner wooden lid) and cook until the shrimp turn pink, 2 or 3 minutes. Cool in the liquid and peel, leaving the tails on.

To assemble the dish, arrange the ingredients, drained· where necessary, in a layer box in rows, or heaps, or if preferred mixed together. Serve from the box placed in the center of the table with each guest having a small bowl and chopsticks. Each guest should taste some of everything.

This dish can be made 2 or 3 days ahead and kept in the refrigerator. The cooking method produces beautifully flavored vegetables with a very juicy texture. Serves 8.

X

The tenth ingredient kuwai (arrowhead, *Sagittaria sagittifolia*) is very hard to find in the U.S. except in markets in California and Hawaii. If available, 8 of the fat little corms (bulblike underground stems) about 1½ inches long are peeled, keeping ½ inch of stalk, then soaked in cold water for 1 hour. Put in a pan with fresh water. Boil, skimming if necessary, changing the water twice, and cook until tender. Soak in cold water overnight. Put into a pan with ¾ cup soup stock and 1 tablespoon sugar and cover with an *otoshibuta* (inner wooden lid). Bring to a boil, reduce the heat to low and cook until the liquid is reduced to half. Add 1 tablespoon *sake,* 1 tablespoon sugar, ½ teaspoon salt and 1 teaspoon soy sauce and cook until the liquid is again reduced to half, still using an *otoshibuta.* Add 1 tablespoon *mirin* and cook, uncovered, until the liquid has evaporated.

Glossary

Aburaage, deep-fried bean curd sold in packages in Japanese markets. Will keep, refrigerated. Freezes well.

Aemono, literally, mixed things, such as poultry, fish and vegetables in a sauce or dressing. Served as an accompaniment to a main course or as a salad.

Agemono, deep-fried foods, including **tempura.**

Aji-no-moto, msg (monosodium glutamate) powder used to enhance flavor. The Chinese call it **mei jiung.** Sold in supermarkets under the name of the compound and under brand names which are more expensive. Widely available in Japanese and other markets.

Ajitsuke warabi, fernbrake, bracken, fiddleheads, seasoned with soy sauce, sugar, msg, etc. Available in vacuum-sealed plastic bags in Japanese markets.

Azuki bean (*Phaseolus angularis*), an Asian species of legume called **adzuki** in Chinese markets, varies in color from dark red to black, mottled and cream. Available in Japanese and Chinese markets and in health food stores.

Beni-shōga, red pickled ginger, available bottled or in vacuum-sealed plastic bags in Japanese markets. Will keep, refrigerated.

Chopsticks, hashi in Japanese, made of wood, bamboo, plastic, ivory and sometimes metal, are used for both cooking and eating in the kitchens of the Orient. In Japanese markets 8-inch-long bamboo chopsticks are sold in joined pairs in individual paper wrapping and must be broken apart for use. Almost all Japanese food is eaten with chopsticks of this type. They can, of course, be washed and re-used. Chopsticks of various lengths, up to about 12 inches, with small holes at the top ends so they can be loosely tied together in pairs with kitchen string, are used in cooking. Eggs are stirred with chopsticks instead of being beaten, and chopsticks are used to turn foods when frying and for mixing foods together, taking the place of cooking spoons and forks. Five or 6 chopsticks, held in a bunch in the right hand, are used to stir certain dishes. They are so useful for any type of cooking that it is worth the small effort required to learn how to use them.

Daikon (*Raphanus sativus*), the Oriental white radish is a large, cylindrical root sold fresh in Japanese markets usually as **daikon** or as Oriental radish in other markets. It varies in size and may be as large as 6 inches in diameter and weigh as much as 50 pounds. It is sold by the piece and is used both cooked and raw, often grated as a garnish, and added to sauces. It will keep, refrigerated, for as long as 2 weeks.

Dashi is the basic Japanese soup and cooking stock made from **kombu** (kelp) and preflaked **katsuobushi** (dried bonito). An instant version requiring only the addition of water is available, packaged, in Japanese markets.

Donabe, lidded earthenware casserole unglazed outside, glazed inside. Comes in various sizes and can be used over direct heat. The larger sizes are used for one-pot dishes cooked at the table, such as **shabu shabu** (simmered beef and vegetables). The casseroles should be heated and cooled slowly to prevent cracking. Available in Japanese markets. (Other domestic and imported fireproof casseroles are usable if the Japanese variety is unobtainable.)

Donburi, large individual ceramic bowl, often with a lid, used for noodle and rice dishes. Available in Japanese markets.

Fu, wheat gluten cake available in Japanese markets, packaged in a number of sizes and shapes. Used mainly as a garnish in soups and one-pot dishes. **Shonaifu,** perhaps the most useful, is packaged in sheets which may be cut to the size needed.

Ganmodoki, fried bean curd balls, available packaged in Japanese markets.

Ginnan, ginkgo (or gingko) nuts, available in Oriental markets and specialty food stores, cooked and bottled or canned. The nuts will keep, refrigerated in a closed container, for several weeks.

Gobō, the root of burdock (*Arctium lappa* of the daisy family) is a long, slender root sold fresh in Japanese markets usually under its Japanese name. It will keep, refrigerated, for up to 2 weeks. It can also be bought canned in Oriental markets. A coarse biennial indigenous to temperate Eurasia, burdock grows wild in most temperate parts of the United States where it is generally regarded as a weed. It is cultivated in Hawaii as well as in Japan. Not all varieties are edible.

Goma, sesame seed, both black (**kuro goma**) and white (**shiro goma**) are available, boxed, in Japanese markets. White sesame seed is sold in the spice section of supermarkets.

Hakusai, Chinese cabbage or celery cabbage, sold fresh by the pound in Japanese and Chinese markets and often in supermarkets. It has broad-ribbed pale green leaves 12 to 16 inches long, and will keep, refrigerated in a plastic bag, for a week or more. It is used a great deal in Japanese cooking.

Harusame, literally "spring rain," bean gelatin noodles, also called cellophane or transparent noodles. Available packaged in Chinese and Japanese markets.

Hijiki, flaked dried seaweed which looks rather like dry tea leaves. Sold packaged in Japanese markets.

Hiyamugi, thin pink, white and green wheat-flour noodles usually eaten cold in summer dishes. Available packaged in Japanese markets.

Ika, squid, cuttlefish, available in fish stores and in Japanese markets.

Itazuri is the method of cutting a slice off the ends of cucumbers, then rubbing the cut surfaces with the slices, after which the cucumber is rolled in salt. This is to remove any bitter taste.

Kabocha, Japanese pumpkin. Any winter squash or West Indian pumpkin available in Caribbean markets are the best substitutes.

Kamaboko, fish sausage made from pounded white fish mixed with cornstarch, formed into a sausage shape and cooked. It is sold ready-made in Japanese markets and comes in many shapes and sizes. Some are colored pink or green.

Naruto-maki, a popular fish sausage, has a spiral pattern in pink or yellow running through it, very attractive when sliced. **Naruto** means whirlpool, the spiral pattern. There are whirlpools off the coast at Naruto, hence the poetic name of the sausage. **Chikuwa,** another type of fish sausage, has a hole running through its length. For practical purposes any fish sausage will substitute for another.

Kanpyō, dried gourd strips. Available packaged in Japanese markets.

Kanten (*Gelidium amansii*), a red alga high in gelatin, is manufactured into colorless **kanten** (agar-agar) and used as gelatin in Japanese cooking. Available packed in Japanese markets and in Chinese markets as agar-agar.

Karashina, mustard greens (genus *Brassica* of the crucifer family). Available in Japanese markets and frequently available in supermarkets.

Karashi, mustard, imported from Japan, is sold dried and ground in small cans in Japanese markets. It is mixed with boiling water to form a stiff paste and is very hot. Dried, ground English mustard is the best substitute.

Katakuriko, starch made from the root of the Japanese dog-toothed violet (*Erythronium japonicum*), closely resembles arrowroot. Available in Japanese markets, often incorrectly labeled potato starch.

Katsuobushi, dried bonito fillet, used for **dashi** (soup stock) and as a garnish. Looks like a piece of wood, and is traditionally shaved into flakes with a **kezuriki,** a special box with sharp blades in the top. This is a tedious chore with the special tool, almost impossible without it. However, preflaked bonito is sold in Japanese markets in boxes or plastic bags as **hanakatsuo** or **hanagatsuo,** the spelling varying slightly from brand to brand. Keeps indefinitely unrefrigerated.

Kikurage, jelly mushroom, available dried in Chinese and Japanese markets.

Kinome, Japanese pepper leaf, used as a garnish. Not usually available, no substitute leaf. See **kona sansho.**

Kinako, soy bean flour, available packaged in Japanese markets.

Kinugoshi tōfu, silky bean curd, a custardlike cake made from white soy beans, sold fresh from refrigerator section of Japanese markets. Must be kept refrigerated in water which is changed daily. Will keep for several days. This is the most delicate of all the forms of bean curd.

Kiriboshi daikon, dried white radish strips, available in Japanese markets.

Kishimen, broad, flat wheat-flour noodles.

Kisu, smelt. Japanese varieties are available frozen in some Japanese markets, otherwise use local smelt.

Knives. Japanese kitchen knives **(hocho)** are magnificent tools, and though good sharp Western knives can well be used for cutting in the Japanese manner, a set of 4 **hocho** is worth investing in as they can be used for cutting in any cuisine. There is a **sashimi** knife for slicing raw fish; a boning knife for fish, meat or poultry; a slicing knife for fish, meat or poultry; and a cutting knife for vegetables. Available made of stainless steel in sets from specialty and Japanese stores.

Kōji, malted rice, available in Japanese markets.

Kombu, kelp, sometimes spelled **konbu** (*Laminaria japonica*), also called tangle and Japanese kelp, is a large marine plant which plays an important role in the Japanese kitchen. The leathery fronds of the seaweed, sold dried in packaged sheets in Japanese markets, are used principally in **dashi,** the basic soup and cooking stock. The seaweed is also sold flaked and shredded, see **hijiki** and **tororo kombu.**

Kona sanshō, Japanese pepper, used as a table condiment, is made from the ground leaf of the prickly ash, (*Zanthoxylum piperatum* of the citrus family). Available, packaged, in Japanese markets. **Kinome,** the pretty pinnate leaf, is used whole as a garnish but is seldom available. The ground version may be used instead.

Konnyaku, translucent oblong cake made from the tubers of an aroid also known as Devil's Tongue or Snake Palm, sold packaged in Japanese markets. Will keep, refrigerated, for several days.

Koshi-an, red (**azuki**) bean paste in powder form, available packaged in

Japanese markets.

Kōyadōfu, freeze-dried bean curd also called **kōridōfu. Kōya** is the name of the place where it was first made, **kōri** is ice, hence the two names. Available in Japanese markets.

Kushi, small bamboo or metal skewers. Available in Japanese markets.

Kuwai is the edible corm (bulbous root) of *Sagittaria sagittifolia* of the arrowhead family, and is sometimes found in markets in Hawaii and California as well as in Japanese markets. The cylindrical corm is small, usually only a few inches long. When cooked its pale yellow flesh is rather like the white sweet potato.

Kuzu shirataki, dried green bean noodles, used in **sukiyaki** instead of **shirataki.** Available, packaged, in Japanese markets.

Kuzuko, arrowroot starch, available in supermarkets, health food stores and Japanese markets.

Kyūri Narazuke, Nara-style pickled cucumber. Available in vacuum-sealed plastic bags in Japanese markets.

Matsutake (*Armillaria edocles*), the pine mushroom, found in Japan's pine forests in autumn. The large mushroom is highly prized as a delicacy. Sometimes available canned in Japanese markets.

Mirin, sweet rice wine used in cooking. Available in Japanese markets. No substitute.

Miso, paste made from fermented, cooked soy beans. Two main vari-

eties, **aka miso** (red bean paste) and **shiro miso** (white bean paste), are available in vacuum-sealed plastic bags in Japanese markets. When **miso** appears in a recipe without specifying red or white, either may be used according to taste.

Misozuke, meat, fish, or vegetables pickled in bean paste.

Mitsuba (*Cryptotaenia canadensis* of the carrot family), trefoil, an herb with a distinctive flavor, used in soups and as a garnish. Sometimes available in Japanese markets. Substitutes are indicated in recipes.

Mochi, rice cakes, available packaged in Japanese markets.

Mochigome, sweet, or glutinous, rice available in Chinese and Japanese markets.

Momen tōfu, cottony bean curd, custardlike cake made from white soy beans, sold fresh from refrigerator section of Japanese markets. Must be kept refrigerated in water which is changed daily. Will keep for several days. This variety is firmer than the delicate **kinugoshi tōfu** (silky bean curd) and is the most used of all forms of bean curd.

Momiji-oroshi, literally autumn leaves with grated radish, is used to describe the technique of stuffing a slice of **daikon** (white radish) with a dried hot pepper and grating them together so that the white radish is flecked with red, reminiscent of the color of autumn leaves.

Moromi miso, soy beans and malted rice, available bottled in Japanese markets.

Mushimono, one-pot cookery. An

electric skillet or a fireproof earthenware casserole (**donabe**), heavy skillet, or shallow round cast-iron pot (**sukiyaki-nabe**) on an electric or gas table heater, or a charcoal-burning **hibachi** can all be used for these dishes where the food is cooked at the table.

Nagashikan, resembles an aluminum loaf pan with an inserted sideless tray that lifts out, making it easy to remove and slice delicate custards and similar dishes that would be hard to unmold. Available in Japanese markets in various sizes.

Namaage, type of fried bean curd, available in Japanese markets.

Nama Udon, fresh noodles, ready-cooked in 7-ounce packages needing only to be reheated in hot water. Also uncooked **nama udon,** to be cooked in the same way as dry noodles. Available in the refrigeration section of Japanese markets.

Na-no-hana, rape blossoms, the yellow flowers found on sprigs of *Brassica napus* of the crucifer family, known as broccoli di rapa, colza, rape, or rape greens. Available in Italian markets especially in summer and fall, in Chinese and Japanese markets, and sometimes in supermarkets.

Natto, fermented soy beans, eaten as a garnish with rice. Available packaged in Japanese markets.

Nimono, simmered or boiled foods, stews.

Nori, purple laver seaweed pressed into thin sheets, greenish black in color, is used principally as a garnish and for **sushi.** Available packaged in Japanese markets. Keeps indefinitely.

Oshiwaku, oblong wooden box about 6 by 4 inches with a removable top and bottom used for pressing vinegared rice when making certain kinds of **sushi.** Available in Japanese markets.

Otoshibuta, an inner wooden lid that fits closely on top of the food being cooked in a saucepan. Made in several sizes, they are sometimes available in Japanese markets. A smaller saucepan lid or a plate may be used as a substitute.

Ponzu, pon vinegar, made from **dai dai,** a limelike Japanese citrus fruit. Available bottled in Japanese markets. Use lime or lemon juice as a substitute.

Renkon, lotus root, available fresh in specialty food stores and Chinese and Japanese markets. The root may be up to 4 feet in length and 3 inches in diameter. It is sold in sections, and is also available canned. The root is perforated throughout its length and when sliced looks like a flower with ten petal-shaped holes.

Sakanayaki, top-of-the-stove grill that goes directly over gas or electric burners. Available in Japanese markets.

Sake, rice wine, the traditional drink, usually served slightly warm in small, handleless cups (**sakazuki**), poured from a small china flask. **Sake** is available from liquor stores, and **sake** flasks and cups are available in Japanese markets.

Sashimi, sliced raw fish.

Sato-imo, taro, the name given to a

diverse group of tropical root vegetables of the arum family. Available in Japanese markets as **sato-imo,** they are sometimes called Japanese potatoes and in fact do look rather like medium-sized potatoes with a rough brown skin marked by prominent rings. Widely available in Latin American and Caribbean markets most usually as **yautía, dasheen** or **tannia.**

Satsuma-age, oval fish cakes available packaged in Japanese markets.

Satsuma-imo, sweet potato, one of the white- or yellow-fleshed varieties, not the orange (Louisiana yam) sweet potato. Widely available in Latin American and Caribbean markets often as **boniato.** Also available in Japanese markets and sometimes in supermarkets.

Seri, water dropwort (*Oenanthe stolonthe*), belonging to the same family as celery, is best described as a kind of aquatic parsley. Sometimes available in Japanese markets. Flat Italian parsley is the best substitute.

Shamoji, round wooden spatula used for stirring and serving rice. It does not break up the rice grains.

Shichimi-tōgarashi, seven-flavor spice, a seasoning powder made from ground hot red peppers, ground Japanese pepper leaf, sesame, mustard, rape and poppy seeds, and dried tangerine peel. Available in containers in Japanese markets. Used as an on-the-table condiment.

Shiitake, Japanese mushrooms, available dried (**hoshi-shiitake**) in Japanese markets. To use, soak the mushrooms for 30 minutes in lukewarm water with a pinch of sugar, and remove the tough stems. When fresh mushrooms (**nama-shiitake**) are called for in a recipe, use either fresh local mushrooms or Japanese dried ones.

Shirataki, literally ''white waterfall,'' translucent noodles made from the tubers of the Devil's Tongue, or Snake Palm plant called **konnyaku** in Japan, a member of the arum family. Available waterpacked in cans or vacuum-sealed plastic bags in Japanese markets.

Shiratama-ko, rice cake flour available packaged in Japanese markets.

Shiso, *Perilla frutescens* of the mint family, commonly known as the beefsteak plant. The leaves are used mainly as a garnish and in pickles. Sometimes available fresh in Japanese markets. Grows easily from seed. Substitutes where possible are indicated in recipes.

Shōga, ginger. Fresh ginger root is sold in Oriental, Caribbean, and many other specialty food markets. Will keep, refrigerated, for some weeks. To make ginger juice, grate finely and squeeze out the juice which freezes well.

Shōyu, soy sauce, available in Japanese markets and in supermarkets, is lighter and less salty than Chinese soy sauce.

Shungiku, the edible or Garland chrysanthemum (*Chrysanthemum coronarium*), whose leaves are used, principally as a garnish, in Japanese cooking. Often available in Japanese markets. (This plant is not to be confused with the Western garden-varieties of chrysanthemum, which are inedible.)

Soba, buckwheat noodles, available packaged in Japanese markets.

Soboro, also called **dembu,** cooked, pink-colored fish- or shrimp-sweetened garnish sold packaged or in jars in Japanese markets.

Sōmen, thin wheat-flour noodles available packaged in Japanese markets.

Stir fry, a Chinese cooking technique also used in the Japanese kitchen in which cut-up food is fried in shallow fat over high heat while being stirred constantly and quickly.

Sudare, a bamboo mat made of thin slats of bamboo very like a bamboo place mat, used for rolling omelettes, **sushi** and vegetables.

Sukiyaki-nabe, a round cast iron pan used for cooking **sukiyaki.** A cast-iron skillet is a good substitute.

Suribachi, serrated earthenware mortar used with a **surikogi,** wooden pestle. Makes grinding nuts and other foods easy. Use chopsticks to scrape down the sides.

Su, rice vinegar, available bottled in Japanese markets, specialty food stores and often in supermarkets. Cider vinegar is the best substitute.

Sunomono, foods in a vinegared dressing, salads. This category sometimes overlaps with **aemono.** Both types of dishes are served as accompaniments to main courses.

Sushi, vinegared rice dishes.

Sushioke, also called **bandai,** is a round, shallow wooden dish for **sushi** (vinegared rice dishes).

Takegushi, small bamboo skewers resembling large toothpicks. Available in Japanese markets.

Takenoko, bamboo shoots. Canned whole shoots are available in Chinese and Japanese markets and in specialty food stores; often sliced and canned shoots can be found in supermarkets. Will keep, refrigerated in a covered container in the liquid from the can, for about a week. For Japanese recipes the whole canned bamboo shoots are to be preferred.

Tamago-yaki nabe, rectangular skillet used especially for making rolled omelettes. Available in Japanese markets. Though any skillet may be used, the oblong shape makes rolling the omelettes easier and gives them a neater look.

Tempura pan, round iron pan for deep-fat frying with a built-in draining rack on one side. Ideal for all **agemono** (fried) dishes. Available in Japanese markets. A deep-fat fryer, or a heavy iron skillet, or a fireproof casserole may be used instead.

Teriyaki, the technique of glazing foods in a soy sauce and **mirin** mixture either in a skillet or on a grill.

Tōfu, soy bean curd, usually refers to **momen tōfu.**

Tōgarashi, whole dried hot red peppers. When ground and put into containers the peppers are called **tōgarashi-ko** and are used as an on-the-table condiment. Available in Japanese markets. Any dried hot red chili pepper may be used. For the ground pepper, cayenne is a good substitute.

Tori-sasamī, bamboo-leaf chicken breasts. These are the two smaller fillets of the skinned and boned whole chicken breast and in Japan are considered the best part. Save the two larger fillets for another use.

Tororo kombu, shredded kelp (seaweed), sold packaged in Japanese markets. Keeps indefinitely.

Toso, cold spiced **mirin,** a traditional New Year drink. In modern Japan, **toso** made with **sake,** giving a much drier drink, is becoming increasingly popular.

Tsukemono, pickled vegetables available bottled or in vacuum-sealed plastic bags in Japanese markets.

Udon, medium-sized wheat-flour noodles, available packaged in Japanese markets.

Umeboshi, small pickled plums available bottled in Japanese markets. Will keep indefinitely refrigerated.

Uni, sea urchins, available in Japanese markets as a prepared paste in jars. Used as a stuffing for **onigiri** (rice balls).

Usukuchi shōyu, light soy sauce available bottled in Japanese markets.

Uzura tamago, quail eggs, ready-cooked and canned, available in Japanese markets.

Wakame, lobe-leaf seaweed sold dried in packages in the form of long, dark green strands that expand rapidly in water. Used in soups and salads. Will keep indefinitely. Available in Japanese markets.

Warabi, the young edible sprouts of fernbrake, bracken or fiddleheads. Sometimes pickled or salted, used in soups and salads and available in vacuum-sealed plastic bags in Japanese markets and sometimes, canned, in specialty food stores.

Wasabi (*Eutrema wasabi* of the cabbage family), Japanese horseradish. In Japan the freshly grated root, used to make a pungent condiment rather like horseradish, is preferred. However, the dried powdered form, which is mixed with water to make a green paste, is also used and is available packaged or canned in Japanese markets.

Yakidōfu, broiled or grilled soy bean curd, available in Japanese markets.

Yakimono, grilled or broiled foods.

Yamaimo, sticky yam, long, fairly thin cylindrical root with a brown skin and crisp white flesh that can be eaten raw in salad. When grated it turns into a sticky white foam. Available in Japanese markets.

Yuba, dried soy bean curd packaged in rolls or in flat sheets. Available in Japanese markets.

Yuzu, a limelike citrus fruit, used in Japanese cooking. Use lime or lemon juice as a substitute.

List of Stores for Foods and Utensils

CALIFORNIA

Maruichi Oriental Food, 580A Grand Ave., Carlsbad, Cal. 92008

Harborside Ranch Mart, 1105 Broadway, Chula Vista, Cal. 92011

Woo Chee Chong #2, 1415 Third Ave., Chula Vista, Cal. 92011

Fukuda's, 2412 S. Escondido Blvd., Escondido, Cal. 92025

Nori's Market, 1119 W. Texas St., Fairfield, Cal. 94533

Meiji, 1569 W. Redondo Beach Blvd., Gardena, Cal. 90247

Okazaki Co., 20 S. Main St., Lodi, Cal. 95240

Enbun Co., 2313 W. Jefferson Blvd., Los Angeles, Cal. 90018

Enbun Co., 248 E. First St., Los Angeles, Cal. 90012

Ginza Market, 2600 W. Jefferson Blvd., Los Angeles, Cal. 90018

Granada Market, 1820 Sawtelle Blvd., Los Angeles, Cal. 90025

Rafu Bussan Co., 344 E. First Street, Los Angeles, Cal. 90012

Safe and Save Japanese Market, 2030 Sawtelle Blvd., Los Angeles, Cal. 90025

Nakagawa Co., 306 C St., Marysville, Cal. 95901

Nak's Oriental Market, 1151 Chestnut St., Menlo Park, Cal. 94025

Kyoto Gift and Food #1, 2303 Highland Ave., National City, Cal. 92050

Kyoto Gift and Food #2, 559 Greenbrier Dr., Suite B, Oceanside, Cal. 92054

Penryn Fish Market, P.O. Box 75, Penryn, Cal. 95663

Genji Import, 12845 Poway Rd., Poway, Cal. 92064

A B C Fish and Oriental Food, 1911 Portrero Way, Sacramento, Cal. 95822

Food Center Market, 1912 Fruitridge Rd., Sacramento, Cal. 95822
Senator Fish Market, 2215 10th Street, Sacramento, Cal. 95818
10th Street Market, 2030 10th St., Sacramento, Cal. 95818
Eiko Shoten, 6082 University Ave., San Diego, Cal. 92115
Oriental Grocery, 418 Island Ave., San Diego, Cal. 92101
Washington Fish, 3131 University Ave., San Diego, Cal. 92104
Woo Chee Chong #1, 633 16th St., San Diego, Cal. 92101
Yutaka Import, 6393 Balboa Ave., San Diego, Cal. 92111
Aloha Super Market, 14146 Almaden Rd., San Jose, Cal. 95118
K. Sakai Co., 1656 Post St., San Francisco, Cal. 94115
Jacks Food Center, 519 E. Charter Way, Stockton, Cal. 95206
Star Fish Market, 320 S. El Dorado St., Stockton, Cal. 95203
Waki's Fish Market, 1335 S. Lincoln St., Stockton, Cal. 95206
Omori's, 2700 N. Santa Fe, Vista, Cal. 92083

DELAWARE

Oriental Grocery, 1705 Concord Pike, Wilmington, Del. 19803

FLORIDA

Tomiko's Oriental, 441 Bryn Athyn Blvd., Mary Esther, Fla. 32569
Tropi Pak Food Products, 3663 N.W. 47th St., Miami, Fla. 33142
Oriental Imports, 54 N. Orange Ave., Orlando, Fla. 32801
Stubbs Oriental Food Store, 807 East Ave., Panama City, Fla. 32401
Schillers Delicatessen, 3417 S. Manhattan Ave., Tampa, Fla. 33609

GEORGIA

Asian Trading Co., 2581 Piedmont Rd. N.E., Atlanta, Ga. 30324
Oriental Market, 2306 Lumpkin Rd., Augusta, Ga. 30906
Oriental Food and Gift Center, 5104 Buena Vista Rd., Columbus, Ga. 31907
Makoto, 1067 Oaktree Rd., Decatur, Ga. 30906

ILLINOIS

Diamond Trading Co., 913 W. Belmont, Chicago, Ill. 60657
Franklin Food Street, 1309 East 53rd Street, Chicago, Ill. 60615
Star Market, 3349 North Clark Street, Chicago, Ill. 60657
Toguri Mercantile Co., 5324 North Clark Street, Chicago, Ill. 60640
York Super Food Market, 3240 North Clark Street, Chicago, Ill. 60657

MARYLAND

Asia Food, 2433 St. Paul St., Baltimore, Md. 21218
Far East House, 33 W. North Ave., Baltimore Md. 21201
Fumi Oriental Mart, 11301 Grandview Ave., Wheaton, Md. 20902

NEW JERSEY

Aki, 1635 Lemoine Ave., Fort Lee, N.J. 07024

NEW YORK

Marumiya, 318 W. 231st St., Bronx, N.Y. 10463
Mitsuba Trading Co. Ltd., 59-10 92, Elmhurst, N.Y. 11373
Main Street Food Inc., 41-54 Main St., Flushing, N.Y. 11355
Mei Di Ya Stores, 18 N. Central Park Ave., Hartsdale, N.Y. 10530
Nippon-Do, 82-69 Parsons Blvd., Jamaica, N.Y. 11432
Katagiri & Co., Inc., 224 E. 59th St., New York, N.Y. 10022
Japanese Food Mart, Inc., 239 W. 105th St., New York, N.Y. 10025
Japanese Foodland, 2620 Broadway, New York, N.Y. 10025
Oriental Food Shop, 1302 Amsterdam Ave., New York, N.Y. 10027
Southeast Asia Food Trading Co., 68A Mott St., New York, N.Y. 10013
Tanaka K. Co., 326 Amsterdam Ave., New York, N.Y. 10023
Tokyo Shoten, 189 Brook St., Scarsdale, N.Y. 10583
AC Gifts New York, Inc., 2642 Central Park Ave., Yonkers, N.Y. 10710

NORTH CAROLINA

Japonica, 3903 E. Independence Blvd., Charlotte, N.C. 28205
Oriental Market, 307 Marine Blvd., Jacksonville, N.C. 23540
Oriental Food Mart, 803 N. Main St., Spring Lake, N.C. 28390

PENNSYLVANIA

Euro-Asian Imports, 1727 N. 3rd St., Harrisburg, Pa. 17102
Oriental Food Mart, 909 Race St., Philadelphia, Pa. 19107
Bando Trading Co., 2126 Murray Ave., Pittsburgh, Pa. 15217

SOUTH CAROLINA

Piggly Wiggly, 5960 Rivers Ave. N., Charleston, S.C. 29405
Oriental House Imperial Imports, Trenholm Plaza Shopping Center, 3022
    Two Notch Rd., Columbia, S.C. 29204
Top of Tokyo, 1510 Asheville Highway, Spartanburg, S.C. 29303

VIRGINIA

Super Asian Market, 2719 N. Wilson Blvd., Arlington, Va. 22201
Mel Trading 7 Day Shop, 2121 Ivy Rd., Charlottesville, Va. 22903
Mekong International, 13754-B Warwick Blvd., Newport News, Va. 23602
Chinese American Trading Co., 313 Reservoir Ave., Norfolk, Va. 23504
Lee's Oriental Foods, 7616-5 Sewells Point Rd., Norfolk, Va. 23513
Oriental Food Center, 6322 Rigsby Rd., Richmond, Va. 23226
Safeway International, 3507 W. Cary St., Richmond, Va. 23221

WASHINGTON, D.C.

House of Hana, 7838 Eastern Ave. N.W., Washington, D.C. 20012
Mikado, 4709 Wisconsin Ave. N.W., Washington, D.C. 20016
Safeway International, 12th & F St. N.W., Washington, D.C. 20004

WEST VIRGINIA

Michaels Food Mart, 27 Delaware Ave., Charleston, W. Va. 25302
The Kroger Co. Supermarkets, in most big towns in W. Va.

Index

Salmon
  Glazed salmon, 92
  Grilled marinated salmon, 91
  Pressed vinegared rice with
    shrimp and salmon, 84-85
  Rice balls, 54-55
  Salmon and vegetable casserole,
    126
  Salmon steamed with bean curd,
    90-91
Sardines
  Glazed dried sardines, 219
Sasagaki, 2, 6
Sashimi, 23, 108-111
Sato-imo To Toriniku No Umani,
  167
Satsuma-age, 116-117
Satsuma-Jiru, 45
Sawara No Teriyaki, 93
Saya-Ingen No Goma-ae, 169
Saya-Ingen No Kuro Goma-ae, 169
Saya-Ingen No Kurumi-ae, 169
Saya-ingen No Miso-ae, 168
Saya-Ingen No Peanuts-ae, 169
Saya-Ingen No Shōyuni, 168
Scallops
  Broiled scallops with Japanese
    pepper, 24
Seaweed, 4
  Clear soup with bean curd and
    lobe-leaf seaweed, 38
  Cucumber salad with lobe-leaf
    seaweed, 184
  Miso soup with lobe-leaf sea-
    weed, 46
  Seaweed and cucumber salad,
    182-183
  Sticky yam salad with seaweed,
    180
  Vinegared rice rolled in seaweed,
    76-78

Sekihan, 57
Sencha, 217
Sengiri, 6
Seri, 234
Serving platters, 15
Shabu Shabu, 132-133
Shamoji, 5, 12, 234
Shiitake, 17, 234
Shiitake No Tsumeage, 29
Shimetama No Sumashi, 39
Shiromizakana No Suimono, 42-43
Shiso, 19, 234
Shōga-Jōyu, 153
Shōga No Suzuke, 210-211
Shrimp
  Batter-fried shrimp and vegeta-
    bles, 112-113
  Chilled noodles with shrimp, 65
  Foil wrapped fish, shrimp and
    vegetables, 101
  Fried shrimp coated with bean
    gelatin noodles, 117
  Garnished rice, 51
  Noodle-coated shrimp, 31
  Noodle-coated shrimp with fried
    sole, 114
  Noodles with eggs, shrimp, fish
    sausage and chicken, 66-67
  Omelette with shrimp and mush-
    rooms, 205
  Pressed vinegared rice with
    shrimp and salmon, 84-85
  Rice with deep-fried shrimp and
    green beans, 60
  Shrimp omelette, 200-201
  Three-color *Soboro*, 59
Shungiku. See Chrysanthemum.
Smelt
  Clear soup with smelt, 44
  Glazed smelt, 97
  Pickled smelt, 96-97